Temperature Conversion Table

American Oven Temperature Terms	Degrees Fahrenheit	Degrees Centigrade (Celsius)
	160 170	71 77
	200 212	93 100
Very Slow	225 230 250	107 110 121
Slow	275 300 302	135 149 150
Moderately Slow.	320 325	160 163
Moderate	350 356 375	177 180 190
Hot	390 400	200 205
	425 428	218 220
	437 450	225 232
Very Hot	475 500	246 260
Broil.	525 550	274 288

TEMPERATURE

Volume 3

Bre–Car

WOMAN'S DAY ENCYCLOPEDIA OF COOKERY

1979 Edition
For WOMAN'S DAY

JEANNE VOLTZ, *Food Editor*

For FUNK & WAGNALLS, INC.

Supervising Editor—**NORMA H. DICKEY**
Production Editor—**KATHIE L. ATTLEE**
Production Executive—**EDWARD HAAS**
Editorial Staff—**DONNA L. AMOS, JUNE V. ROOK**
Art Director—**MURRAY KESHNER**
Layout Artists—**HERBERT ASCHER, MARTIN GORDON,
ERLA SIGURDARDOTTIR**

Special Project Staff:

Contributing Editors—**INEZ M. KRECH, JAMES W. TRAGER**

Original Edition

Prepared and edited by the Editors of WOMAN'S DAY

GLENNA MCGINNIS, *Food Editor*

Special Project Staff:

Editor—**NIKA STANDEN HAZELTON**
Associates—**L. GERALDINE MARSTELLER, HELEN FEINGOLD,
SUSAN J. KNOX**

First Revised Edition

Special Project Staff:
Editor—**MARIE ROBERSON HAMM**
Associate Editor—**ISABEL CORNELL**

Copyright © 1966, 1973, 1979 by CBS Publications,
the Consumer Publishing Division of CBS, Inc.,
All Rights Reserved.
Distributed by Funk & Wagnalls, Inc.

HIGHLIGHTS

Volume 3

Bread–Carp

Arranged alphabetically, the articles in this volume fall between the two words listed above. Among the interesting and informative entries found in this volume, several sections are worthy of special attention. We have listed these below for your convenience.

BREAD COOKBOOK	10
BREAKFAST COOKBOOK	32
TIPS FOR THE YOUNG-BRIDE COOK by Paula Jones	36
BUSY DAY DINNERS	50
CAKE COOKBOOK	66
WHEN A COOK GOES CAMPING by Lelia Carson Cox	86
CANADIAN COOKERY	89
CANDY COOKBOOK	98
CARIBBEAN STEWS by Shirley Sarvis	118
50 MENUS	124

How to use the Woman's Day Encyclopedia of Cookery

The twenty-two volumes of the Woman's Day Encyclopedia contain a wealth of alphabetically arranged information. If you wish to prepare Apple Pie, look under Apple in volume 1. But to find all of the information in all of the volumes, you should use the twenty-third volume, the Index. Composed of five separate indexes, volume 23 includes: meal and menu planning; information on nutrition and diet; techniques of cookery and equipment use; a listing by author; and an alphabetical listing by ingredients.

This Encyclopedia contains many individual entries that supplement one another. Meal and Menu Planning, for instance, is treated throughout the Encyclopedia in many different entries. The first index in volume 23 collects these entries and lists volume and page numbers for such diverse items as Busy Day Dinners and Low Cost Meals. How to entertain or cook in different national styles will be simplified by consulting such items as Parties or Mexican Cookery. If you want to cook for a crowd or make up a Christmas menu, this index shows you where to find Quantity Cooking and three separate styles of Christmas meals.

If you are learning to cook or beginning to plan diets for a family, two other indexes offer assistance. The Encyclopedia entries that contain information on nutrition and diet are listed in one index, and techniques of cookery and equipment are listed in the other. If you want to know which foods are necessary in your child's diet or how to cut down on cholesterol, see the second index. If you want to find out which pan is appropriate for a layer cake, see Bake in the third index.

The fourth index in volume 23 is a listing by author of all the special articles in the Encyclopedia. Here you will find titles and location of articles by noted cookbook authors and food and health authorities.

A major part of volume 23 is the listing of all the recipes contained in the Encyclopedia, arranged alphabetically by main ingredient and by one or more menu categories. Thus, an Abalone Chowder recipe in volume 1 is listed in this Index under ABALONE and under SOUPS. A Crabmeat Dip recipe appears under CRABS, under DIPS, APPETIZER, and under APPETIZERS.

These volumes offer helpful advice on cooking, meal planning, food budgeting, and entertaining. Brimming with tempting recipes, mouthwatering photos, and interesting tid-bits about the origin and history of some of the ingredients, the Woman's Day Encyclopedia of Cookery is indeed a browsing library for food lovers.

BREAD COOKBOOK

BREAD

BREAD—Defined simply as a food made from flour or meal by moistening, kneading, and baking, bread, in its various forms, has been one of the most universal foods, indeed the staff of life, since prehistoric times. It has inspired prayer and poetry. The Puritans admitted that "Brown bread and the Gospel is good fare." For sheer love of life who could want more than, "A Book of Verses underneath the Bough, A Jug of Wine, a Loaf of Bread and Thou." And we all know Little Tommy Tucker, who sang for his supper and got white bread and butter.

Bread has made history, too. Bread riots unseated emperors in ancient Rome. The French revolutionists of 1789 cried for bread and received the unthinking reply: "Let them eat cake." In more recent times Mussolini asked his people to "love bread, the heart of home." In all ages, governments in time of stress have hesitated before taking the final, desperate step of rationing bread.

The bread of primitive man was unleavened and perhaps, as the story goes, the discovery of a leavening agent by a cook of ancient Egypt was pure chance. However it came about, the Egyptians baked some of the finest bread in the ancient world in cone-shape ovens. Flattened and perhaps coarse to present-day taste, the ancient round or triangular loaves unearthed at Deir-el-Bahari were a great improvement over the open-air baking of earlier times. Bread, the symbol of the bounty of the Nile, was cast upon its waters as a tribute to the gods; it was placed in tombs to feed the departed spirits. Egyptians literally earned their daily bread: workers were given bread at the end of the day as wages.

It was the practical-minded Romans who developed the circular millstone and enlarged the baking oven to mass-production capacity. The commercial baker, in business by 168 B.C., carefully put his mark on each loaf. The ruins of Pompeii reveal beehive-shape ovens, as well as the remains of bread baked in them. Pliny states that bread *sine pondere* (without heaviness) is best, revealing an early preference for light, white bread.

In the Middle Ages, as the cities and towns grew, trade guilds were established for bakers. Millers and bakers were not always highly respected, for they were suspected, and in many cases rightly so, of taking some of the grain or dough for themselves. A London baker devised a method for taking dough under the watchful eyes of his customers. His kneading board had a small hole in the middle through which pieces of dough were pulled by a boy hidden under the table.

During the Revolutionary War, bread was so important a part of our diet that the Continental Congress appointed a "Superintendent of Bakers and Director of Baking in the Grand Army of the United States." Latecomers though we were in the long history of bread-making, we were fast to learn, and a breakfast menu for first-class passengers, at the height of riverboat luxury, offered a choice of twelve kinds of hot bread. Yet Greece of the 2nd century A.D. offered as many as fifty different breads, including a cheese bread similar to our modern cheese bread.

It wasn't until 1834 that the roller mill was invented to crush grain more rapidly and economically between its revolving cylinders, completely removing the outer covering and germ. The customers were happier with their snowwhite bread and millers and bakers were happier, too, because without the germ the flour kept longer. It wasn't until recently that we realized that nutritional elements were lost in the process, necessitating the enrichment of bread with additional B vitamins and iron.

There are two basic kinds of bread: yeast breads, which are leavened by yeast and quick breads which are leavened by baking soda or baking powder.

YEAST BREADS AND ROLLS

Yeast breads are made from non-sweet or sweet doughs. The former are used to make what we commonly call bread. The sweet doughs are made into sweet loaves, coffeecakes, kuchens, and buns of many different kinds.

Yeast comes in two types: dry granular or compressed. Each requires a different temperature of water in which to dissolve properly. For best results, use a small room thermometer or a candy thermometer to test the temperature.

In making a yeast bread, sugar, warm water, and salt are added to the yeast, stimulating its growth and starting fermentation. During the process of fermentation a gas is released which is trapped within the elastic structure which flour gives to dough, causing the bread to rise. Kneading the dough causes the development of these elastic strands, formed from the gluten in the flour. Extra milk, eggs, sugar, butter or fat add tenderness, color, and flavor to the bread.

Since yeast hates the cold, all ingredients used should be heated slightly or be at room temperature, and bread doughs should be allowed to rise in a warm draft-free spot. Breads should be baked quickly in a hot oven and allowed to cool on a rack away from drafts.

Baked breads can be stored in moistureproof wrappings and freeze well.

Making Yeast Breads—The amount of all-purpose flour used is variable, depending on variations in the size of eggs and the amount of moisture in the flour itself. Add flour to the dough until, after beating well, the dough pulls off the spoon cleanly. Knead on a lightly floured board, adding more flour until dough no longer sticks. Kneading is simple. Fold the dough toward you and push the outer edge of the dough down, and away from you with the heel of your hand give dough a slight turn and repeat. Keep repeating until dough is smooth and feels bouncy.

Let dough rise in a greased bowl, turning the dough or slightly greasing the top to keep surface of dough from drying out. Allow to rise until double in bulk, or until, when the top is pressed, a dent remains. If you wish a finer, more even-textured loaf, push dough down firmly and allow to rise once again.

To shape a loaf of bread, roll out dough into an oblong, *three inches* wider than the length of the pan and *three times* longer than the width of the pan (a pan 9 x 5 x 3 inches requires an oblong 12 x 15 inches). Starting at the narrow edge, roll up as for a jelly roll. Seal ends and fold over one inch at either end. Place in a greased loaf pan and allow to rise until double in bulk.

Brush loaf with beaten egg for a shiny crust, and with milk or butter for a soft crust.

When baked, the loaf has a hollow sound when tapped and is well browned.

FREEZING YEAST BREADS AND ROLLS

All freezing must be done in freezer, since refrigerator frozen-food compartment temperatures are not cold enough. It is preferable to freeze baked yeast breads and rolls rather than unbaked ones.

To Freeze, Unbaked—Plain yeast dough, prepared as usual, does not rise well even after a short time in the freezer. Consequently, if yeast dough is to be prepared for freezing, double the amount of yeast in the recipe and make a rich dough with additional sugar, shortening, and egg (depending on the kind of bread or roll made). Divide the dough into proper amounts to use at one time. Shape, if desired. Pack or wrap dough in any moisture-vaporproof wrapping material or container, excluding as much air as possible. Freeze quickly to stop yeast action.

To bake dough which has been frozen, leave freezer package in refrigerator overnight to thaw. Or unwrap and place in a greased bowl to thaw. Then knead dough, shape it, and allow to rise until double in bulk, as for fresh dough. Punch down. Bake as directed in recipe.

Storage life: 2 weeks

To Freeze, Baked—Cool baked breads or rolls thoroughly on a rack. Wrap in moisture-vaporproof wrapping material, excluding as much air as possible. Thaw in wrapper for 15 to 30 minutes. To freshen or warm, heat in preheated slow oven (300°F.) for 15 to 20 minutes. If original wrapper is unsuited to oven heat, transfer to paper bag and heat.

Storage life: 3 to 6 months, depending on bread.

QUICK BREADS

The person who first named these popular members of the bread family remains a mystery. *Why* they are so-named is obvious; they are easier to make and take less time than the ones made with yeast. *What* they are requires some special definition, for there are so many of them and they are also called "hot breads," or by the name of the specific recipe in mind.

Quick breads can be classified by the type of leavening agent used. For example: *biscuits, griddle cakes, scones,* and *shortcake* are leavened by baking powder or baking soda. *Popovers* and *Yorkshire pudding* are leavened by steam.

Quick breads can also be grouped according to the thickness or thinness of the batter used to make them. There are "pour" batters, "drop" batters, and "soft" doughs which are to be rolled, patted out, or shaped. *Popovers* and *waffles* are made with pour batters. *Corn bread, loaves, spoon breads,* and *dumplings* are made from drop batters, while some *muffins* and *gingerbread* are made from pour batters, others from drop. *Scones, coffeecakes, tea breads,* and *doughnuts* are made from soft doughs, and *biscuits* can be made from either drop batters or soft doughs.

Although these result in completely different breads, all are made of almost the same ingredients. They vary only because of the proportions used, and the way they are mixed and baked or cooked.

Further variety in quick breads comes from the diversity of cereal products used: wheat, whole-wheat, rye, and corn flours, and bran, oatmeal, or cornmeal. Any of these can be made into muffins, for example, yet the final baked products will taste and look different.

MIXING QUICK BREADS

There are two methods used for mixing quick breads:

1. The Muffin Method. Most instructions in recipes follow a pattern. The dry ingredients are mixed together and sifted into a mixing bowl, and a depression or "well," as it is often called, is made in the center of this. Then the liquid specified in the recipe is combined with melted fat, and with beaten eggs if they are required. This, in turn, is poured into the "well" and the batter stirred *only enough* to mix it. About 15 strokes is usually sufficient. This caution is almost always included in the recipe, for overmixing will result in disappointments: tunnels, tough texture, and crust with high peaks in muffins, for example. Popovers are an exception to this rule because although they are mixed by the muffin method too, they do not contain baking powder or soda (the leavening depends on eggs) and they must be well beaten so the mixture will have enough gluten to hold the steam which forms during baking and makes them "pop."

2. The Biscuit Method. For light, flaky biscuits, a solid fat is "cut" into the flour and the other dry ingredients in the mixing bowl, with a pastry blender, two knives, or the fingers. When the mixture looks fine and even, the liquid is added all at once. This is stirred until all ingredients are wet, then turned out on a floured board, formed into a ball with floured fingers, and folded over and over or kneaded 10 to 20 times, until the dough is smooth and uniform. Finally, it is patted or rolled out, cut into the desired shapes, and baked.

Biscuits—The standard for baking biscuits is doubled volume, straight sides, level tops, uniform browning, smooth tender crust, flaky layers with fine even cells, and a creamy white color free from yellow or brown spots.

Drop biscuits have a crispier crust and crumblier texture than rolled biscuits; more liquid is used in the recipe and biscuits are dropped from a spoon onto a cookie sheet.

Biscuits made with soda differ in flavor and texture from those made with baking powder. Fortunately, there are enough recipes to give everyone a biscuit to his taste.

Popovers—Thin hollow shells, crisp, yet tender, and moist inside, popovers are golden brown with enlarged, rounded peaked tops, rather like a chef's hat in shape. The flavor is mild and the pleasure of eating is partly this, partly the crisp crust. Although mixed by the muffin method, the batter requires more liquid and more beating, and the eggs in the mixture allow the batter to expand with the steam formed. A very hot oven is required to do this and to set the batter before the steam escapes.

Griddle Cakes—These should be evenly browned on both sides, of fairly even shape and uniform thickness, with a smooth and tender crust. Inside they should be

BREAD

moist but not sticky, evenly grained, and pleasantly flavored. Much of the success in griddle or pancakes lies in correct recipe proportions, proper mixing, uniformity of griddle temperature, and freshly mixed batter.

Waffles—Crisp, light buttercakes with a tender crust, waffles are imprinted with the crisscross of the iron in which they are baked to a golden brown. When mixing, be sure not to overstir; this will make them tough and heavy. When baking, watch the temperature of the iron and measure the batter carefully; then pour.

Muffins—These delicate quick breads have an evenly rounded and browned top with a slightly pebbly appearance. The crust is crisp and tender, and inside they should be moist, evenly fine-grained with no long tunnels. They are tender and have a fine flavor. There are many kinds of muffins and many recipes for them. In making them watch out for overmixing; the batter is mixed only enough to blend the dry and the moist ingredients.

FREEZING QUICK BREADS

Quick breads may be frozen both unbaked and baked.

Storage life of frozen unbaked biscuits and muffins: 2 weeks; if frozen baked, 4 to 9 months.

All storage must be done in freezer, because refrigerator frozen-food compartment temperatures are not cold enough.

To Freeze, Unbaked—Make doughs as usual. Wrap in moisture-vaporproof wrapping material, excluding as much air as possible. If a batter, freeze in baking container such as paper cups. Unmold and then wrap for freezing. See below for additional directions for the quick breads most frequently frozen unbaked.

Biscuits

Shape dough into biscuits. Wrap as above, separating the biscuits with a double layer of wrapping material.

To bake unthawed: Remove wrapping. Put frozen biscuits on greased cookie sheet. Bake in preheated hot oven (425°F.) for 15 to 25 minutes, depending on thickness of biscuit, or until golden brown.

To bake thawed: Unwrap to make sure the biscuits won't stick together during thawing. Thaw at room temperature. Bake thawed biscuits in preheated hot oven (425°F.) for 10 to 12 minutes or until golden brown.

Muffins

Spoon batter into paper baking cups and put cups in freezer. When batter is frozen, keep in paper baking cups and wrap in moisture-vaporproof wrapping material, excluding as much air as possible. Return to freezer.

To bake unthawed: Unwrap. Put paper cups with frozen batter into ungreased muffin pans. Bake in preheated slow oven (300°F.) until well risen. Finish baking in hot oven (425°F.) for 15 to 25 minutes, depending on size of muffins, or until golden brown.

To bake thawed: Unwrap. Put paper cups with frozen batter into ungreased muffin pans. Thaw for 1 hour at room temperature. Bake in preheated hot oven (425°F.) for 15 to 25 minutes, depending on size of muffins, or until golden brown.

To Freeze, Baked—Bake as usual. Cool thoroughly on a rack. Wrap in moisture-vaporproof wrapping material, excluding as much air as possible. See below for additional directions for the quick breads most frequently frozen baked.

Storage life of frozen baked biscuits, muffins, and waffles: 2 months

Biscuits

Do not thaw frozen baked biscuits. To heat them: Unwrap. Bake in preheated slow oven (300°F.) for 20 minutes or until golden brown.

Muffins

When ready to use, frozen baked muffins can be heated unthawed or thawed.

To heat unthawed: Unwrap. Put muffins into greased muffin pans. Heat in preheated slow oven (300°F.) for 10 to 25 minutes, depending on size of muffins, or until golden brown.

To heat thawed: Unwrap and thaw at room temperature. Put muffins into greased muffin pans. Heat in preheated slow oven (300°F.) until warmed through. Baking time depends on size of muffins.

Waffles

Waffles are always baked before being frozen. To freeze baked, see general directions above. When wrapping, separate waffles with double layers of wrapping material.

To heat: Unwrap. Put in waffle iron or toaster until heated through.

YEAST BREADS

WHITE BREAD

¼ cup water*
1 package active dry yeast or 1 cake compressed yeast
2 cups milk, scalded
¼ cup butter or margarine
2 tablespoons sugar
2 teaspoons salt
6 cups sifted all-purpose flour

*Use very warm water (105°F. to 115°F.) for dry yeast; use lukewarm (80°F. to 90°F.) for compressed. Sprinkle dry yeast or crumble cake into water. Let stand for a few minutes; then stir until dissolved. Pour hot milk over butter, sugar, and salt in large mixing bowl. Cool to lukewarm and add yeast and 3 cups flour. Beat well. Add remaining flour and mix well. Turn out on floured pastry cloth or board and knead until smooth and satiny. Put in greased bowl; turn once, cover, and let rise until

doubled, about 1½ hours. Punch down; let rise for 30 minutes. Shape into 2 loaves and put in greased pans 9 x 5 x 3 inches. Let rise until doubled, about 45 minutes. Bake in preheated hot oven (400°F.) for about 35 minutes.

Individual Loaves

Use recipe for White Bread above. After first rising, cut half of dough into 6 pieces. Shape into small loaves and put in greased pans 4¾ x 2⅝ x 1½ inches. Let rise until doubled, about 30 minutes. Brush with melted butter and bake in preheated hot oven (425°F.) for about 20 minutes. Shape remaining dough into 1 loaf and put in greased loaf pan. Let rise and make as in directions for White Bread.

FRENCH BREAD

Water*
1 package active dry yeast or 1 cake compressed yeast
1 tablespoon shortening
2 teaspoons salt
1 tablespoon sugar
6 cups sifted all-purpose flour
1 egg white

*Use very warm water (105°F. to 115°F.) for dry yeast; use lukewarm (80°F. to 90°F.) for compressed. Sprinkle dry yeast or crumble cake into ¼ cup water. Let stand for a few minutes; then stir until dissolved. Pour 1 cup boiling water over shortening, salt, and sugar in large mixing bowl. Add ¾ cup cold water and cool to lukewarm. Add yeast and gradually beat in enough flour to form a stiff dough. Turn out on floured pastry cloth or board and knead until smooth and satiny. Put in greased bowl; turn once, cover, and let rise until doubled, about 1½ hours. Shape into 2 oblong loaves about 14 inches long. Put on greased cookie sheets. Let rise until doubled, about 1 hour. Brush with beaten egg white and, with knife, make 3 slashes across top. Sprinkle with poppy, or sesame seeds, if desired. Bake in preheated hot oven (425°F.) for 30 minutes. Reduce heat to moderate (350°F.); bake for 20 minutes more.

Braided French Bread

Divide dough for each loaf into 3 parts. Shape into balls and roll lightly in flour, then roll to form ropes about 10" long. For each loaf, braid 3 ropes into a loaf and place on greased cookie sheet. Brush with beaten egg white. Sprinkle with poppy or sesame seeds, if desired. Bake as above.

WHITE BATTER BREAD

2¾ cups water*
2 packages active dry yeast or 2 cakes compressed yeast
6½ cups sifted all-purpose flour
3 tablespoons sugar
3 teaspoons salt
2 tablespoons soft shortening

*Use very warm water (105°F. to 115°F.) for dry yeast; use lukewarm (80°F. to 90°F.) for compressed. In large bowl of electric mixer, sprinkle dry yeast or crumble cakes into water; let stand for a few minutes, then stir until dissolved. Add 3¼ cups flour, the sugar, salt, and shortening. Blend at low speed; then beat for 2 minutes at medium speed (or beat by hand). Beat in remaining flour by hand. Cover and let rise until doubled, about 45 minutes. Stir batter, beating hard for half minute. Spread in 2 greased loaf pans 9 x 5 x 3 inches. Let rise until doubled, about 20 minutes. Bake in preheated moderate oven (375°F.) for 40 to 50 minutes.

HOT CASSEROLE BREAD

Water*
1 package active dry yeast or 1 cake compressed yeast
4 cups sifted flour (preferably unbleached)
1 tablespoon sugar
2 teaspoons salt
Butter

*Use very warm water (105°F. to 115°F.) for dry yeast; use lukewarm (80°F. to 90°F.) for compressed. Sprinkle dry yeast or crumble cake into 1 cup water. Let stand a few minutes; then stir until dissolved. Combine flour, sugar, and salt in bowl. Add water and yeast, and mix. Add more water, ¼ to ½ cup, to make a soft dough. Cover and let rise until doubled. Beat down and divide dough between two round 1-quart heatproof glass casseroles that have been buttered generously. Let rise until doubled; then bake in preheated hot oven (400°F.) for 40 minutes. Remove from casseroles and brush crust with butter.

CHEESE BREAD

¼ cup water*
1 package active dry yeast or 1 cake compressed yeast
2 tablespoons sugar
1½ cups skim milk
2½ cups shredded sharp Cheddar cheese
¼ cup grated raw carrot
3 tablespoons cooking oil
1¼ teaspoons salt
5 to 6 cups sifted all-purpose flour

*Use very warm water (105°F. to 115°F.) for dry yeast; use lukewarm (80°F. to 90°F.) for compressed. Sprinkle dry yeast or crumble cake into water. Let stand for a few minutes; then stir until dissolved. Heat remaining ingredients except flour to lukewarm. Pour over yeast. Add about half of flour and mix well. Add enough more flour to make a stiff dough that will not stick to bowl. Turn out on floured pastry cloth or board and knead until smooth and satiny. Put in greased bowl; turn once, cover, and let rise until doubled. Punch down and shape into 2 loaves. Put in greased loaf pans 9 x 5 x 3 inches. Let rise until doubled. Bake in preheated moderate oven (350°F.) for about 40 minutes.

BREAD

DARK RYE BREAD

1 cup dark molasses
4 cups water*
2 packages active dry yeast or 2 cakes compressed yeast
  Cooking oil (about ⅔ cup)
2 tablespoons salt
4 egg yolks
2 cups riced hot cooked potato
2 cups nonfat dry-milk powder
2 cups rye meal or rye flour
7 cups dark rye flour
3½ to 4½ cups all-purpose flour

*Add molasses to very warm water (105°F. to 115°F.) for dry yeast or lukewarm (80°F. to 90°F.) for compressed yeast. Sprinkle or crumble yeast into water and let stand for 10 minutes. Beat ½ cup oil, the salt, egg yolks, and potato together and add to yeast mixture. Mix in dry ingredients, adding enough white flour to make a stiff dough that pulls from the spoon after it has been beaten. Brush top lightly with oil and allow to rise until double. Punch down and let rise again. Shape into 4 round loaves and put in well-greased 2-quart heat-proof glass casseroles. Let rise until double in size. Bake in preheated hot oven (400°F.) for 15 minutes. Reduce heat to moderate (350°F.) and bake for about 40 minutes more.
Note: Recipe can be halved, if desired. Or, if four 2-quart casseroles are not available, bread can be baked in loaf pans (9 x 5 x 3 inches).

ONION BREAD

1 cup water*
1 package active dry yeast or 1 cake compressed yeast
2 teaspoons sugar
2 teaspoons salt
3¼ cups sifted all-purpose flour (about)
2 tablespoons melted butter or margarine
½ cup coarsely chopped onion
2 teaspoons paprika

*Use very warm water (105°F. to 115°F.) for dry yeast; use lukewarm (80°F. to 90°F.) for compressed. Sprinkle dry yeast or crumble cake into water; stir until dissolved. Add sugar, 1 teaspoon salt, and 2 cups flour. Stir, then beat well. Stir in ½ cup more flour, reserving ½ cup for kneading. Sprinkle about ¼ cup flour on pastry cloth or board. Turn dough out on flour; knead until smooth and satiny, adding remaining flour as needed. Put in greased bowl; turn once, cover, and let rise until doubled, about 1 hour. Punch down and divide. Pat each half into a greased 9-inch round layer-cake pan or 8-inch square-pan. Brush with butter and sprinkle with onion. Punch onion down into dough so surface looks dented. Let rise until doubled, about 45 minutes. Sprinkle each with ½ teaspoon salt and 1 teaspoon paprika. Bake in preheated very hot oven (450°F.) for about 20 minutes. Cut into wedges or strips and serve hot with butter. (Good with roast beef.)

SENNEBEC HILL BREAD

2 cups water*
2 packages active dry yeast or 2 cakes compressed yeast
½ cup molasses
4 egg yolks
2½ teaspoons salt
⅓ cup cooking oil
1 cup nonfat dry-milk powder
½ cup regular rolled oats
½ cup yellow cornmeal
½ cup wheat germ
1 cup rye meal or rye flour
2 cups whole-wheat flour
3 cups all-purpose flour (about)

*Use very warm water (105°F. to 115°F.) for dry yeast; use lukewarm (80°F. to 90°F.) for compressed. Sprinkle dry yeast or crumble cakes into water in large bowl of electric mixer; add molasses. Let stand for a few minutes; then stir until dissolved. Add egg yolks, salt, oil, dry milk, oats, cornmeal, and wheat germ. Beat on low speed until well mixed. (Or beat with rotary beater.) By hand, add rye meal, whole-wheat flour, and enough all-purpose flour to make a stiff dough. Mix well and brush lightly with oil. Cover and let rise until doubled. If punched down and allowed to rise again, this bread will have a finer texture, but this is not necessary. Turn out on floured pastry cloth or board and knead gently. Shape into 4 loaves. Put in 4 greased pans 7½ x 3½ x 2½ inches, or two pans 9 x 5 x 3 inches. Let rise until doubled. Bake in preheated moderate oven (375°F.) for 25 minutes. Reduce heat to 350°F. and bake for about 20 minutes longer. This bread is excellent for toast. Makes 4 medium or 2 large loaves.

INDIVIDUAL WHOLE-WHEAT BATTER LOAVES

1¼ cups water*
1 package active dry yeast or 1 cake compressed yeast
2 tablespoons honey, firmly packed brown sugar, or molasses
1 cup whole-wheat flour
2 cups sifted all-purpose flour
2 teaspoons salt
2 tablespoons soft shortening

*Use very warm water (105°F. to 115°F.) for dry yeast; use lukewarm (80°F. to 90°F.) for compressed. In large bowl of electric mixer, sprinkle dry yeast or crumble cake into water. Let stand for a few minutes; then stir until dissolved. Add honey, about half of each of the flours, the salt, and shortening. Blend at low speed, then beat for 2 minutes at medium speed. (Or beat by hand.) Stir in remaining flours with spoon. Cover and let rise until doubled, about 30 minutes. Stir down and spread evenly in 6 greased pans (4¾ x 2⅝ x 1½ inches). Smooth and shape tops of loaves with floured hand. Let rise until batter reaches tops of pans, about 40 minutes. Bake in preheated moderate oven (375°F.) for about 30 minutes. Cool.

BUTTERMILK CHEESE BREAD

- 1 cup buttermilk
- ⅓ cup butter
- ¼ cup sugar
- 2½ teaspoons salt
- 1 package active dry yeast
- ½ teaspoon baking soda
- 1½ cups shredded sharp Cheddar cheese
- 5 to 5½ cups all-purpose flour

Heat buttermilk and 1 cup water with the butter until butter melts. Stir in sugar and salt and cool to about 120°F. In large bowl of electric mixer, combine next 3 ingredients with half the flour. Add first mixture and beat at low speed ½ minute, then beat on medium-high speed 3 minutes. With wooden spoon, stir in enough more flour to make a soft but firm dough and turn out on floured board. Knead 7 to 10 minutes, or until smooth and elastic. Put in greased bowl and turn greased side up. Cover and let rise in warm place 1 hour, or until doubled. Punch down and shape in 2 loaves. Put in greased 9 x 5 x 3 inch loaf pans and let rise 30 to 40 minutes, or until doubled. Bake in preheated hot oven (400°F.) 30 to 40 minutes. Turn out on cake racks and cool before cutting.

WHEAT GERM BREAD

- Water*
- 2 packages active dry yeast or 2 cakes compressed yeast
- 3 tablespoons sugar
- 2½ teaspoons salt
- Butter or other shortening
- ⅓ cup molasses
- ¾ cup milk, scalded
- 1 cup wheat germ
- 4 cups whole-wheat flour
- 2 cups all-purpose white flour

*Use very warm water (105°F. to 115°F.) for dry yeast; use lukewarm (80°F. to 90°F.) for compressed. Measure ¼ cup water into large bowl. Sprinkle dry yeast or crumble cakes into water. Let stand a few minutes; then stir until dissolved. In saucepan mix 1¼ cups water, sugar, salt, ⅓ cup butter, and molasses. Heat until butter melts. Cool to lukewarm. Pour scalded milk over wheat germ. Let stand until liquid is absorbed and mixture is lukewarm. To yeast, stir in the lukewarm molasses mixture and the lukewarm wheat-germ mixture. Mix whole-wheat and white flours. Add half to yeast mixture and beat until smooth. Stir in the remaining flour mixture. Turn the dough out on a lightly floured board. Knead quickly and lightly until smooth and elastic. Place in a greased bowl and brush the top lightly with melted shortening or butter. Cover with a clean damp towel. Let rise in a warm place, free from draft, until doubled in bulk, about 1½ hours; punch down and divide into 2 equal portions. Shape into loaves and place in 2 greased loaf pans (9 x 5 x 3 inches). Cover with a clean damp towel. Let rise in a warm place, free from draft, until doubled in bulk, for about 1¼ hours. Bake in preheated oven (400°F.) for about 50 minutes.

PUMPERNICKEL

- 1½ cups cold water
- ¾ cup yellow cornmeal
- 1½ cups boiling water
- 1½ teaspoons salt
- 2 tablespoons sugar
- 2 tablespoons shortening
- 1 tablespoon caraway seeds
- ¼ cup water*
- 2 packages active dry yeast or 2 cakes compressed yeast
- 2 cups mashed potatoes
- 4 cups rye flour
- 4 cups whole-wheat flour

Stir cold water into cornmeal in a saucepan, add boiling water, and cook, stirring constantly, until thick. Add salt, sugar, shortening, and caraway seeds and let stand until lukewarm. *Use very warm water (105°F. to 115°F.) for dry yeast; use lukewarm (80° to 90°F.) for compressed. Sprinkle dry yeast or crumble cakes into water. Let stand for a few minutes; then stir until dissolved. Add yeast and mashed potatoes to the cornmeal; mix well. Stir in flours. Turn out on floured pastry cloth or board and knead until smooth and satiny. Put in greased bowl; turn once, cover, and let rise until doubled. Divide dough into 3 portions, form into balls, and let rest for a few minutes. Roll each loaf twice as long and twice as wide as the pan in which it is to be baked. Fold ends into center and overlap slightly. Press sides to seal and then fold over in similar fashion to fit pan. Put each one in a greased pan with seam side down. Let rise until doubled. Bake in preheated moderate oven (375°F.) for about 1 hour.

PETAL BREAD

- 1 cup very warm water
- 1 package active dry yeast
- 2 tablespoons sugar
- Butter or margarine
- 1 egg
- 1 teaspoon salt
- 3¼ cups all-purpose flour

Put water (105°F. to 115°F.) in large bowl of electric mixer (or other bowl if mixer is not available). Sprinkle with yeast. Let stand a few minutes, then stir until dissolved. Add sugar, 2 tablespoons softened butter, egg, salt and 1½ cups flour. Beat at medium speed 2 minutes, scraping sides and bottom of bowl occasionally, or beat hard with wooden spoon until smooth. With spoon, stir in remaining flour to make a firm dough that clears sides of bowl. Put in greased bowl and turn to grease top. Cover and let rise in warm place 45 minutes, or until light and almost doubled. Punch dough down and knead a few turns on lightly floured board. Roll to 18-inch by 12-inch rectangle and cut in about 30 diamonds with knife or cutter. Dip each in ½ cup melted butter to coat both sides. Arrange in large tube pan (if loose-bottomed, set pan on jelly-roll pan as some of butter may run out). Cover and let rise in warm place 30 minutes, or until doubled. Bake in preheated hot oven (400°F.) 25 minutes, or until golden

BREAD

brown. Let stand a few minutes, then turn out on rack or plate. Serve whole and pull off petals as desired.

OATMEAL BREAD

- 1 cup quick-cooking rolled oats (not instant)
- 2 cups milk, scalded
- ½ cup water*
- 1 package active dry yeast or 1 cake compressed yeast
- ½ cup molasses
- 2 teaspoons salt
- ¼ teaspoon ground ginger
- 4½ cups all-purpose flour

Put oats in large bowl and cover with milk. Stir and let stand until lukewarm. *Use very warm water (105°F. to 115°F.) for dry yeast; use lukewarm (80°F. to 90°F.) for compressed. Sprinkle or crumble yeast into water. Let stand a few minutes; then stir until dissolved. Add yeast mixture, molasses, salt, and ginger to oat mixture. Stir in 4½ cups unsifted flour. Cover and let rise in warm place until double in bulk, about 1 hour. Knead down on well-floured board and put into 2 greased loaf pans 9 x 5 x 3 inches. Let rise until almost double, about 45 minutes. Bake in preheated moderate oven (350°F.) for 45 to 50 minutes. Makes 2 loaves.

SALLY LUNN

- ½ cup water*
- 1 package active dry yeast or 1 cake compressed yeast
- 1 cup milk, scalded
- ½ cup sugar
- 2 teaspoons salt
- ½ cup butter or margarine
- 3 eggs, well beaten
- 4½ cups unsifted all-purpose flour

*Use very warm water (105°F. to 115°F.) for dry yeast; use lukewarm (80°F. to 90°F.) for compressed. Sprinkle dry yeast or crumble cake into water. Let stand for a few minutes; then stir until dissolved. Pour milk over ¼ cup sugar, the salt, and butter in large bowl. Cool to lukewarm and add yeast, eggs, and flour. Beat until smooth. Cover and let rise until doubled, about 1 hour. Stir down; pour into 2 well-greased 8-inch square cake pans. Cover and let rise until doubled, about 30 minutes. Sprinkle each loaf with 2 tablespoons sugar and bake in preheated hot oven (400°F.) for 25 minutes. Makes 2 loaves.

BUTTER BRAID

- 1 cup milk
- ½ cup butter
- ⅓ cup sugar
- 2 teaspoons salt
- 2 packages active dry yeast or 2 cakes compressed yeast
- ¼ cup water*
- 3 whole eggs, beaten
- 6 to 7 cups sifted all-purpose flour
- Poppy or sesame seeds
- 1 egg white

Scald milk and pour it over butter, sugar, and salt. *Use very warm water (105°F. to 115°F.) for dry yeast; use lukewarm (80°F. to 90°F.) for compressed. Sprinkle or crumble yeast into water. Let stand a few minutes, then stir until dissolved. Stir into the cooled milk mixture. Add whole eggs and 3 cups of flour. Beat until smooth. Stir in remaining 3 to 4 cups flour or enough to make a stiff dough. Turn onto a lightly floured board and knead well. Put in a greased bowl. Cover and let rise until double in bulk. Punch down and turn out onto board. Divide in half. Cut one half of dough into 3 equal pieces and roll out into strips about 18 inches long. Braid. Place on greased cookie sheet. Divide two thirds of the remaining dough into 3 equal pieces, and braid. Place over the first braid. Form remaining dough into braid and lay over the first two. Brush all with melted butter and sprinkle with poppy seeds. Let rise until double. Brush with a mixture of egg white and 1 tablespoon water. Bake in preheated moderate oven (375°F.) for 30 to 35 minutes, or until done. Brush twice with egg and water mixture while baking.

BACON BATTER BREAD

- ½ cup water*
- 2 packages active dry yeast or 2 cakes compressed yeast
- ¼ cup firmly packed brown sugar
- 1½ cups milk, scalded
- 2 teaspoons salt
- 2 tablespoons bacon fat
- 1 egg, beaten
- 4 cups sifted all-purpose flour
- 1 cup whole wheat flour
- ¼ teaspoon ground coriander
- ⅓ cup crumbled cooked bacon

*Use very warm water (105°F. to 115°F.) for dry yeast; use lukewarm (80°F. to 90°F.) for compressed. Combine yeast, 2 tablespoons brown sugar, and water. Combine milk, salt, 2 tablespoons brown sugar, and bacon fat. Cool. When yeast mixture is bubbly add to the cooled milk mixture. Add egg and flours. Beat thoroughly for 3 minutes. Put in greased bowl. Cover and let rise for about 45 minutes. Stir in coriander and crumbled bacon. Beat for 2 minutes and pour into greased 2-quart glass casserole or two greased glass loaf pans 9 x 5 x 3 inches. Let rise until the batter reaches top of the pans. Score top with knife. Bake in preheated moderate oven (375°F.) for 35 to 40 minutes.

POTATO BREAD

- ½ cup butter
- 1½ cups cooked potato, put through a sieve
- 2 tablespoons sugar
- 2 teaspoons salt
- 1 cup milk, scalded
- ⅓ cup water*
- 2 packages active dry yeast or 2 cakes compressed yeast
- 5½ cups sifted all-purpose flour
- 1 egg white
- Sesame seeds

Add butter to hot potatoes and stir until melted. Add sugar, salt, and milk. *Use very warm water (105°F. to 115°F.) for dry yeast; use lukewarm (80°F. to 90°F.) for compressed. Sprinkle or crumble yeast into water. Let stand a few minutes; then stir until dissolved. Add to milk mixture. Stir in 3 cups of flour and beat until smooth. Gradually stir in remaining 2½ cups flour, or enough to make a firm dough. Knead for 10 minutes. Put in a greased bowl, cover, and let rise until double in bulk. Punch down and let rise again. Punch down and shape dough into a large braid, or into 2 smaller braids. Put on greased cookie sheet or into 2 greased loaf pans 9 x 5 x 3 inches. Cover and let rise. Brush with egg white which has been slightly beaten with 1 tablespoon of water. Sprinkle heavily with sesame seeds. Bake in a preheated hot oven (400°F.) for 10 minutes. Lower heat to moderate (350°F.) and bake for 30 to 35 minutes longer. Makes 1 large braid or 2 smaller braids.

COFFEECAKES AND RINGS MADE WITH YEAST

STREUSEL COFFEECAKE

- 2 tablespoons water*
- 1 package active dry yeast or 1 cake compressed yeast
- Sifted all-purpose flour (about 2½ cups)
- 1⅓ cups sugar
- 1 teaspoon salt
- Butter or margarine (about ⅔ cup)
- 3 eggs
- ½ cup dairy sour cream
- 1 teaspoon vanilla extract
- Cinnamon
- ½ cup seedless raisins

*Use very warm water (105°F. to 115°F.) for dry yeast; use lukewarm (80°F. to 90°F.) for compressed yeast. Sprinkle dry yeast or crumble cake into water. Let stand for a few minutes; then stir until dissolved. Sift 2½ cups flour, ½ cup sugar, and the salt into bowl. Cut in ½ cup butter. Add yeast, eggs, sour cream, and vanilla. Beat hard for 3 minutes. Let rise until bubbly, about 30 minutes. Beat hard one or two minutes, and chill overnight. Roll to a rectangle ¼ inch thick. Sprinkle with a mixture of ½ cup sugar, 1 tablespoon cinnamon, and the raisins. Roll up and fit into buttered 9-inch tube pan. Don't worry if roll breaks. Sprinkle with mixture of 2 tablespoons flour, 2 tablespoons butter, remaining ⅓ cup sugar, and ½ teaspoon cinnamon. Let rise until light, about 1½ hours. Bake in preheated slow oven (325°F.) for about 45 minutes.

FINNISH COFFEE BRAIDS

- 2¼ cups water*
- 1 package active dry yeast or 1 cake compressed yeast
- 1 cup, plus 3 tablespoons sugar
- 4 egg yolks
- 2½ teaspoons salt
- Melted butter or margarine
- 10 cardamom seeds, finely ground, or 1 teaspoon ground cardamom
- ⅔ cup nonfat dry milk powder
- 7 cups all-purpose flour

*Use very warm water (105°F. to 115°F.) for dry yeast; use lukewarm (80°F. to 90°F.) for compressed. Sprinkle dry yeast or crumble cake into water in large bowl of electric mixer; add 1 cup sugar. Let stand for a few minutes; then stir until dissolved. When lukewarm, add 2 egg yolks, salt, ½ cup butter, the cardamom, and dry milk. Beat with electric mixer on low speed while adding 3 cups flour. (Or beat with rotary beater.) Add remaining flour or enough to make a stiff dough, mixing well by hand. Cover and let rise until doubled. Roll out on floured board to rectangle 18 x 12 inches and cut into nine strips 12 x 2 inches. Dough will be soft. Brush each strip with melted butter. On lightly greased cookie sheet, braid 3 strips into a long (about 12-inch) coffee loaf. Repeat, making 3 loaves. Bake in preheated hot oven (400°F.) for 10 minutes. Remove from oven and quickly brush loaves with 2 egg yolks beaten with 1 teaspoon water. Sprinkle with remaining sugar. Bake in moderate oven (375°F.) for about 15 minutes.

APPLE DANISH PASTRIES

- ¼ cup water*
- 2 packages active dry yeast or 2 cakes compressed yeast
- ¾ cup milk, scalded
- Sugar
- 2 teaspoons salt
- 1⅓ cups butter or margarine
- ½ teaspoon lemon extract
- 3 eggs, beaten
- 4½ cups all-purpose flour
- 1 can (1 pound, 4 ounces) sliced apples
- 3 teaspoons cinnamon

*Use very warm water (105°F. to 115°F.) for dry yeast; use lukewarm (80°F. to 90°F.) for compressed. Sprinkle dry yeast or crumble cakes into water. Let stand a few minutes; then stir until dissolved. Pour hot milk over ⅓ cup sugar, the salt, and ⅓ cup butter. Cool to lukewarm. Add the yeast mixture. Stir in the lemon extract and eggs. Add the flour gradually. Place the dough in a greased pan 13 x 9 x 2 inches. Chill for 1 to 2 hours. Turn the chilled dough out onto a floured board. Roll into a rectangle 16 x 12 inches. Spread ⅓ cup butter or margarine over two thirds of the dough. Fold the unspread portion of the dough over half the covered portion. Fold the third section over the first two. Roll the dough to its original size and repeat this process twice, using the remaining butter. Return the dough to the refrigerator and chill overnight. Next day, divide the dough in half. Roll each half into a rectangle 14 x 9 inches. Cut into strips 14 x ¾ inches. Twist and form each strip into a spiral roll. Put a few drained apple slices in center of each. Sprinkle with the cinnamon mixed with ½ cup sugar. Cover. Let rise in a warm place, free from draft, until doubled in bulk. Bake in preheated moderate oven (375°F.) for about 12 minutes. Makes about 2 dozen.

BREAD

CINNAMON LOAF

- 2 tablespoons water*
- 1 package active dry yeast or 1 cake compressed yeast
- ⅔ cup milk, scalded
- ½ cup sugar
- 1 teaspoon salt
  Butter or margarine
- 2 eggs
- 3 cups sifted all-purpose flour
- 1½ teaspoons ground cinnamon
- 2 tablespoons melted butter or margarine

*Use very warm water (105°F. to 115°F.) for dry yeast; use lukewarm (80°F. to 90°F.) for compressed. Sprinkle dry yeast or crumble cake into water. Let stand for a few minutes; then stir until dissolved. Pour hot milk over ¼ cup sugar, the salt, and ¼ cup butter; cool to lukewarm. Add eggs, yeast, and half of flour. Beat with rotary beater or electric beater until smooth. Beat in remaining 1½ cups flour with spoon. Cover and let rise until doubled, about 1 hour. Punch down and knead lightly. Roll out on floured pastry cloth or board to a rectangle 18 x 9 inches. Spread with 2 tablespoons butter; sprinkle with remaining ¼ cup sugar mixed with the cinnamon. Roll up tightly from narrow end and put in greased loaf pan 9 x 5 x 3 inches. Brush with melted butter and let rise until doubled, about 45 minutes. Bake in preheated moderate oven (350°F.) for about 30 minutes. Cool.

YEAST ROLLS

CINNAMON ROLLS

- 2¼ cups water*
- 1 package active dry yeast or 1 cake compressed yeast
- ½ cup granulated sugar
- 2 egg yolks
  Cooking oil
- 2½ teaspoons salt
- 1 cup nonfat dry milk powder
- 7 to 8 cups sifted all-purpose flour
- 1½ cups firmly packed light brown sugar
- 1 tablespoon ground cinnamon

*Use very warm water (105°F. to 115°F.) for dry yeast; use lukewarm (80°F. to 90°F.) for compressed. Sprinkle sugar and dry yeast or crumble cake into water in large bowl of electric mixer. Let stand for a few minutes; then stir until dissolved. Add egg yolks, ⅓ cup oil, the salt, dry milk, and 2 cups flour. Beat at low speed. (Or beat with rotary beater.) Add enough of remaining 5 to 6 cups flour to make a stiff dough. Mix well. Cover and let rise until doubled. Divide dough into halves; roll each half on a floured board to form a rectangle 14 x 10 inches. Using a pastry brush, brush with oil. Sprinkle half the brown sugar and cinnamon over each rectangle. Roll up as for jelly roll. Pinch dough firmly together and brush all over with oil. Cut into 1-inch slices and place in greased pan. Cover and let rise until doubled. Bake in preheated hot oven (400°F.) for about 20 minutes. Makes about 28 rolls.

PARKERHOUSE ROLLS

- ½ cup water*
- 1 package active dry yeast or 1 cake compressed yeast
- ⅔ cup butter or margarine (about)
- ¼ cup sugar
- ½ cup boiling water
- 1 egg, beaten
- 3 cups all-purpose flour
- 1 teaspoon salt

*Use very warm water (105°F. to 115°F.) for dry yeast; use lukewarm (80°F. to 90°F.) for compressed. Sprinkle dry yeast or crumble cake into warm water. Let stand for a few minutes; then stir until dissolved. Put ½ cup butter, the sugar, and boiling water in bowl and stir until butter is melted. Cool to lukewarm; then add yeast and egg. Add flour and salt; mix well, cover and put in refrigerator for at least 24 hours. Roll on lightly floured board to ¼-inch thickness and cut with floured 2½-inch cutter. With handle of wooden spoon, make a crease in each circle to one side of center; flatten smaller half of round slightly by rolling handle of spoon toward edge. Brush with melted butter; fold thicker half over thinner half; press edges together. Put on cookie sheets and brush again with butter. Bake in preheated hot oven (400°F.) for 12 to 15 minutes. Makes about 3 dozen.

SQUASH ROLLS

- 1 cup water*
- ¾ cup sugar
- 1 package active dry yeast or 1 cake compressed yeast
  Cooking oil
- 2 teaspoons salt
- 1 cup strained, cooked winter squash
- ½ cup nonfat dry-milk powder
- 5 cups sifted all-purpose flour (about)

*Use very warm water (105°F. to 115°F.) for dry yeast; use lukewarm (80°F. to 90°F.) for compressed. Put water and sugar into large bowl of electric mixer. Sprinkle dry yeast or crumble cake into this and allow to stand for 5 minutes. Add 3 tablespoons oil, salt, squash, and dry milk. Beat well at low speed. Gradually beat in 2 cups of the flour. (Or beat with rotary beater.) Scrape beaters and add the remaining 3 cups flour by hand, mixing well. Let rise. Knead gently on a floured board. Roll to 1-inch thickness. Cut with floured 2½-inch biscuit cutter. Roll edges lightly in oil so that the baked rolls will separate readily. Put into greased pan 13 x 9 x 2 inches and allow to double in size. Bake in preheated hot oven (400°F.) for about 20 minutes. Makes about 15.

BREAD

CROISSANTS

- 3 cups all-purpose flour
- 1 teaspoon salt
- ¼ cup sugar
- ½ cup butter (or part margarine)
- 1 yeast cake or 1 envelope active dry yeast
- ½ cup water*
- 1 egg, well beaten with ½ cup milk
- ¼ pound (1 stick) butter.
- 1 egg
- 1 tablespoon milk

Sift dry ingredients. Add ½ cup butter softened to room temperature and work with fingers or pastry blender as for piecrust. Add yeast dissolved in water. Use very warm water (105°F. to 115°F.) for dry yeast; use lukewarm (80°F. to 90°F.) for compressed yeast. Then add egg beaten with milk. Mix well with hands or spoon. Cover bowl well and let stand in refrigerator at least 3 to 4 hours before using. Using a floured rolling pin, roll all the raised dough into a rectangle about ¼ inch thick on floured board. Using large shredder or kitchen grater, shred half a 4-ounce stick of cold butter over surface. Press into place with lightly floured hands, then gently fold ends of rectangle until they meet in center. Fold dough in half where edges meet. This makes an envelope (the French call it a turn). Re-flour counter and, turning narrow end of envelope toward you, roll dough in another rectangle. Shred rest of stick of butter over this and make another turn. Roll out third time, trying to keep edges straight and not letting cold butter break through soft dough. Roll gently; do not pull. After making third turn, wrap dough in waxed paper and put back in refrigerator at least 20 minutes before rolling out. You can prepare dough a day or two before you want to make the croissants. When ready to bake, roll dough in 20 by 15 inch rectangle —you should not reroll, so try to keep edges straight. Cut in 5 inch squares and cut each square in half diagonally, making triangles. Starting at wider edge, roll up each triangle. Place 2 inches apart, center point down, on lightly buttered cookie sheet and curve ends to form crescent. Brush tops with egg mixed with milk and let rise in warm room until very light, 2 to 2½ hours, depending on time of year and temperature of dough. Bake in preheated hot oven (400°F.) 15 minutes, or until rolls are golden brown. Remove from oven and serve warm or cool. Makes about 2 dozen.

CHEESE-FILLED ROLLS

- 2 tablespoons water*
- 1 package active dry yeast or 1 cake compressed yeast
- Milk (about ⅔ cup)
- Sugar (about ½ cup)
- ½ teaspoon salt
- ⅓ cup butter or margarine
- 2 eggs
- 1 teaspoon grated lemon rind
- 3¼ cups sifted all-purpose flour
- 4 ounces cream cheese
- 1 teaspoon ground cinnamon

*Use very warm water (105°F. to 115°F.) for dry yeast; use lukewarm (80°F. to 90°F.) for compressed. Sprinkle dry yeast or crumble cake into water. Let stand for a few minutes; then stir until dissolved. Scald ½ cup milk and pour over ⅓ cup sugar, the salt, and butter. Cool to lukewarm. Stir in yeast, 1 whole egg, 1 egg yolk, and lemon rind. Beat in 1½ cups flour; then stir in remaining 1¾ cups. Cover and let rise until doubled, about 1½ hours. Punch down. Roll on floured surface to form a rectangle, 14 x 10½ inches. Cut into twelve squares. Soften cheese with 1½ tablespoons milk. Spread 2 teaspoons on each square; fold each over into a triangle. Put on greased cookie sheets and let rise until light, about 30 minutes. Brush with 1 egg white beaten with 2 teaspoons water. Sprinkle with 2 tablespoons sugar mixed with cinnamon. Bake in preheated moderate oven (350°F.) for 10 to 15 minutes. Makes 12 rolls.

POTATO ROLLS

- 1 cup water*
- 1 package active dry yeast or 1 cake compressed yeast
- 2 eggs
- ⅓ cup sugar
- 3 teaspoons salt
- Cooking oil
- 1½ cups riced warm cooked potato
- ½ cup nonfat dry-milk powder
- 4½ to 5 cups sifted all-purpose flour

*Use very warm water (105°F. to 115°F.) for dry yeast; use lukewarm (80°F. to 90°F.) for compressed. Sprinkle or crumble yeast into water. Let stand for 10 minutes; then stir until dissolved. Into large bowl of electric mixer put the eggs, sugar, salt, ⅓ cup oil, potato, milk, and yeast mixture. Beat at low speed until well blended. (Or beat with rotary beater.) Gradually add 2 cups flour and beat well. Add remaining 2½ to 3 cups flour by hand. Mix until the dough forms a ball away from the sides of the bowl. Let rise until double in size. Roll out on a floured board until about 1½ inches thick. Cut with floured 2¼-inch biscuit cutter. Roll edges lightly in oil and put into baking pan 13 x 9 x 2 inches. Allow to rise again. Bake in preheated hot oven (400°F.) for about 25 minutes. Makes about 20.

Potato Rolls

BREAD

REFRIGERATOR SESAME BREAKFAST BUNS

- 1 package active dry yeast
- 1 teaspoon salt
- 2 cups whole-wheat flour
- ½ cup wheat germ
- 2½ cups all-purpose flour
- ¼ cup margarine
- 2½ cups milk
-   Vegetable oil
- 1 egg, slightly beaten
-   Sesame seed

Combine first 5 ingredients in mixing bowl and stir to blend. Melt margarine in small saucepan over low heat, add milk and heat to lukewarm (105°F. to 115°F.). Pour over dry ingredients and stir to blend. Turn dough out on floured board and knead until smooth and elastic. Shape in a roll and cut in 12 equal pieces. Shape each piece with palm of hand, using a little flour if necessary, in a round bun, then in oblong bun. Put on lightly oiled baking sheet. Brush well with oil. Cover loosely with plastic wrap and refrigerate overnight or 24 hours. Let stand at room temperature while heating oven to 400°F. Cut a deep slit lengthwise in each roll with sharp knife. Brush with egg and sprinkle with sesame seed. Bake 25 to 30 minutes, or until light brown and done. Cool, covered with towel if a soft crust is desired, on rack. Makes 12.

LITTLE BRIOCHES

- ¼ cup water*
- 2 packages active dry yeast or 2 cakes compressed yeast
- ¾ cup milk, scalded
- 1 cup butter or margarine
- ½ cup sugar
- 2 teaspoons salt
- 6½ cups sifted all-purpose flour
- 5 eggs
- 1 tablespoon cold water

*Use very warm water (105°F. to 115°F.) for dry yeast; use lukewarm (80°F. to 90°F.) for compressed. Sprinkle or crumble yeast into water. Let stand a few minutes; then stir until dissolved. Pour hot milk over butter, sugar, and salt; cool to lukewarm. Add 2 cups flour and beat well. Add yeast and beat. Cover and let rise until bubbly. Stir down. Add 4 eggs and beat well. Add remaining 4½ cups flour using just enough to make a soft dough. Turn out on floured pastry cloth or board and knead until smooth and satiny. Put into greased bowl, cover and let rise until doubled, about 1½ hours. Punch down and divide dough into 24 pieces. From each piece, cut a small piece. Shape large pieces into balls and put into well-greased 2¾-inch muffin cups. Shape small pieces in balls. Make indentation in center of each large ball by pressing with thumb. Press small balls into indentations. Let rise until doubled, about 45 minutes. Mix 1 egg and cold water. Brush rolls with mixture. Bake in preheated moderate oven (375°F.) for 15 minutes. To freeze, wrap in foil. Reheat, wrapped, in slow oven (300°F.).

NEW-WORLD RECIPES FOR OLD-WORLD BREADS

The fabulous breads you can't buy anymore, made with hearty, wholesome flours and grains by all-new methods and with an innovative twist here and there.

OLD-FASHIONED OATMEAL MUFFINS

- ¾ cup regular rolled oats
- ¾ cup plus 2 tablespoons all-purpose flour
- 2 tablespoons firmly packed light-brown sugar
- 1½ teaspoons baking powder
- ½ teaspoon baking soda
- ½ teaspoon salt
- 1 teaspoon cinnamon
- ¼ cup butter or margarine
- 1 egg
- ¾ cup buttermilk
-   Sugar-cinnamon mixture

Combine first 7 ingredients in mixing bowl and mix well. Cut in butter. Beat egg and buttermilk together and pour over first mixture. Mix only until dry ingredients are moistened. Put 12 2½-inch paper-lined foil muffin cups on baking sheet and fill two thirds full. Sprinkle tops with sugar-cinnamon mixture. Bake in preheated hot oven (425°F.) 15 to 20 minutes. Serve warm with butter.

Note: Muffins can be baked in greased muffin cups, if preferred.

SWEDISH WHOLE-WHEAT RUSKS [Grahamsskorpor]

- 1 package active dry yeast
- ¼ cup warm water (105°F. to 115°F.)
- 2 tablespoons shortening
- 2 cups milk
- 1 teaspoon salt
- 4 cups whole-wheat flour
- 2 cups all-purpose flour
- ½ cup margarine
- 1 cup firmly packed light-brown sugar

Dissolve yeast in water in mixing bowl. Melt shortening over low heat in saucepan. Add milk and heat to warm (105°F. to 115°F.). Add to yeast with salt, whole-wheat flour and 1 cup all-purpose flour. Stir to blend. Turn out on lightly floured board and knead until smooth and elastic. Put back in greased bowl, cover and let rise in warm place 1 hour. Meanwhile cream margarine and sugar until light; beat into risen dough. Turn out on heavily floured board, using remaining flour. Knead until smooth and elastic. Divide dough in 4 equal pieces. Shape each in long roll and cut in 10 pieces. Shape in round even buns and then in oblongs slightly tapered at ends. Put on baking sheets and let rise in warm place 30 minutes, or until very light. Bake in preheated hot oven (400°F.)

12 to 15 minutes, or until light brown. Put on rack, cover with towel and cool. Split with fork in 2 halves. Put on sheets, split side up, and score lightly crosswise about 3 times. Toast in preheated hot oven (425°F.) 6 to 7 minutes, or until well browned. Turn off heat, put rusks in large roasting pan, return to oven and dry with oven door ajar 3 hours, or until completely dry. Store tightly covered. Good with butter and honey for tea. Makes about 80.

FINNISH-STYLE HEALTH BREAD

1 package active dry yeast
¼ cup very warm water (105°F. to 115°F.)
2¼ cups buttermilk
1 teaspoon salt
1¼ cups rye flour, or rye meal
1¼ cups whole wheat flour
    Wheat germ
2 cups all-purpose flour

Dissolve yeast in water in mixing bowl. Add next 4 ingredients and ¼ cup wheat germ and stir with wooden spoon until well blended. Gradually add all-purpose flour, beating until smooth. Turn out on floured board and knead until smooth and elastic. Cover loosely and let rest on board 30 minutes. Divide dough in 2 equal pieces and pat each in round cake 6 inches in diameter. Brush with water and press top into wheat germ. Put on lightly greased baking sheet. Let rise 1 hour, or until doubled in bulk. Cut a crisscross pattern on top with very sharp knife. Bake in preheated hot oven (400°F.) 30 minutes, or until done. Cool on rack.

SWEDISH STEAMED RYE LOG
[Kubb]

1 package active dry yeast
1¼ cups warm water (105°F. to 115°F.)
1 teaspoon salt
¾ cup molasses
4 cups whole-rye flour
1 cup all-purpose flour

Dissolve yeast in water in mixing bowl. Add next 3 ingredients and stir with wooden spoon until well blended. Gradually add all-purpose flour, beating until smooth. Turn out on floured board and knead until smooth and elastic. Shape dough in a ball and press into well-greased 2-quart vegetable-shortening can (3 pound size) or other metal can of similar shape and volume. Cover with plastic wrap and let rise in warm place 2½ hours, or until almost doubled in bulk. Cover can tightly with foil, place on rack in deep kettle and fill kettle with warm water up to two thirds the height of can. Cover with lid and bring to boil. Reduce heat and simmer 2½ hours. Replace water during cooking if needed. Turn out gently and cool well wrapped in clean towel. To serve, cut lengthwise in 4 wedges and thinly slice each wedge crosswise. Good with butter or for open tea sandwiches.

FENNEL RYE CAKES

2 packages active dry yeast
3 cups very warm water (105°F. to 115°F.)
¼ cup margarine, softened
1 teaspoon salt
1 tablespoon light fennel seed, lightly crushed
2 tablespoons molasses
4 cups whole-rye flour
3½ cups all-purpose flour
1 tablespoon butter or margarine

Dissolve yeast in water in large mixing bowl. Add next 5 ingredients and stir with wooden spoon until well blended. Gradually add all-purpose flour, beating until smooth. Turn out on floured board and knead until smooth and elastic. Divide dough in 4 equal parts. Roll each to a round cake about 8½ inches in diameter. Cut out a 1¼ inch hole in center and add scraps to next piece of dough before rolling out. Put on lightly greased baking sheets and prick with fork. Let rise in warm place 50 to 60 minutes. Bake in preheated hot oven (425°F.) 15 minutes, or until well browned and done. Brush with butter mixed with small amount of hot water. Cool on rack covered with a clean towel. Cut in wedges, split and serve with butter, if desired. Makes four 8½ inch cakes.
Note: Hole in center can be pulled instead of cut, if preferred.

RAISED CURRANT MUFFINS

1 package active dry yeast
¼ cup very warm water (105°F. to 115°F.)
¼ cup butter or margarine, melted
½ teaspoon salt
¼ cup sugar
½ cup dry currants
2 eggs, slightly beaten (2 tablespoons reserved)
¼ cup yellow cornmeal
    Milk
    Wheat germ
2¼ cups all-purpose flour

Dissolve yeast in water in mixing bowl. Add next 6 ingredients, 1 cup milk and ¼ cup wheat germ and stir with wooden spoon until well blended. Gradually add all-purpose flour, beating until smooth. Cover loosely with plastic wrap and let rise in warm place 1 hour, or until doubled in bulk. Beat well and fill 18 well-greased 2½-inch muffin cups two thirds full. Let rise 20 to 30 minutes, or until muffin cup is full. Beat reserved egg with 2 tablespoons milk. Brush tops carefully and sprinkle with wheat germ. Bake in preheated moderate oven (375°F.) 15 to 20 minutes, or until well browned and done. Cool on rack 5 minutes. Loosen carefully around edges and turn out. Split and serve slightly warm with butter. Good with tea, coffee or milk. Makes about 18 muffins.

BUCKWHEAT-BANANA BISCUITS

¼ cup buckwheat flour
1¾ cups whole-wheat flour
¼ cup all-purpose flour
3 teaspoons baking powder
½ teaspoon baking soda
1 teaspoon sugar
½ teaspoon salt
½ cup butter
½ cup dairy sour cream
½ cup (about 1 medium) mashed ripe banana
¼ cup milk

BREAD

Combine first 7 ingredients in mixing bowl. Cut in butter until mixture resembles cornmeal. Add remaining ingredients and stir just to moisten dry ingredients. Turn out on lightly floured board and knead 10 turns. Roll gently to ½ inch thickness, prick with fork and cut in rounds with 2¼ inch cutter. Reroll scraps and cut. Put on ungreased baking sheet and bake in preheated very hot oven (450°F.) 12 to 15 minutes, or until well browned. Split and serve warm with butter and cheese, or jam, if desired. Makes about 1½ dozen biscuits.

SESAME AND WHEAT-GERM CORN STICKS

- ¼ cup all-purpose flour
- 3 tablespoons sugar
- ½ teaspoon salt
- ¾ teaspoon baking soda
- 1 cup yellow cornmeal
- ½ cup wheat germ
- ¼ cup sesame seed
- 1 cup buttermilk
- ⅓ cup vegetable oil
- 1 egg

Mix thoroughly dry ingredients in medium bowl. Combine buttermilk and oil and blend in egg; add all at once to dry ingredients and stir just until dry ingredients are moistened. Turn into well-greased corn-stick or muffin pans, filling cups about two thirds full. Bake in preheated moderate oven (350°F.) about 20 minutes. Makes 1 dozen.

WHOLE-WHEAT ENGLISH MUFFINS

- 1 cup milk
- 2 tablespoons sugar
- 1 teaspoon salt
- 3 tablespoons margarine
- 1 cup warm water (105°F. to 115°F.)
- 1 envelope active dry yeast
- 1½ cups whole-wheat flour
- 3½ cups all-purpose flour (about)
- Cornmeal

Scald milk and stir in next 3 ingredients; cool to warm (105°F. to 115°F.). Put water into large warm bowl. Sprinkle with yeast, then stir until dissolved. Stir in milk mixture, then stir in whole-wheat flour and 1½ cups all-purpose flour. Beat with spoon until smooth. Add enough additional flour to make a stiff dough. Turn out onto floured board and knead 2 to 3 minutes, or until dough can be formed into ball (dough may be slightly sticky). Put in greased bowl, turning to grease top. Cover and let rise in warm place 1 hour, or until doubled. Punch dough down and divide dough in half. On board heavily sprinkled with cornmeal, pat each half to ½ inch thick. Cut with 3 inch cutter and put about 2 inches apart on ungreased baking sheets. Let rise in warm place ½ hour, or until doubled. Cook on lightly greased medium-hot griddle or skillet about 10 minutes on each side until well browned on both sides. Cool on racks. To serve, split muffins and toast. Makes about 18.

WHOLE-WHEAT SCONES

- 2½ cups whole-wheat flour
- 2 cups all-purpose flour
- 1 teaspoon salt
- 2 tablespoons sugar
- 5 teaspoons baking powder
- ½ cup margarine
- 2 cups buttermilk
- Finely chopped nuts, grated Parmesan cheese, sesame seed or dillweed

Combine first 5 ingredients in mixing bowl. Cut in margarine until well distributed. Add buttermilk and stir just until moistened. Spoon dough onto greased baking sheets in 4 inch to 6 inch round cakes. Mark each cake in quarters with floured knife. Sprinkle with nuts, cheese, etc. and press down into dough. Bake in preheated very hot oven (450°F.) 12 minutes, or until well browned. Cool slightly on rack and break each in 4 pieces. Serve split, with butter and marmalade. Makes 16.
Note: Especially good toasted.

QUICK BREADS

RICH MUFFINS

- 2 cups sifted all-purpose flour
- 2½ teaspoons baking powder
- 2 tablespoons sugar
- ¾ teaspoon salt
- ½ cup shortening
- 1 egg, well beaten
- ¾ cup milk

Sift dry ingredients together. Cut in shortening. Combine egg and milk and add all at once to flour mixture. Then stir only until dry ingredients are dampened. Turn into greased muffin pans, filling each about ⅔ full. Bake in preheated hot oven (400°F.) for about 25 minutes. Makes about 10 muffins.

Cranberry Muffins

Use recipe for Rich Muffins. Chop 1 cup cranberries, sprinkle with 2 tablespoons sugar, and fold into batter. Bake as directed. Makes 12 muffins.

Bacon Muffins

Use recipe for Rich Muffins. Add ½ cup crumbled crisp bacon to flour mixture. Bake as directed.

Apricot Muffins

Use recipe for Rich Muffins. Add ½ cup cut dried apricots to flour mixture. Bake as directed.

BREAD

DOUBLE-CORN MUFFINS

1⅓ cups all-purpose flour
3 teaspoons baking powder
1 teaspoon salt
2 tablespoons sugar
¾ cup yellow cornmeal
2 eggs, beaten
1 cup milk
¼ cup butter or margarine, melted
¼ teaspoon dried rosemary
1 cup cut fresh corn

Sift first 4 ingredients. Add remaining ingredients and mix only enough to dampen dry ingredients. Fill greased 2½-inch muffin cups about ⅔ full. Bake in preheated hot oven (400°F.) about 25 minutes. Makes 12 muffins.

PINWHEEL ONION ROLLS

4 onions, thinly sliced
2 tablespoons butter
2¼ teaspoons salt
Dash of cayenne
2 cups sifted all-purpose flour
3 teaspoons baking powder
¼ cup shortening
⅔ cup milk
1 egg, beaten
⅓ cup undiluted evaporated milk

Cook onions in butter until golden; cool. Add ¾ teaspoon salt and cayenne. Sift flour, baking powder, and 1 teaspoon salt. Cut in shortening. Add milk; mix only enough to dampen dry ingredients. Roll into rectangle 12 x 8 inches. Spread with onions; roll up as for jelly roll. Cut into eight 1-inch slices. Put flat side down, in greased pan 13 x 9 x 2 inches. Mix egg, evaporated milk, and remaining ½ teaspoon salt. Brush over rolls. Bake in preheated hot oven (400°F.) about 25 minutes.

RICH POTATO BISCUITS

1 cup prepared instant mashed potato (2 servings, prepared as directed on label)
2 cups all-purpose flour
1 teaspoon salt
1 cup butter or margarine
2 tablespoons dairy sour cream
4 egg yolks
Sesame or caraway seed

Refrigerate potato until cold. Mix flour and salt and cut in butter. Add sour cream, 3 unbeaten egg yolks and potato. Stir with fork until blended. Knead 2 or 3 turns, then roll thin on floured board and fold in quarters. Chill 30 minutes, then roll again and fold. Repeat 3 times. Then roll ¼ inch thick and cut with floured 2½ inch cutter. Put on ungreased baking sheet and brush with remaining egg yolk slightly beaten. Sprinkle with seed and bake in preheated hot oven (400°F.) 15 to 20 minutes. Makes about 3 dozen.

RAISIN BRAN MUFFINS

3 tablespoons soft butter or margarine
¼ cup molasses
1 egg
1 cup shredded bran cereal
¾ cup buttermilk
1 cup sifted all-purpose flour
1 teaspoon baking powder
½ teaspoon each baking soda and salt
⅓ cup seedless raisins

Cream butter and molasses. Add egg and beat well. Add bran and buttermilk and let stand for 5 minutes. Add to sifted dry ingredients and mix only enough to dampen. Add raisins. Fill greased 2¾-inch muffin cups ⅔ full. Bake in preheated hot oven (400°F.) for about 25 minutes. Makes 9 large muffins.

BAKING POWDER BISCUITS

2 cups sifted all-purpose flour
2½ teaspoons baking powder
¾ teaspoon salt
⅓ cup shortening
¾ cup milk

Sift flour, baking powder, and salt together. Cut in shortening. Add milk and stir with fork until soft dough is formed. Turn out on lightly floured board and knead 20 turns. Pat or roll lightly ½-inch thick. Cut with floured 2-inch cutter. Bake on ungreased cookie sheet in preheated very hot oven (450°F.) for 12 to 15 minutes. Makes about 14 biscuits.

FRUIT BUNS

2 cups buttermilk baking mix
1 tablespoon sugar
⅛ teaspoon ground nutmeg
¾ cup milk
½ cup soft butter or margarine
Fruit Filling

Combine mix, sugar, and nutmeg. Add milk and stir until mixture stiffens. Turn out on floured board and roll ⅛-inch thick. Spread with ¼ cup butter, fold dough in half, and roll out again. Spread with remaining ¼ cup butter. Fold and roll into a rectangle 18 x 6 inches. Cut into twelve 3-inch squares. Put squares in greased large muffin pans and fill with Fruit Filling. Pull corners of dough together; pinch to seal. Bake in preheated moderate oven (375°F.) for about 25 minutes.

Fruit Filling. Beat 1 egg, ½ cup sugar, 1 teaspoon fresh lemon juice, and ½ teaspoon ground cinnamon. Stir in 6 chopped drained cooked dried apricots, 3 chopped pitted cooked prunes, and 1 chopped cooked dried peach. (Or use ⅔ cup any drained stewed fruit.)

Coffee Cakes and Buns

POPOVERS

- 2 eggs
- 1 cup milk
- ½ to 1 tablespoon melted butter
- 1 cup sifted all-purpose flour
- ¼ teaspoon salt

Beat eggs slightly; add milk and butter; then add flour and salt. Beat vigorously for 2 minutes. Pour batter into very hot greased custard cups or iron popover pans, filling ⅔ full. Bake in preheated hot oven (425°F.) for about 40 minutes. Serve at once. Makes 6 large popovers.

Cheese Popovers

Use recipe for Popovers. Sprinkle filled pans with ¼ cup grated sharp Cheddar cheese before baking.

Whole-Wheat Popovers

Use recipe for Popovers. Add 2 teaspoons melted butter to eggs and milk. Substitute ½ cup whole-wheat flour for half of white flour. Mix and bake.

Almond Popovers

Use recipe for Popovers. Add ⅓ cup ground blanched almonds to sifted flour and salt. Mix and bake.

BUTTERMILK WAFFLES

- 3 eggs, separated
- 1½ cups buttermilk
- ⅓ cup melted shortening
- 2 cups sifted cake flour
- 2 teaspoons baking powder
- ½ teaspoon baking soda
- ¾ teaspoon salt
- 1 tablespoon sugar

Beat egg yolks; add buttermilk and shortening. Add to sifted dry ingredients; mix only enough to dampen dry ingredients. Fold in stiffly beaten egg whites. Bake in hot waffle iron. Makes 6 servings.

APPLE-BUTTERMILK WAFFLES

Use recipe for Buttermilk Waffles. Add to batter 2 finely chopped peeled apples and 1 teaspoon ground cinnamon. Serve with maple-flavored syrup or honey.

BACON-BUTTERMILK WAFFLES

Use recipe for Buttermilk Waffles. Dice and cook 6 slices of bacon. Substitute bacon fat for equal part of shortening. Add bacon to batter. Serve with syrup.

BREAD

CURRANT SCONES

- 2 cups all-purpose flour
- 1½ teaspoons cream of tartar
- ¾ teaspoon baking soda
- 1 teaspoon salt
- ½ cup soft butter or margarine
- ½ cup dry currants
- 1 whole egg
- 1 cup buttermilk (about)
- 1 egg yolk
- water
- Sugar

Sift flour, cream of tartar, soda, and salt into bowl. Cut in butter. Add currants, whole egg, and enough buttermilk to make a soft dough. Mix and turn out on well-floured board. Knead a few times, then roll ½-inch thick. Cut into 2-inch diamonds. Put on cookie sheets and prick tops several times with fork. Beat egg yolk with a little cold water and brush on scones. Sprinkle with sugar. Bake in preheated hot over (425°F.) about 15 minutes. Makes about 2 dozen.

SESAME-SEED DIPS

- 2¼ cups sifted all-purpose flour
- 1 tablespoon sugar
- 3½ teaspoons baking powder
- 1½ teaspoons salt
- 1 cup milk
- ⅓ cup butter or margarine
- Sesame seed

Sift dry ingredients into bowl. Add milk and mix well. Turn out on well-floured board and sprinkle lightly with flour. Knead about 10 turns. Roll out, making a rectangle about 12 x 8 inches. With floured knife, cut strips ½ x 4 inches. Meanwhile, melt butter in pan 13 x 9 x 2 inches in preheated very hot oven (450°F.). Remove pan from oven and dip strips into butter, covering all sides. Lay in rows in the same pan, sprinkle with sesame seed, and bake about 15 minutes. Makes 48.

PANCAKES

- 1¼ cups sifted all-purpose flour
- 1½ teaspoons baking powder
- ¾ teaspoon salt
- 1 tablespoon sugar
- 1 egg, well beaten
- 1 cup milk
- 3 tablespoons shortening, melted
- fat for frying

Sift dry ingredients. Mix egg and milk; add to dry ingredients with the shortening. Mix only enough to dampen dry ingredients. Batter will be lumpy. Bake on hot greased griddle until browned on both sides. Turn only once. Serve hot with butter and syrup. Makes 10 to 12. For thinner pancakes, increase milk.

Cheese Pancakes

Use recipe for Pancakes. Add ½ cup grated Cheddar cheese to batter.

Bran Pancakes

Use recipe for Pancakes, but reduce flour to 1 cup and add ¾ cup bran flakes to dry ingredients. Makes 8 to 10 pancakes.

SWEET BREADS

COCONUT BREAD

- 3 cups sifted all-purpose flour
- 3 teaspoons baking powder
- ½ teaspoon salt
- 1 cup sugar
- 1 cup shredded coconut
- 1 egg, beaten
- 1 cup milk
- 1 teaspoon vanilla extract

Sift dry ingredients and add coconut. Mix thoroughly. Combine liquid ingredients and stir into the dry ingredients. Blend carefully. Let stand for 20 minutes. Pour into well-greased loaf pan 9 x 5 x 3 inches. Bake in preheated moderate oven (350°F.) for 45 to 50 minutes.

ORANGE NUT BREAD

- 2½ cups sifted all-purpose flour
- 3 teaspoons baking powder
- 1 teaspoon salt
- 1 cup sugar
- ¼ cup shortening
- ¾ cup milk
- ¼ cup fresh orange juice
- 1 egg
- 1 tablespoon grated orange rind
- 1 cup chopped nuts

Sift dry ingredients into bowl. Cut in shortening with pastry blender or 2 knives. Add milk, orange juice, and egg. Mix only enough to dampen dry ingredients. Add grated rind and nuts. Pour into greased loaf pan 9 x 5 x 3 inches; spreading batter to corners and leaving a slight depression in center. Let stand for 20 minutes. Bake in preheated moderate oven (350°F.) for about 1 hour. Let stand for 5 minutes; then turn out on rack to cool. Store overnight before slicing.

BREAD

CORN BREADS

CORN STICKS

1 cup sifted all-purpose flour
¾ cup yellow cornmeal
2 teaspoons baking powder
¾ teaspoon salt
2 tablespoons sugar
1 egg, beaten
¾ cup milk
¼ cup melted shortening or cooking oil

Sift dry ingredients. Add egg, milk, and shortening. Stir until just blended. Mix only enough to dampen dry ingredients. Heat greased corn-stick pans; pour in batter. Bake in preheated very hot oven (450°F.) for about 20 minutes. Makes 8 large corn sticks.

CUSTARDY CORN BREAD

¾ cup white cornmeal
¼ cup sifted all-purpose flour
1 to 2 tablespoons sugar
½ teaspoon salt
1 teaspoon baking powder
1½ cups plus 2 tablespoons milk
1 egg, well beaten
2 tablespoons butter

Sift dry ingredients; stir in 1 cup plus 2 tablespoons milk and the egg. Mix only enough to dampen dry ingredients. Melt butter in 8-inch square pan and pour mixture into pan. Pour remaining ½ cup milk over batter; do not stir. Bake in preheated hot oven (400°F.) for about 30 minutes. Serve as you would spoon bread. Makes 4 to 6 servings.

PINEAPPLE UPSIDE-DOWN CORN BREAD

1 can (1 pound 4½ ounces) sliced pineapple, drained
½ cup firmly packed brown sugar
2 tablespoons butter or margarine
1 cup all-purpose flour
1 cup cornmeal (not water-ground)
4 teaspoons baking powder
¼ cup granulated sugar
½ teaspoon salt
1 egg
1 cup milk
¼ cup soft shortening

Arrange pineapple slices in greased 9 inch square pan, cutting slices in half if necessary to fit. Blend brown sugar and butter and sprinkle on pineapple. Mix flour and next 4 ingredients. Add egg, milk and shortening and mix well. Pour over pineapple and bake in preheated hot oven (425°F.) about 25 minutes. Let stand a few minutes, then turn out and cut in squares.

HUSH PUPPIES

2 cups water-ground cornmeal
1½ teaspoons salt
1 teaspoon sugar
2 teaspoons baking powder
1 tablespoon instant minced onion
2 eggs, beaten
½ cup milk
Fat for deep frying

Mix first 5 ingredients. Add eggs and milk; mix well. Shape into balls the size of a large walnut. Fry in hot deep fat (375°F. on a frying thermometer) until well browned and done, turning once. Drain on absorbent paper. Makes 4 servings.

DATE-NUT CORN BREAD

1 cup all-purpose flour
1 cup cornmeal (not water-ground)
4 teaspoons baking powder
¼ cup sugar
½ teaspoon salt
1 egg
1 cup milk
¼ cup soft shortening
½ cup each chopped dates and nuts

Mix first five ingredients. Add egg, milk, and shortening and mix well. Stir in dates and nuts and pour into greased 9 inch square pan. Bake in preheated hot oven (425°F.) 25 minutes.

LITTLE BREADS, JIFFY BREADS, AND PASTRIES

ANISE CASSEROLE BREAD

1 package (13¾ ounces) hot-roll mix
¼ cup warm water (105°F. to 115°F.)
¼ cup margarine
½ cup milk
¼ teaspoon salt
¼ cup sugar
1½ teaspoons aniseed, lightly crushed
2 eggs, slightly beaten

In mixing bowl, dissolve yeast (from hot-roll mix) in water. Melt margarine, add milk and heat to warm (105°F. to 115°F.); add yeast mixture with salt, sugar, 1 teaspoon aniseed, eggs and hot-roll mix. Beat with wooden spoon until smooth. Pour into well greased deep 1-quart casserole and sprinkle top with remaining ½ teaspoon seed. Cover loosely and let rise in warm place 40 minutes. Bake in preheated hot oven (400°F.) about 15 minutes; reduce heat to 350°F. and bake 20 to 25 minutes longer. Turn out and cool on rack. Serve in ½-inch slices with butter and jam. Good toasted.

BREAD

WALNUT-FILLED "DANISH" PASTRIES

- ¾ cup minced walnuts (use knife or chop in blender)
- ½ cup granulated sugar
- 1 egg white, slightly beaten
- 1 package (13¾ ounces) hot-roll mix
- ¼ cup warm water (105°F. to 115°F.)
- ½ cup milk
- 1 whole egg, slightly beaten
- 2 sticks margarine, well chilled and sliced ⅛ inch thick
- 1 egg yolk beaten with 2 teaspoons milk or cream
- Crushed slivered unblanched almonds
- Confectioners' sugar frosting or confectioners' sugar

Blend walnuts, granulated sugar and egg white; set aside. In mixing bowl, dissolve yeast (from hot-roll mix) in water, add milk, whole egg and hot-roll mix and stir until blended. Turn out on lightly floured board and knead until smooth. Roll into rectangle 12 x 10 inches. Cover two-thirds of rectangle with slices of margarine, leaving a 1-inch border. Fold uncovered third of dough over margarine on center third, then over on margarine on remaining third. Align long side of dough with front edge of board; roll dough gently into rectangle 12 x 10 inches; fold in thirds, turn and repeat rolling, folding and turning once more. Wrap in plastic and chill 45 minutes. Divide dough in half. Roll each half on lightly floured board into rectangle 25 x 5 inches; cut into 20 2½-inch squares. Put ½ to ¾ teaspoon walnut mixture in center of each square. Fold corners to center, pinching points together. Or shape in triangles by folding squares almost double, pinching edges together; or let only 2 opposite corners meet in the center. Put on baking sheets and let rise at room temperature 1 hour, or until very light. Brush tops with egg-yolk mixture and sprinkle with almonds. Bake in preheated hot oven (425°F.) 10 minutes, or until golden brown. Remove to rack to cool. Spread with Confectioners'-Sugar Frosting or sift confectioners' sugar over tops. Best served freshly baked. Makes about 40.

Note: Pastries can be wrapped, frozen and reheated, if desired. Any kind of nuts can be used in filling, or fill with preserves.

LEMONY CURRANT AND CREAM-CHEESE BUNS

- 1 package (13¾ ounces) hot-roll mix
- ¾ cup warm water (105°F. to 115°F.)
- 1 egg, slightly beaten
- 1 package (8 ounces) cream cheese, softened
- Grated rind of 1 lemon
- ½ cup dry currants
- 1 cup sifted confectioners' sugar
- 1 tablespoon lemon juice

In mixing bowl; dissolve yeast (from hot-roll mix) in water. Mix in egg and hot roll mix. Turn out on lightly floured board and knead until smooth. Put dough in lightly greased mixing bowl. Cover and let rise in warm place 30 minutes, or until light. Meanwhile combine cream cheese, lemon rind and currants and mix well; set aside. Turn dough out on floured board and knead until smooth. Roll rectangle 20 x 10 inches and spread with cream-cheese mixture. Starting from long side, roll up tightly. Cut in 20 slices, place in greased 13 x 9 x 2 inch baking pan, cover and let rise in warm place 40 minutes, or until almost doubled. Bake in preheated moderate oven (350°F.) 30 minutes, or until done. Cool on rack. Beat confectioners' sugar with lemon juice until smooth and spread on buns.

WHEAT GERM AND SESAME SQUARES

- Margarine, softened
- 4 tablespoons sesame seed
- 1 package (13¾ ounces) hot-roll mix
- 1 cup warm water (105°F. to 115°F.)
- 1 egg, slightly beaten
- ½ cup wheat germ

Grease a 13 x 9 x 2 inch baking pan with margarine. Sprinkle bottom with 2 tablespoons sesame seed and set aside. In mixing bowl, dissolve yeast (from hot-roll mix) in water. Stir in 2 tablespoons margarine, egg, wheat germ and hot-roll mix. Turn out on lightly floured board and knead until smooth. Roll to a rectangle and press into bottom of prepared pan. Brush top with 1 tablespoon melted margarine and sprinkle with remaining 2 tablespoons seed. With pastry wheel or sharp knife, cut in 15 pieces. Cover and let rise in warm place 45 minutes, or until light. Bake in preheated hot oven (400°F.) 20 minutes, or until done. Cool slightly on rack, then break in squares.

BREAD

CHEESE-FILLED RING

1 (13¾ ounces) hot-roll mix
¾ cup warm water (105°F. to 115°F.)
1 teaspoon each dried oregano and dried basil
1 whole egg, slightly beaten
1 cup coarsely shredded sharp Cheddar cheese
  Grated Parmesan cheese
  Parsley flakes
  Paprika
1 egg yolk beaten with 2 teaspoons milk or cream

In mixing bowl, dissolve yeast (from hot-roll mix) in water. Mix in herbs, whole egg and hot-roll mix. Turn out on lightly floured board and knead until smooth. Put dough in lightly greased mixing bowl. Cover and let rise in warm place 30 minutes, or until light. Turn out on floured board and knead until smooth. Roll into rectangle 15 x 10 inches. Sprinkle with Cheddar cheese, 3 tablespoons Parmesan cheese, parsley flakes and paprika to taste. Starting from long side, roll up tightly. Arrange on greased baking sheet, seam side down, in a ring, pinching ends together. Cut slashes ½ inch deep on top at 2-inch intervals. Let rise in warm place 30 to 40 minutes, or until light. Brush with egg-yolk mixture and sprinkle with 1 to 2 tablespoons Parmesan cheese. Bake in preheated moderate oven (350°F.) 30 to 35 minutes, or until done. Remove to rack to cool slightly. Serve in thin wedges with soups or salads. Makes 8 servings.

QUICKIES MADE WITH REFRIGERATOR CRESCENT ROLLS

Several brands of refrigerator crescent rolls are widely available throughout the country. One type weighs 8 ounces and contains 4 rectangles. The other, 7 ounces, contains 3 thicker rectangles. Both types should be unrolled and separated in rectangles. Each rectangle has a seam that divides it into two triangles. Pinch the seams together. If the triangles are already separated, put them together in pairs to form rectangles, pinching edges. The thicker rectangles of the 7-ounce package should be flattened slightly before proceeding with recipe.

CINNAMON SNAILS

Spread each rectangle with soft butter and sprinkle generously with granulated sugar and cinnamon. Roll up, starting at long side. Cut in 1¼-inch pieces and place, cut side up, on ungreased baking sheet. Brush tops with beaten egg, if desired. Bake in preheated moderate oven (375°F.) 10 to 12 minutes. Remove to rack. Makes about

BUTTER-NUT COMBS

Melt 2 tablespoons butter, stir in 1 teaspoon vanilla extract and set aside. Combine 3 tablespoons each finely chopped pecans and coarse or regular granulated sugar. With pastry wheel, cut each rectangle in 4 or 5 strips crosswise; fold strips in half lengthwise and cut 3 or 4 slips ½-inch deep along fold. Dip strips first in vanilla butter and then in nut mixture. Arrange on ungreased baking sheet in slight curve with slits separated. Bake in preheated moderate oven (375°F.) 10 to 12 minutes. Makes about 16.

WALNUT-RAISIN SWEETS

Combine ¼ cup each finely chopped walnuts, chopped golden raisins, and sugar with 2 tablespoons heavy cream and mix well. Spread filling in lengthwise strip down center of rectangles. Fold dough in thirds lengthwise. Turn upside down and cut in 1-inch pieces with serrated knife. Brush tops with beaten egg and dip in mixture of finely chopped walnuts and sugar. Bake in tiny individual baking cups in moderate oven (375°F.) 10 to 12 minutes. Cool on rack. Makes about 2 dozen.

ALMOND TWISTS

Melt ¼ cup butter or margarine. Combine ¼ cup each sugar, and slivered unblanched almonds or chopped nuts. Open package of rolls, but do not unroll. Cut in ¼ inch slices with serrated knife. Pinch center of slices and twist once. Dip one side in butter and then press firmly into sugar-nut mixture. Bake on ungreased baking sheet in moderate oven (375°F.) 8 to 10 minutes. Remove to rack. Makes about 2 dozen.

BREAD

HERB BISCUITS

- 2 cups buttermilk baking mix
- 1/8 teaspoon ground nutmeg
- 1/2 teaspoon dried sage
- 1 teaspoon caraway seed
- 3/4 cup milk

Combine mix, nutmeg, sage and seed. Add milk all at once and stir to mix fairly well. Drop by tablespoonfuls onto greased cookie sheet and bake in preheated very hot oven (450°F.) about 10 minutes. Serve hot with butter. Makes 12.

PLUM COFFEE ROLLS

- 1 can (1 pound) purple plums
- 8 refrigerated buttermilk biscuits
- 2 tablespoons soft butter or margarine
- 2 tablespoons all-purpose flour
- 2 1/2 tablespoons sugar
- 2 tablespoons grated Parmesan cheese
- Grated Cheddar cheese

Drain plums and, if whole, halve and pit. Cut each biscuit in thirds. Spread each piece into a 2-inch round. Mix next 4 ingredients and 1/2 cup grated Cheddar. Spread biscuits with the mixture and top each with plum half, cut side down. Sprinkle with more grated Cheddar and bake in preheated hot oven (400°F.) 8 to 10 minutes. Serve hot. Makes 2 dozen.

CELERY ROLLS

- 1 tablespoon soft butter
- 1/4 teaspoon celery salt
- 6 brown-and-serve dinner rolls

Mix butter and celery salt. Make a lengthwise slit in each roll. Spread 1/2 teaspoon mixture in slit and over top of each roll. Bake in preheated hot oven (400°F.) about 12 minutes.

SNOWFLAKE ROLLS

- 12 brown-and-serve cloverleaf rolls
- 1/2 cup raspberry or strawberry jam
- 2 tablespoons butter, melted
- 2 tablespoons flaked coconut

Partially separate sections of rolls, being careful not to break bottom crust. Insert 2 teaspoons jam in center of each roll, push sections firmly together and put in greased muffin cups. Bake in hot oven (400°F.) 12 minutes, or until rolls are browned. Brush tops preheated with butter and at once sprinkle each with 1/2 teaspoon coconut.

JEWEL BUNS

- 12 brown-and-serve dinner rolls
- 2/3 cup jelly or preserves
- 1 1/2 cups sifted confectioners' sugar
- 1 1/2 tablespoons milk
- 1/4 teaspoon vanilla extract

Cut halfway through the center of each roll with a 1 inch round cutter, using a twisting motion. Remove center of rolls. Fill centers with jelly just to the top. Put on cookie sheet and bake in preheated hot oven (400°F.) about 10 minutes. Mix sugar, milk and vanilla and spread on tops of hot rolls around jelly centers.
Note: Frosting can be tinted in a pastel color to match the jelly, if desired.

BREAD, TO—To coat a food with bread or other crumbs, either directly or after dipping it first into beaten egg or milk. Breading is done prior to cooking the food; the cooking method is usually frying. Breading preserves the juices and provides a crust for texture. The crumbs used can be flavored with herbs, spices, cheese, etc., all ground fine. Some breading is done with dry crumbs, some with fresh crumbs, depending on the taste and texture desired.

Sesame Biscuit Ring

BREAKFAST COOKBOOK

Breaking the fast is not the only function of breakfast. To be a good breakfast, the meal should be high in protein. The reason: protein is essential for building and maintaining healthy bodies and is best utilized when distributed evenly throughout the day. In addition to protein, a good breakfast should contain from one fourth to one third of all the other food values needed daily: carbohydrates, fats, vitamins, and minerals.

Today the typical morning meal has become orange juice, bacon and eggs or cereal, buttered toast and jam, and milk or coffee. But there is no law that says this menu must be served morning after morning. In fact, where indifference to breakfast is a problem, variety may be the answer. Any food enjoyed at lunch or dinner can be served at breakfast too. Vary the fruit one week, the cereal the next, etc., and gradually build up new menus.

A few years ago, breakfasts had fallen into a dismal decline. What should have been a happy morning treat had developed into a hastily gulped meal which had little chance of ending with a chorus of "Oh, What a Beautiful Mornin'!" We use the past tense warily, but ever so hopefully, for we believe that today's homemakers, heeding the warnings of doctors and nutritionists, are providing more nourishing breakfasts for their families.

To enliven your table in the mornings, we suggest a look at some American regional breakfasts, those which carry on the good-eating traditions of our forefathers in various parts of the country. In order to perform their mighty chores, these men who built America started their days with appropriately mighty meals, including favorite dishes from their homelands across the sea and also products local to their own regions.

WESTERN BREAKFAST

Fresh Fruit Compote*
Buttermilk Pancakes*
Bacon   Ham   Sausage
Maple Syrup   Honey   Sour Cream
Boysenberry Syrup   Preserves
Whipped Butter   Apple Butter
Coffee, Tea, or Milk

Fresh Fruit Compote—This is simply a combination of the fruits in season, cut up, lightly sugared, and served with all the juices. Oranges, pineapple, grapefruit, bananas, papayas, apples, pears, and summer fruits and berries can be used. Two or more fruits are usually included.

Buttermilk Pancakes—This recipe makes about 30 large pancakes. Sift together 4 cups sifted all-purpose flour, 1 teaspoon salt, 2 teaspoons soda, and 2 tablespoons sugar. Beat 4 eggs; add 1 quart buttermilk and ¼ cup melted butter. Combine with dry ingredients and stir just enough to blend. Cook by the tablespoonfuls on a buttered griddle or skillet over low heat. Turn when cakes rise and are bubbly.

CHARLESTON BREAKFAST

Papaya with Lime
Shrimp Paste*   Hominy Grits*
Waffles, Creamed Chicken
and Virginia Ham (all optional)
Beaten Biscuits   Honey or Preserves
Coffee

Shrimp Paste—Put 4 cups small cooked and peeled shrimps through the grinder, then pound them in a mortar, or whirl in a blender, with 1 cup butter. When a smooth paste, season with freshly grated nutmeg, salt, and pepper or hot pepper sauce to taste. Pack in a well-buttered bread pan and bake in moderate oven (350°F.) for 30 minutes. Chill and serve cold, sliced. Makes 6 servings. (Some cooks don't bake it, merely pack the mixture in the pan and chill; easier and just as good.)

Hominy Grits—Follow package directions. Serve them very hot with butter.

CALIFORNIA BRUNCH

Strawberries with Orange Juice*
or Curaçao
Hangtown Fry*   Bacon
Smothered Onions*   Cherry Tomatoes*
Toast   Dates and Cheddar*   Coffee

Strawberries with Orange Juice—This is just what it says. Hull the berries and sugar them if they need it. Have them at room temperature, and pour over them cold orange juice.

Hangtown Fry—Drain 1 pint medium-sized oysters; dry and flour, and then dip them into 1 egg beaten slightly with 1 tablespoon milk. Roll in cracker crumbs and allow to dry for at least 15 minutes. Melt 6 tablespoons butter in a large skillet and brown the oysters lightly on both sides. Add 8 eggs that have been beaten with ¾ teaspoon salt and a little pepper. Stir once or twice, then allow to set. Fold like an omelet onto a plate or carefully turn to brown other side before serving. Serve with smothered onions or fried green peppers. Makes 6 servings.

Smothered Onions—Peel and slice 2 pounds onions and sauté very slowly in ¼ cup butter. When they begin to brown, "smother" them by covering. Cook until golden.

Cherry Tomatoes—These may be served raw or they may be hulled and just heated in butter, then sprinkled with a dash of thyme.

Dates and Cheddar—Fresh dates, preferably. Pit and stuff them with cheese, or just serve whole with cubed cheese.

BREAKFAST

Western Breakfast

NEW ENGLAND BREAKFAST
*Strawberries and Country Cream
Fried Brook Trout*   Bacon
Popovers   Wild Honey   Coffee*

Strawberries—You'll probably have to settle for cultivated instead of tiny, wild ones, but do have them small, ripe, and *not* iced. As for the cream, just get the heaviest you can find.

Fried Brook Trout—Don't let anyone tell you that they're better any other way, and we include *truite au bleu!* Clean the fish, the smallest and freshest you can find, dip them into cornmeal, and sauté in butter or bacon fat until crisply brown on both sides. Serve with crisp bacon.

Popovers—See section on Quick Breads

PENNSYLVANIA-DUTCH BREAKFAST
*Canned or Stewed Plums
Scrapple*   Creamed Eggs* (optional)
Fried Apples*
Schnecken*   (cinnamon roll)   Coffee*

Scrapple—Cook 4 fresh pigs' feet and 2 pounds of pork shoulder (including bone or other inexpensive cut) in 2 quarts boiling water and 1 tablespoon salt, until the meat literally falls from the bones. Strain broth into a saucepan; pick meat from bones and grind. Bring broth to a boil and stir in ½ cup chopped onions and 1½ cups cornmeal. Cook for 2 minutes, add meat, and correct seasoning, adding salt and pepper to taste. Cook until thick, pour into a loaf pan, and chill. At serving time, slice ½ inch thick and fry crisp on both sides. (Add shortening to skillet only if needed.) Makes 6 servings.

Creamed Eggs—Hard-cook 10 eggs and dice the whites. Combine with 1 cup of cream sauce, and pour over 6 slices of buttered toast on a platter. Press the hard-cooked yolks through a sieve and drift over the creamed egg whites. Sprinkle with minced parsley. Makes 6 servings.

Cream Sauce—For each cup of cream sauce, melt 2 tablespoons butter, add 2 tablespoons flour, and cook, stirring, for 1 minute. Pour in 1 cup light cream and mix thoroughly, Season with salt and pepper to taste and turn heat very low, so that sauce will cook, without burning, for at least 5 minutes. Or cook over hot water. This will

33

BREAKFAST

remove any raw taste of flour. Add 2 tablespoons heavy cream and use as indicated for Creamed Eggs.

Fried Apples—Core apples and slice across about ⅜ inch thick. Fry in butter or bacon fat until brown on both sides, sprinkling with sugar when they begin to color.

Schnecken—Use recipe for Basic Sweet Dough (see below) and, after the first rising, roll into a rectangle about 18 inches square. Spread lightly with melted butter; then sprinkle with the following mixture: 1 cup sugar, 1 tablespoon ground cinnamon, ½ cup seedless raisins, ½ cup chopped almonds, and ¼ cup chopped citron or candied fruits (optional). Roll like a jelly roll and slice ½ inch thick. Put on buttered cookie sheets, flat side down, and let rise until double in bulk. Bake in preheated moderate oven (350°F.) for 20 minutes, or until nicely browned. Remove from the pan while still warm. Makes about 36.

Basic Sweet Dough—Use very warm milk (105°F. to 115°F.) for dry yeast; use lukewarm milk (80°F. to 90°F.) for compressed. Crumble 1 yeast cake into ⅔ cup warm milk, and stir. Add 2 tablespoons sugar, ½ teaspoon salt, ¼ cup soft butter, 1 egg, and 1 cup sifted all-purpose flour. Beat well until elastic. Now add another 1 cup flour and work in well. If it's still sticky add up to 1 cup more flour. The dough should be soft but easy to handle. Turn out on a lightly floured board and knead until the dough is smooth, shiny, and elastic. Put in well-buttered bowl, turn to grease top, cover and let rise in a warm place until double in bulk. Punch down, turn onto a lightly floured board, knead for ½ minute or so, then use as directed to make Schnecken.

NORTHERN BREAKFAST

Canned or Stewed Prunes
Ham with Cream Gravy*
Corn Fritters*
Toast   Apple Butter   Beverage

Ham with Cream Gravy—This is a country dish. Have 1½ pounds uncooked or tenderized ham sliced thick or thin, as you like, and brown it on both sides in its own fat. Remove to a hot platter. To 1½ tablespoons fat in skillet add 1½ tablespoons all-purpose flour and 2 cups thin cream. Cook quickly, stirring, until slightly reduced and thickened; add pepper to taste and salt, if necessary, and pour over the ham. Makes 6 servings.

Corn Fritters—There are several kinds of corn fritters. Because this is a family breakfast, we give you the easiest, although none is difficult. Combine 2 cups chopped cooked or raw corn, ½ cup all-purpose flour, 1 teaspoon baking powder, 1 teaspoon salt, and 2 eggs, beaten until thick. Fry, by the tablespoonful, in hot butter, turning to brown both sides. Makes 6 servings.

New England Breakfast

ONE DISH BREAKFASTS

CHICKEN CRÊPES IN CASSEROLE

- 2 cups cooked chicken, in chunks
- 1 can (10½ ounces) condensed cream of chicken soup
- 2 tablespoons chopped parsley
- 5 water chestnuts, sliced
- 1 jar (15 ounces) small onions, drained
- Pimento strips
- 8 to 10 crêpes

Mix first 6 ingredients. Line buttered shallow 2-quart baking dish with crepes, letting some hang over edges. Fill with chicken mixture and fold edges of crepes over chicken. Put in preheated moderate oven (350°F.) 25 minutes, or until heated. Makes 6 servings.

CRÊPES

Sift ½ cup sifted all-purpose flour and ¼ teaspoon salt. Mix 1 egg, 1 egg yolk and ¾ cup milk; add to dry ingredients and beat until smooth. Let stand in refrigerator 1 hour or longer. Butter hot skillet about 6 inches in diameter. Pour in a scant ¼ measuring cup of batter and quickly tilt and rotate pan so that batter runs to edges and covers bottom with a thin layer. Allow to set and then turn carefully. Repeat with remaining batter. Makes about 12 crêpes. Cook and dice chicken. Make crêpe batter and refrigerate.

Note—Crêpes freeze very well.

PRUNE-NOODLE CASSEROLE

- 1 cup dairy sour cream
- 1 package (8 ounces) cream cheese, softened
- 1 pound pitted prunes, snipped
- 1 tablespoon lemon juice
- 1 teaspoon grated lemon rind
- 1 package (8 ounces) wide noodles, cooked and drained
- ½ cup cornflake crumbs
- 2 tablespoons butter, melted
- 1 tablespoon sugar
- ½ teaspoon ground cinnamon
- ¼ teaspoon ground nutmeg

Mix well first 5 ingredients and toss gently with noodles. Put in buttered shallow 2-quart baking dish. Mix remaining ingredients and sprinkle on top. Bake in preheated hot oven (400°F.) about 50 minutes. Good with bacon or ham. Makes 6 to 8 servings.

Note. Assemble night before and refrigerate. Bake 15 minutes longer.

CHEESY SCALLOPED POTATOES AND CORNED BEEF

- 1 can (10½ ounces) condensed Cheddar cheese soup
- ⅓ cup milk
- 1 pimiento, chopped
- 2 tablespoons chopped parsley
- 3 cups sliced cooked potatoes
- 1 can (12 ounces) corned beef, sliced
- 1 cup shredded Cheddar cheese

Mix first 4 ingredients. Arrange potatoes and beef in greased shallow 2-quart baking dish. Pour soup mixture over top and sprinkle with cheese. Bake in preheated moderate oven (350°F.) 40 to 45 minutes. Makes 4 to 6 servings.

UPSIDE-DOWN SAUSAGE CORN-BREAD

- 1 package (8 ounces) brown-and-serve sausages
- 1 can (1 pound) tomato wedges
- 1 can (8 ounces) whole kernel corn, drained
- 1 package (12 ounces) corn-muffin mix
- 2 eggs

Arrange sausage links in 8 inch square glass baking dish. Bake in preheated hot oven (400°F.) 15 minutes, or until lightly browned. Pour off any accumulated fat. Drain tomatoes, reserving juice. Add tomatoes and corn to sausages. Prepare muffin mix as directed on package, using eggs and ⅔ cup tomato juice for the liquid. Pour over ingredients in baking dish. Bake in preheated moderate oven (350°F.) about 30 minutes. Cut in squares or spoon out to serve. Makes 4 to 6 servings.

APPLES AND SMOKED PORK CHOPS

- ⅓ cup wheat germ
- ⅓ cup firmly packed brown sugar
- 1 can (1 pound 4 ounces) pie sliced apples
- 1 can (1 pound) sliced small potatoes, drained
- 1 can (11 ounces) mandarin orange slices, drained
- 4 smoked pork chops

Mix wheat germ and brown sugar. Reserve 2 tablespoons and mix remainder with fruits and potatoes. Turn into buttered shallow 1½-quart baking dish. Top with pork chops and sprinkle with reserved sugar-wheat germ mixture. Bake in moderate oven (350°F.) about 35 minutes, or until chops are tender. Makes 4 servings.

PUDDING FOR BREAKFAST

Puddings, rich in eggs, milk and bread or cereal, qualify as well-fortified breakfast food. Fresh fruits and berries in season, frozen or canned out of season make luscious impromptu toppings.

BRIDE'S COOKING HINTS

APPLE-OATMEAL PUDDING

2 cups milk
3 tablespoons firmly packed brown sugar
1 tablespoon butter or margarine
¼ teaspoon salt
¼ teaspoon ground cinnamon
1 cup rolled oats, regular or instant
1 cup diced peeled apple
½ cup seedless raisins
Cream

Put milk, 2 tablespoons sugar, butter, salt and cinnamon in saucepan. Scald milk. Add oats, apple and raisins and heat until bubbles appear at edge of pan. Turn into lightly buttered 1½-quart casserole and bake in preheated moderate oven (350°F.) about 30 minutes. After 15 minutes, stir and sprinkle with remaining 1 tablespoon sugar. Serve with cream. Serves 4.

PINEAPPLE AND COTTAGE-CHEESE PUDDING

Graham-cracker crumbs
1 pound (2 cups) cottage cheese
1 cup undiluted evaporated milk
½ cup sugar
½ cup dry nonfat milk powder
3 eggs
¼ cup all-purpose flour
2 tablespoons lemon juice
¼ teaspoon salt
2 teaspoons vanilla extract
1 can (1 pound, 4½ ounces) crushed pineapple, drained

Butter 9 x 9 x 2-inch baking pan and sprinkle with crumbs. Sieve cottage cheese or beat with an electric mixer until smooth. Beat in next 8 ingredients, then stir in pineapple. Spoon into prepared baking pan. Bake in preheated slow oven (300°F.) 1 hour. Serves 6.

BREAKFAST SANDWICHES

HEARTY HASH SANDWICHES

1 small onion, minced
1 tablespoon butter or margarine
1 can (1 pound) corned-beef hash
Pepper
1 cup diced sharp Cheddar cheese
8 large slices rye bread
Chili sauce

Sauté onion lightly in the butter in skillet. Add hash and brown quickly, stirring frequently. Season with pepper. Add cheese, cover and cook slowly 2 minutes over low heat. Toast bread and spread half the slices with hash mixture. Top with a little chili sauce and remaining toast slices.

POACHED EGGS ON CHICKEN MUFFINS

1 can (4¾ ounces) chicken spread
½ teaspoon ground thyme
3 English muffins
6 eggs
Chopped chives (optional)

Mix first 2 ingredients. Split and toast muffins and spread with chicken mixture. Keep warm in oven while poaching eggs. Top each muffin half with an egg, and sprinkle with chives, if desired. Makes 6 servings.

CUBED STEAK SANDWICHES

¾ pound cube steaks, cut in strips
All-purpose flour
Salt and pepper
2 tablespoons butter or margarine
4 frankfurter rolls

Dredge steak strips with seasoned flour and brown quickly on both sides in hot butter in skillet. Serve steak strips in toasted rolls. Makes 4 servings.

PORK SAUSAGE AND APPLE SANDWICHES

8 to 12 brown-and-serve sausage links
1 tablespoon butter or margarine
1 tablespoon sugar
¼ teaspoon ground cinnamon
8 slices fresh apple ¼ inch thick
8 frozen waffles, 4 x 3 inches

Heat sausage as directed on label; keep warm. Put next 3 ingredients in skillet and mix. Add apple slices and sauté just until apple is tender, turning once. For each sandwich, overlap 2 apple slices on a waffle, top with 2 or 3 sausage links and cover with second waffle. Makes 4 servings.

TIPS FOR THE YOUNG-BRIDE COOK
By Paula Jones

To cook frozen steak without defrosting, turn the broiler to high. Place the steak on a rack on the broiler pan and broil enough so that the fat can be slit around the edges to prevent curling. Broil 7 to 10 minutes on each side. The meat will be tender and juicy.

When you freeze chickens, accumulate the necks and giblets in a freezer bag in the freezer until you have enough for soup or a rice dish. Without the giblets tucked inside, you can easily and fairly quickly roast the chicken from its frozen state. Place it in a large casserole with ½ cup water, sprinkle with salt, pepper and your choice of herbs. Cover tightly and roast in a preheated 500°F. oven for 15 minutes. Reduce the heat to 325°F. and continue to roast for another hour.

BRIDE'S COOKING HINTS

Do the same with a frozen roast. Preheat the oven to 500°F. Roast the meat for 15 minutes; turn the heat down to 350°F. and continue to roast until the meat thermometer tells you that the roast has nearly reached required doneness. Remove it just before done since it will continue to cook by itself while "resting" for the 10-minute period recommended before carving.

MEAT LOAF

- 1 can (1 pound) stewed tomatoes
- 1 garlic clove
- 2 tablespoons chopped parsley
- 1 egg
- 1 pound ground beef
- 1 cup fine bread crumbs
- 1 teaspoon salt

Pour tomatoes in blender, add garlic, parsley and egg; blend a few seconds or mash garlic and mix with fork. Mix bread crumbs, salt, meat and half the tomato mixture. Mix lightly, then put in 9 x 5 x 3-inch loaf pan and pour remaining tomato mixture over top. Bake in preheated moderate oven (350°F.) about 1 hour. Makes 4 servings.

Note: Put leftover dry bread crusts in blender to make crumbs.

BRIDE'S DINNER MENUS AND RECIPES

Avocado and Blue-Cheese Dip*   Crackers
Rock Cornish Hens   Wild Rice Stuffing
Cherry Sauce*
Buttered Asparagus
Baby Carrots
Key Lime Pie*

AVOCADO AND BLUE-CHEESE DIP

- 1 ripe medium avocado
- ¼ cup mashed blue cheese
- 1 tablespoon lemon juice
- Salt and pepper to taste
- Crackers

Peel avocado and mash fine. Add remaining ingredients, except crackers, and mix well. Chill and serve with crackers. Makes about 1 cup.

ROCK CORNISH HENS, WILD RICE STUFFING, CHERRY SAUCE

- ¼ cup raw wild rice, or ¾ cup cooked
- 1 small onion, chopped
- Butter or margarine
- ⅓ cup each finely diced ham and mushrooms
- 4 frozen Rock Cornish hens, thawed to room temperature
- Salt and pepper
- Cherry Sauce

Cook rice according to package directions. Sauté onion in 2 tablespoons butter 5 minutes in small skillet or until tender but not browned. Add ham, mushrooms and rice. Wash Cornish hens inside and out and pat dry with paper towel. Sprinkle lightly inside and out with salt and pepper. Fill with stuffing. Put in greased shallow baking dish and roast in preheated moderate oven (350°F.) 1 hour or until tender, brushing several times with melted butter. Pour Cherry Sauce over top. Or pass sauce separately. Makes 4 servings.

Cherry Sauce—In saucepan, mix 4 teaspoons cornstarch; ¼ cup sugar; ¼ teaspoon each salt, dry mustard and ginger. Drain 1 can (1 pound) waterpack red sour pitted cherries, reserving liquid. Add liquid, ½ cup orange juice, ¼ cup red-currant jelly and a few drops red food coloring to mixture in saucepan. Cook over medium heat, stirring, until mixture boils and thickens. Add cherries and heat through.

KEY LIME PIE

- 3 egg yolks
- Cup sugar
- 1 package (3 ounces) lime-flavor gelatin
- 1 cup warm water
- 2 limes, rind and juice
- 3 drops green food coloring
- 1 cup heavy cream
- 1 Baked 9-inch pastry shell, chilled
- 4 egg whites
- ¼ teaspoon cream of tartar

In top part of double boiler, mix egg yolks, ½ cup sugar, gelatine, water, green food coloring, lime rind and juice. Cook over simmering water, stirring until thickened. Set top part of double boiler in bowl of ice and water and stir until thickened. Whip cream until stiff and fold into lime mixture. Pour into pie shell and chill 1½ hours, or until set. Beat egg whites until frothy, then add cream of tartar and beat until almost stiff. Gradually add ½ cup sugar and beat until mixture is blended and stiff. Pile lightly on pie, spreading to cover edge of pastry. Bake in preheated hot oven (425°F.) 5 minutes, or until golden brown. Chill 2 to 3 hours before serving. Makes 6 to 8 servings.

Chicken Divan*
Fluffy Rice
Waldorf Salad
Packaged Croissants (frozen, brown-and-serve or other, heated)
Twinkies Surprise (mold your favorite ice cream around Twinkies and top with a favorite fruit— strawberry, blueberry, cherry, etc.)

BRIDE'S COOKING HINTS

CHICKEN DIVAN

- 1 package (10 ounces) frozen broccoli spears
- Salt
- 2 boned chicken breasts, split
- 1 can (10½ ounces) condensed cream of chicken soup
- ½ cup mayonnaise
- ½ teaspoon lemon juice
- ½ teaspoon curry powder
- ½ cup shredded Cheddar or process American cheese
- ¼ cup soft bread crumbs
- 2 tablespoons butter, melted
- 2¼ cups hot cooked rice, or ¾ cup raw

Cook broccoli in boiling salted water as directed on package. Drain and arrange in greased shallow 1½-quart baking dish. Simmer chicken in small amount of water 35 minutes, or until tender. Drain and arrange on broccoli. Mix next 4 ingredients and pour over top. Sprinkle with cheese, and bread crumbs mixed with the butter. Bake in preheated moderate oven (350°F.) about 25 minutes. Serve with rice. Makes 2 or 3 generous servings.

*Chinese Beef with
Ginger Rice
Frozen Egg Rolls (dinner size)
Hot Fudge or Marshmallow Sundaes
(sprinkle with slivered toasted almonds)
Hot Tea*

CHINESE BEEF WITH GINGER RICE

- ½ cup onion strips
- ½ cup bias-cut celery strips
- ½ cup green-pepper slices
- 1½ tablespoons vegetable oil
- 1 large or 2 small minute steaks, cut in ¼-inch strips
- 1 can (3 or 4 ounces) sliced mushrooms, drain and reserve liquid
- Water
- 3 tablespoons soy sauce
- 3½ teaspoons cornstarch
- 1 teaspoon sugar
- ½ teaspoon salt
- ⅓ cup thinly sliced water chestnuts
- 1 firm medium tomato, peeled and cut in wedges
- 1½ cups hot cooked rice (½ cup raw)
- Ground ginger

In heavy skillet, quickly stir-fry first 3 ingredients in the oil until crisp-tender. Remove from skillet and set aside. Add meat to hot skillet and brown quickly, then add mushrooms and sauté quickly. Add water to reserved mushroom liquid to make 1 cup; add next 4 ingredients; add to skillet. Cook, stirring, until mixture thickens and bubbles. Add reserved vegetables, water chestnuts and tomato; cook over low heat about 2 minutes. Serve on rice, sprinkled with ginger. Makes 2 servings.

SUNDAY BRUNCH FOR FOUR

*Tomato Juice (with 2 drops Worcestershire and a squeeze of lemon juice in each glass)
Melon in Season (with lemon wedge on colorful toothpick)
Eggs Continental*
Assorted Doughnuts or Corn Muffins with honey*

EGGS CONTINENTAL

- 1 cup sliced onion
- 1 tablespoon butter
- 8 eggs, hard-cooked and sliced
- 2 cups shredded Swiss cheese
- 1 can (10½ ounces) condensed cream of mushroom soup
- ¾ cup milk
- 1 teaspoon prepared mustard
- 1 teaspoon salt
- ¼ teaspoon dillweed (optional)
- ¼ teaspoon pepper
- 6 slices favorite bread (caraway rye is delicious), buttered and cut in triangles.

Sauté onion in the butter until tender but not browned. Put in shallow 2-quart baking dish. Top with egg slices and sprinkle with the cheese. Beat remaining ingredients, except bread, with rotary beater until blended. Pour over cheese and overlap bread slices on top. Bake in preheated moderate oven (350°F.) 30 to 35 minutes. Makes 4 servings.

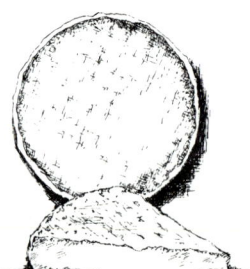

BRIE—This is one of the finest of French cheeses, and one of the most famous. Brie is made from whole milk, and its shape is round and flat. The flavor varies from mild to pungent. The crust is edible. Brie is fully ripened when the texture of the whole cheese is even: soft but not runny.

Brie is not a cooking cheese. It is excellent for appetizers and delicious eaten with fresh fruit. Brie should be allowed to stand at room temperature before serving, to bring out the full flavor of the cheese.

BRILLAT-SAVARIN—Jean Anthelme Brillat-Savarin (1755-1826) was a French magistrate and politician who became the most famous gastronome in the world. His book *La Physiologie du Goût*, also translated into English *(The Physiology of Taste),* is a learned and witty treatise on food, drink, and people, and has been constantly quoted to this day for its amusing and profound comments.

BROCCOLI

BRINE—A strong salt solution used in the preservation of fish, meats, vegetables, and in pickling. To keep foods in brine is one of the very oldest methods of preservation.

BRIOCHE—A light, yet rich cake-bread made with yeast dough, butter, and eggs. The traditional shape of a brioche is round with a little hat, but there are also round, tall and slender, and ring brioches.

Brioche is a French cake-bread, and it goes back for hundreds of years. It is used as a sweet roll, as a cake combined with fruit, or as a shell to hold a hot entrée, such as creamed fish or meats.

A recipe for Little Brioches appears in the section on breads.

BROCCOLI—This dark green vegetable is a member of the *Brassica* family and is closely related to cauliflower, less closely to cabbage and Brussels sprouts. Broccoli has tight small heads called curds, which sit like buds on a thick stem. Both heads and stems are eaten. Broccoli should not be overcooked. It is delicious crisp-tender.

Broccoli, of which more than one hundred million pounds are sold in fresh form each year, is very popular today, but recipe books printed at the turn of the century made little mention of it. Mrs. Hannah Glasse's *Art of Cookery* in 1774 included a recipe "To dress Brokala" and Mrs. Mary Randolph's *Virginia Housewife,* published in 1824, suggested cooking broccoli "as asparagus" and dressing it "in the same manner as the cauliflower." Thomas Jefferson, it is said, grew broccoli at Monticello in the early 19th century.

In Greece and Italy, broccoli has been a favorite vegetable for some 2,000 years. It seems to have looked and tasted much as it does today. Italian families brought broccoli seeds to America and grew these handsome dark-green clusters of buds in the suburbs of New York and Boston long before the vegetable was known throughout the country as a whole. About 1920 commercial growers began producing and distributing broccoli.

Availability—Available all year round with peak crop from October to November. Major crop from California, also from Arizona, New Jersey, New York, Oregon, Pennsylvania, South Carolina, Texas, and Virginia.

Broccoli is also available frozen, in spears or chopped.

Purchasing Guide—It is sold by the bunch and by the pound, sometimes wrapped in transparent film. Look for dark-green or light-purplish heads with tightly closed buds. Stalks should be tender yet firm with unwilted leaves. Yellowish buds or leaves indicate poor quality or overmaturity.

One pound fresh makes 3 to 4 servings.

Storage—Store in vegetable container or in moisture-proof bag in refrigerator.

Refrigerator shelf, raw: 3 to 5 days
Refrigerator shelf, cooked: 1 to 4 days
Refrigerator frozen-food compartment, prepared for freezing: 1 month
Freezer, prepared for freezing: 6 months

Nutritive Food Values—One of the richest vegetable sources of vitamin C, if vegetable is cooked quickly in a small amount of water. Excellent source of vitamin A, riboflavin, iron, and calcium.

3½ ounces, raw = 32 calories
1 cup cooked = 45 calories
1 medium stalk, cooked = 40 calories
1 package (10 ounces) frozen, cooked, drained = 65 calories

Basic Preparation—Wash; cut off only toughest part of stem and larger leaves. To insure quick cooking of stalks more than one inch in diameter, make lengthwise gashes starting at ends of stalks; they will then cook as quickly as the flowerets.

The head may be divided into individual flowerets by slicing lengthwise, starting at base of flower and cutting straight down length of stem.

During cooking, remove cover several times to allow steam to escape. This will keep broccoli green.

To Boil—Cook in skillet or large flat pan in 1 inch of boiling salted water, covered, for 10 to 15 minutes, cooking stem pieces for a few minutes before adding buds.

To Steam—Tie in a bunch and stand upright in deep kettle. Add boiling salted water to base of flowerets. Cook quickly until stem near head is just tender, 10 to 15 minutes. Remove carefully from water.

To Sauté—Cut into thin diagonal slices and sauté quickly in hot oil or other shortening until tender-crisp. Cook stem pieces a little longer than bud pieces.

Season with salt, pepper, and butter. May be eaten hot or cold with hollandaise sauce. Good, too, with a French dressing or with plain lemon juice.

Sprinkle with Parmesan cheese, and a little butter; put under the broiler for a few minutes.

To Freeze—Use dark, compact heads. Cut off heavy stems and break or cut into flowerets. Wash thoroughly in water. Blanch in boiling water: Small flowerets for 3 minutes; Medium for 4; Large for 5. Chill in cold water for 4 to 5 minutes. Drain. Pack in containers with no headspace.

BROCCOLI

To Cook, Frozen Broccoli—Drop unthawed broccoli into ½ cup boiling salted water. Use a fork to break apart after block begins to thaw. When water returns to boil, cover; cook for 8 to 10 minutes, or until tender. One 10-ounce box makes about 3 servings.

To Bake, Frozen Broccoli—Put 1 box (10 ounces) frozen broccoli spears in a 1½-quart casserole. Add 1 tablespoon butter or margarine and ¼ teaspoon salt. Cover and bake in preheated moderate oven (350°F.) about 30 to 40 minutes.

BROCCOLI AND CHICKEN SOUP

- 1 bunch broccoli
- 1½ cups boiling water
- 2 cans (10½ ounces each) condensed cream of chicken soup
- 1 cup light cream
- Salt, pepper, cayenne
- Croutons
- Grated Parmesan Cheese

Cut off and discard large leaves and tough parts of stalks. Wash and chop broccoli coarsely. Add boiling water. Boil rapidly until tender. Using all the liquid, chop broccoli very fine in blender or force through coarse sieve. In saucepan mix soup, cream, and broccoli; season to taste. Heat to simmering. Top with croutons and grated Parmesan cheese. Makes about 1 quart.

BROCCOLI AND CHEESE CUSTARD

- 1 bunch broccoli
- 3 eggs
- ⅔ cup milk
- 1¼ cups grated sharp Cheddar cheese
- Salt and pepper

Broccoli and Cheese Custard

Cut off and discard large leaves and tough parts of stalks. Wash; split stalks into halves or quarters so they cook as quickly as flowerets. Cook, uncovered, in small amount of boiling salted water until barely tender. Drain and put in buttered shallow casserole. Beat eggs; add milk, cheese, salt, and pepper. Mix and pour over broccoli. Set casserole in pan with about 1 inch of hot water. Bake in a preheated moderate oven (350°F.) for 30 minutes, or until firm. Makes 4 servings.

BROCCOLI WITH SPINACH

- 1 package (10 ounces) frozen chopped broccoli, cooked
- 1 package (10 ounces) frozen chopped spinach, cooked
- 1 small onion, finely chopped
- 1 sweet red pepper, slivered
- 3 tablespoons olive oil
- 3 tablespoons cider vinegar
- ½ teaspoon salt

Drain broccoli and spinach well. Sauté onion and pepper in olive oil until just tender. Add broccoli, spinach and remaining ingredients and cook, stirring, until heated through. Serve at once. Makes 4 to 6 servings.

Note: If available, use 2 cups fresh chopped broccoli or spinach, cooked.

Broccoli and Chicken Soup

BROWNIE

today broiling has been reinstated as a favorite cooking method because of the interest in outdoor cooking and the need for methods of quick cooking without many preliminary steps. Basting to prevent drying is the only additional requirement.

To Broil—If using separate broiler, set regulator for broiling. Follow manufacturer's directions for operation of broiler. Place meat on rack of broiler pan. Adjust rack and pan so that top of meat is approximately 2 inches below heat for ¾- to 1-inch cuts, 3 inches for thicker cuts. Broil about half of the time indicated on timetable. Season. Turn. Complete broiling. Season and serve.

To Charcoal Broil—Use charcoal briquettes; start fire 20 to 30 minutes before cooking. Use only a small amount of charcoal and wait until coals are covered with a gray ash before cooking.

Knock gray ash off several times during cooking to achieve maximum radiant heat. Place foods high above coals so they cook slowly and thoroughly and do not burn.

Broccoli Piquant

BROCCOLI PIQUANT

- 1 package (10 ounces) frozen broccoli, cut up
- 2 slices of bacon, diced
- ½ garlic clove, minced
- 2 tablespoons cider vinegar
- ¼ cup soft bread crumbs
- 1 tablespoon butter

Cook broccoli according to package directions. Meanwhile, cook bacon and garlic until bacon is crisp. Add vinegar; heat. Brown bread crumbs in butter. Pour sauce over hot broccoli and sprinkle with crumbs. Makes 3 servings.

Note: Frozen chopped broccoli may be used.

BROCHETTE—This French word describes a small skewer on which meat, fish, or vegetables are cooked. The term *en brochette* means meats cooked, and often served, on a skewer. Like all skewered foods, *en brochette* foods can be grilled over an open fire or under a broiler, or cooked in the oven.

BROIL—To cook directly under or above a source of radiant heat, which may be gas, electricity, charcoal, or an open fire. To grill is the word used in the British Isles for broiling.

Broiling is one of the oldest cooking processes, since it requires little equipment. As new stoves and kitchen appliances became available during the last century, broiling lost its prominent place in the home kitchen. But

BROTH—A thin liquid in which fish, meat, or vegetables have been cooked. Broth is often used interchangeably with bouillon, but it should not be confused with the word stock which denotes a richer extract.

QUICK MUSHROOM BROTH

- 1 tablespoon butter
- ¼ pound mushrooms
- 3 cups water
- 3 cans (10½ ounces each) condensed beef consommé
- ¼ cup sherry, if desired

Melt butter in a saucepan; add chopped mushrooms and cook slightly. Add water and simmer for 10 minutes. Add consommé and heat thoroughly. Add sherry just before serving. Makes 6 servings.

BROWN—In cooking, to brown is to scorch the surfaces of a food, especially meat, in order to seal the juices within and to add flavor. Browning can be done either by exposing the food directly to the heat or by cooking it in a small amount of fat. For browned toppings, place foods under the broiler or in a hot oven.

For additional flavor and color in the finished dish, butter and flour may be browned by cooking, while stirring, over low heat.

BROWNIE—This rich, moist chocolate cookie has a universal appeal. Brownies are easy to make and they keep and ship well. Brownies fall into two main categories: the fudge-type which is very chewy, or cake-type, with a lighter texture. Many brownie recipes include nuts

BROWNIE

and fruits, and some are quite fanciful. Brownies are also sold ready-made, frozen and ready-to-eat, or as a mix.

BROWNIES
[The Fudge Type]

- 1 cup soft butter or margarine
- 2 cups sugar
- 3 eggs
- 1 teaspoon vanilla extract
- 4 ounces (4 squares) unsweetened chocolate
- 1 cup sifted all-purpose flour
- ½ teaspoon salt
- 1 cup chopped nuts

Cream ½ cup of butter with sugar. Add eggs and beat until light. Add vanilla. Melt remaining butter with chocolate; cool, and beat into first mixture. Add flour, salt, and nuts. Mix well and pour into greased and floured pan 13 x 9 x 2 inches. Bake in preheated moderate oven (350°F.) for about 45 minutes. Cool in pan and cut into small squares. Makes 5 dozen.

BLACK AND WHITE BROWNIES
[The Cake Type]

- 1 cup butter or margarine
- 1½ teaspoons vanilla extract
- 2 cups sugar
- 4 eggs
- 2 cups sifted all-purpose flour
- ½ teaspoon salt
- 2 cups chopped nuts
- 2 ounces (2 squares) unsweetened chocolate
- Chocolate Frosting

Cream butter until light and fluffy. Beat in vanilla and sugar. Add eggs, one at a time, beating well after each addition. Add flour and salt and mix until blended. Stir in nuts; divide batter into halves; add cooled melted chocolate to one. Drop batters alternately by teaspoons into greased, floured pan 13 x 9 x 2 inches. Run knife through batter several times to marbleize. Bake in preheated moderate oven (350°F.) for about 45 minutes. Turn out on rack to cool. Frost. At serving time, cut into bars about 3 x 1½ inches. Makes 24 bars.

BROWN SAUCE

BROWN SAUCE—A sauce—A dark basic sauce from which many other sauces are made. For this reason brown sauce, or *Sauce Espagnole,* as a similar sauce is called in French, is considered a *sauce mère,* a "mother sauce," in French cooking. Brown sauce can be made in various ways, some elaborate, some simple, but it should always cook very slowly to become properly flavorful.

Brown sauce freezes well. It will keep four to six weeks.

BROWN SAUCE

- ⅓ cup minced onions
- ⅓ cup minced carrots
- ⅓ cup minced celery
- ¼ cup boiled ham or raw bacon, finely chopped
- ¼ cup butter or cooking oil
- ¼ cup all-purpose flour
- 6 cups boiling hot beef bouillon
- 2 tablespoons tomato paste
- Bouquet garni
- Salt and pepper

Cook onions, carrots, celery, and ham or bacon in hot butter or oil over low heat for 10 minutes. Stir flour into mixture. Cook over moderate heat, stirring constantly, for 10 minutes, until the flour is nut brown. Add bouillon all at once. Stir until smooth. Add tomato paste, *bouquet garni,* and salt and pepper to taste. Simmer, partly covered, over low heat for 2 hours or more. Skim when necessary. If sauce thickens too much, add a little more bouillon. Strain and degrease sauce. If not used at once, store covered in refrigerator, or freeze. Makes about 4 cups sauce.

Demi-Glace for Steaks

Combine ¼ pound mushrooms and ¼ cup sherry in a saucepan. Cook until sherry is reduced by half. Add 2 cups Brown Sauce and 1 tablespoon beef extract. Bring to a boil, reduce heat, and cook for 15 to 20 minutes.

Diable for Grilled Chicken

To 1 cup Brown Sauce, add 1 tablespoon each Worcestershire, cider vinegar, and prepared mustard, a dash of hot pepper sauce, and ¼ cup beef bouillon. Simmer for 10 minutes. Stir in a little chopped parsley.

Fines Herbes for Meats, Poultry, and Eggs

To 1 cup Brown Sauce, add 1 teaspoon each of dried tarragon, chervil, and chives, 1 tablespoon minced parsley, 1 tablespoon chopped green onion, and juice of 1 lemon. Cook for 10 to 15 minutes.

BRUNCH—This meal is a combination of breakfast and lunch, and takes its name from the first two letters of *breakfast* and the last four of *lunch.* Brunches are a convenient form of entertaining, very popular on Sunday and holiday mornings, since they give hosts and guests a chance to sleep late, entertain and be entertained with little trouble (compared to a complete lunch or dinner), and still have a portion of the day for their individual pursuits.

BRUNCH, COUNTRY STYLE
Menu 1

*Raspberry-Rhubarb Compote**
*Ham and Eggs, French Style**
Corn Sticks
Honey Preserves
Coffee   Milk

RASPBERRY-RHUBARB COMPOTE

- 1 package (1 pound) frozen rhubarb
- 1 package (10 ounces) frozen raspberries, thawed overnight in refrigerator
- Dash of ground cinnamon
- Few drops of almond extract

Cook rhubarb according to directions on package. Stir raspberries into rhubarb and add cinnamon and extract. Cool. Makes 4 servings.

HAM AND EGGS, FRENCH STYLE

- 2 tablespoons butter
- 4 thin slices of cooked ham
- 4 eggs
- Pepper
- Salt (optional)

Arrange ham slices in butter melted in heavy skillet. Break 1 egg on each slice. Cook over medium heat so that white becomes solid; about 10 minutes. Sprinkle with pepper, and salt if desired. Makes 4 servings.

Menu 2

Pineapple-Grapefruit Juice
*Sausage Patties   Sautéed Apples**
*Crisp-Fried Noodles**
Coffeecake From Mix
Coffee   Milk

SAUTÉED APPLES

- 1½ tablespoons butter
- 5 apples, peeled, cored, and sliced
- 2 tablespoons sugar
- Ground cinnamon

Melt butter in heavy skillet over low heat. Add apples, stirring, until all are covered with butter. Cover pan, shaking occasionally to keep apples from sticking. Cook for 5 to 10 minutes, or until apples are mushy. Sprinkle with sugar and cinnamon. Makes 4 servings.

BRUSSELS SPROUTS

CRISP-FRIED NOODLES

- 4 teaspoons butter
- ½ package (8 ounces) broad noodles, cooked and drained

Melt butter in heavy skillet over low heat. Cook noodles on one side, without stirring, until browned. Using dinner plate, invert noodles so that browned side is on top. Slip noodles back into pan; cook for another 5 minutes or until bottom is browned. Makes 4 servings.

BRUSSELS SPROUTS—Brussels sprouts are a member of the cabbage family, and they look like miniature cabbages. The plant, instead of making one large cabbage head, produces a number of rows of small heads where the leaves are attached. By pulling away the lower leaves the little heads are given room to develop.

Brussels sprouts appear to be about 400 years old, and they are said, in a vague way, to have originated in Brussels, capital of Belgium. By 1793 they were an article of export from that country.

Until fairly recently, Brussels sprouts were a luxury vegetable, especially in Europe, where the tiny sizes are prized for the delicacy of their taste. They should always be cooked in very little water. A dash of nutmeg is a good seasoning for a sauced or unsauced dish of sprouts.

Availability—Late August through March, with peak in November. Most of the crop comes from California and New York.

Brussels sprouts are also available frozen. One 10-ounce package makes about 3 servings.

Purchasing Guide—Usually marketed in pint-size boxes and sold as a unit. One pint, cooked, makes about 2 to 3 servings.

Sprouts should be firm, compact, and a true green color. Yellow leaves indicate poor quality and flavor. Small to medium-size sprouts are more desirable than large.

Storage—Keep boxes in refrigerator, air vents prevent internal browning. Some of the loose or discolored outer leaves may be discarded before storing, but do not wash until ready to cook.

Refrigerator shelf or vegetable compartment, wrapped: 4 days
Refrigerator frozen-food compartment, prepared for freezing: 1 month
Freezer, prepared for freezing: 11 months

Nutritive Food Values—Brussels sprouts are high in vitamins A and C, and contain fair amounts of iron.
   3½ ounces, raw = 45 calories
   1 cup, cooked = 55 calories

Basic Preparation—Remove loose, discolored outer leaves. Trim off a bit of the stem. Wash thoroughly in cold water. Drop into a small amount of boiling salted water in a saucepan. Cover pan and cook for 5 to 10 minutes, or until just tender. Overcooking may produce strong flavor and cause loss of vitamins. Drain, add seasonings and butter or margarine, and serve.

To Freeze—Select firm, compact heads of good green color. Trim ends and remove coarse outer leaves. Wash and drain. Blanch in boiling water: small heads for 3 minutes, medium for 4, and large for 5. Chill in cold water for 6 to 8 minutes. Drain. Pack in containers, leaving no headspace.

To Cook, Frozen Brussels Sprouts—Cook in a small amount of boiling salted water for 4 to 6 minutes, or until tender. Follow any additional directions on package.

BRUSSELS SPROUTS WITH TARRAGON-MUSTARD SAUCE

- 1 pound Brussels sprouts, washed and trimmed
- Salt
- 2 tablespoons finely chopped onion
- 1½ tablespoons butter or margarine
- 1½ tablespoons all-purpose flour
- ¾ teaspoon dry mustard
- ¼ teaspoon dried tarragon
- 1 cup chicken broth or bouillon
- 1 tablespoon cider vinegar

Cook sprouts in small amount of lightly salted boiling water until just tender and drain and keep hot. Sauté onion in butter until tender but not browned. Stir in flour, mustard and tarragon. Add broth and vinegar and cook, stirring, until smooth and thickened. Serve over sprouts. Makes 4 servings.

BRUSSELS SPROUTS AND CHESTNUTS

Cook 1 package (10 ounces) frozen, or 1 pint fresh, Brussels sprouts until tender. Shell ½ pound chestnuts. To shell, gash end of each nut and cook in boiling water to cover for 15 to 20 minutes. Drain and remove shells and skins with a sharp knife. If not tender enough, cook in boiling salted water for 10 minutes longer. Combine Brussels sprouts and chestnuts and pour over ¼ cup melted butter or margarine. Season to taste. Makes 4 servings.

BRUSSELS SPROUTS AND POTATOES

    2 packages (10 ounces each) frozen Brussels sprouts
    2 beef bouillon cubes
    1 small onion, finely chopped
    2 tablespoons butter or margarine
    ½ cup pecan halves or chopped pecans
    ½ teaspoon Worcestershire
    1 cup diced cooked potato

Prepare Brussels sprouts as directed on package, adding bouillon cubes to liquid. Meanwhile, sauté onion in the butter until golden. Add pecans and cook, stirring, a few seconds. Add remaining ingredients and toss with drained sprouts. Serve at once. Makes 6 servings.
Note: If available, 4 cups fresh Brussels sprouts, cooked, can be substituted for the frozen.

BRUSSELS SPROUTS AND MUSHROOMS

    1 quart (1¾ pounds) Brussels sprouts
      Salt
    ½ pound fresh mushrooms, sliced
    3 tablespoons butter or margarine
      Pepper
      Canned pimiento, cut in strips

Wash and trim sprouts. Put in saucepan with 1 cup boiling water; add salt to taste. Cook, uncovered, 5 minutes. Cover and cook 10 minutes, or just until crisp-tender; drain. Meanwhile, cook mushrooms in the butter until tender and golden brown. Add to sprouts and season with salt and pepper to taste. Put in serving dish and garnish with pimiento strips. Makes 6 servings.
Note: Two boxes (10 ounces each) frozen Brussels sprouts can be substituted for the fresh. Cook as directed on the label.

BRUSSELS SPROUTS IN BROWNED BUTTER

Cook and drain 2 pints fresh, or 2 packages (10 ounces each) frozen, Brussels sprouts. Brown ¼ cup butter or margarine slowly in a heavy skillet. Add juice of 1 lemon, sprouts, salt and pepper; heat. Makes 4 servings.

BUCKWHEAT

BUCKWHEAT—The triangular seeds of this plant are used as a cereal although, botanically speaking, it is an herb of the genus *Fagopyrum*. It is not a member of the family of cereal grasses to which wheat belongs. Buckwheat originates in Central Asia and Siberia, where it grows wild. Its use as a cereal is recent, compared to rice, barley, and millet; it is first mentioned in Chinese writings during the 10th and 11th centuries. Buckwheat was introduced into Europe during the early 15th century, and the first settlers brought it to the New World.

Buckwheat is a plant that likes a cool climate, and it will grow on the poorest and most arid soils. It is the staple grain of Russia and Poland, where millions of acres are put under buckwheat cultivation. The familiar Russian and Polish name for cooked buckwheat is *kasha*, and Jewish cookery, which uses buckwheat extensively, also uses this term.

Buckwheat is also consumed in Germany and France, the French name being *sayrasin*. In the United States, buckwheat is used mainly as flour for pancakes.

Purchasing Guide—Bran is removed and the remainder of the kernel is used to make flour or groats.

Buckwheat groats may be brown or white and also whole-kernel, coarse, medium, or fine; the medium is the most popular.

Storage—Flour, kitchen shelf: 3 months
Groats, kitchen shelf: 1 year
Groats, refrigerator shelf, cooked, covered: 1 week

Nutritive Food Values—High in carbohydrates, with small amounts of vitamins and minerals.
Light flour, 1 cup, sifted = 347 calories
Whole-kernel, 3½ ounces = 335 calories

Basic Preparation—Cook buckwheat groats as you would rice; follow package directions.

Buckwheat flour is used in combination with white flour; anything made of all-buckwheat flour would lack good color and texture.

KASHA

    1 egg, beaten
    1 cup buckwheat groats
    1 teaspoon salt
    ¼ cup shortening
    2 cups water

Combine egg, groats, and salt. Melt shortening in medium-size skillet. Stir in groat mixture and water; bring to a boil and cook, tightly covered, over low heat for about 15 minutes. Serve as a vegetable, in soups, or with gravy. Makes 4 servings.

BUCKWHEAT CAKES

      Water*
    1 package active dry yeast of 1 cake compressed yeast
    2 cups warm milk
    ¼ cup melted butter or sausage drippings
    2 cups buckwheat flour
    1 cup all-purpose flour
    3 tablespoons sugar
    2 teaspoons salt
    ½ teaspoon baking soda

*Use very warm water (105°F. TO 115°F.) for dry yeast; use lukewarm water (80°F. to 90°F.) for compressed. Sprinkle yeast or crumble cake into 1 cup water. Let stand for a few minutes, then stir until dissolved. Add milk and butter. Combine flours, sugar, and salt in a large bowl; add yeast and beat until smooth. Let rise overnight in a warm place; next morning dissolve soda in 1 tablespoon water and stir into raised mixture. Bake on hot griddle, lightly greased if necessary, turning once to brown both sides. Serve with butter and syrup. Makes about 36.

BUFFET

COUNTRY-STYLE BUCKWHEAT GROATS

½ cup buckwheat groats
3 cups milk
½ teaspoon salt
    All-purpose flour
    Buttered maple syrup

Combine buckwheat groats, milk, and salt in a small saucepan. Bring to a boil, stirring occasionally, Spread evenly in an 8-inch square pan; chill. Unmold; cut into 2-inch squares; dredge with flour. Brown on both sides on lightly greased griddle, turning once. Serve with buttered maple syrup. Makes 4 servings.

BAKED BUCKWHEAT PUDDING

2 eggs, beaten
½ cup buckwheat groats
6 cups milk
¾ cup molasses
6 tablespoons sugar
¾ teaspoon salt
1½ teaspoons ground ginger

Combine eggs and groats. Scald 2 cups milk in medium-size frying pan. Stir in groats, cover, and cook over low heat for 10 minutes, stirring occasionally. Blend in 4 cups milk and remaining ingredients. Pour into greased 1½-quart baking dish. Bake, uncovered, in preheated slow oven (325°F.) about 1 hour. Stir in remaining 2 cups milk; continue to bake for 1¼ hours. Serve warm with cream or ice cream. Makes 6 servings.

BUFFET—Literally translated, this French word means a "sideboard" or "cupboard." In French culinary language, a buffet indicates a good-size tiered table on which various dishes have been arranged in a decorative manner and, by implication, a restaurant that has such an arrangement. But even in French-speaking countries, the word is also used for an informal restaurant where a quick meal can be found, such as in *Buffet de la Gare*, "a station restaurant."

In America, the word buffet is used as a term for a meal where the guests help themselves from a table on which the foods are placed in a decorative array.

Buffet entertaining has become popular in recent years for three good reasons. First, fewer people have servants in this modern era, and when the food is good, the table attractive, and the company congenial, a buffet has all the graciousness of a meal that is formally served. The second point in favor of buffets: they permit a hostess to entertain more guests than she can seat comfortably at her dining-room table. And third, informality is the keynote of much of life today, and buffet entertaining, where guests serve themselves and, unconfined by a seating arrangement, can mingle with one another, fits in with this informality. But buffet meals, while they are easier on the hostess at the time of the party, do require careful planning and special equipment.

Planning the Menu—Consider casserole dishes: they come piping hot from oven to table and hold heat well.

Plan menus in terms of a main course that can be served on one plate.

Avoid foods that are hard to cut unless there are tables for all the diners.

Planning the Buffet Table—Make it as attractive as possible, and remember that food is part of the display so it should be considered as part of the color scheme.

Make it easy for guests to serve themselves. Arrange plates, napkins, silver, and serving dishes in the order in which they will be wanted.

Special Equipment—Chafing dishes, candle warmers, and electric warming trays keep hot foods hot.

Epergnes or other tiered serving dishes let you use space vertically if the buffet table is small.

CASSEROLE BUFFET
Menu with recipes for eight servings

Hamburger Casserole*
Tossed Salad   Garlic Bread*
Mixed-Fruit Bowl*
Coffee

HAMBURGER CASSEROLE

2 large onions, chopped
3 green peppers, sliced
⅓ cup butter or margarine
2½ pounds ground beef
3½ teaspoons salt
½ teaspoon pepper
5 cups fresh or canned whole-kernel corn
8 tomatoes, sliced
1 cup soft bread crumbs

Sauté onions and peppers in butter until brown. Add meat, breaking up with fork; cook for a few minutes, or until meat loses red color. Season with salt and pepper. In two 2-quart casseroles, arrange layers of half the corn, meat, and tomatoes. Repeat. Cover with crumbs. Bake in preheated moderate oven (350°F.) for 35 minutes. Makes 8 to 10 generous servings.

GARLIC BREAD

Cream ½ cup butter or margarine. Put 2 garlic cloves, halved, on toothpick and submerge garlic in butter; let stand for about 30 minutes. Remove garlic. Slice French bread loaf not quite through and spread slices with butter. Put slices together and spread a little butter over top; sprinkle with paprika. Heat in preheated hot oven (400°F.) for about 10 minutes.

MIXED-FRUIT BOWL

Chill pear halves, allowing 1 per serving. Add any other frozen or fresh fruit, such as grapefruit and orange sections, melon balls, or berries such as strawberries and blueberries.

BUFFET

ORIENTAL BUFFET
Menu with recipes for twelve servings

Sweet-And-Sour Meatballs*
Chinese Egg Rolls
Plum Sauce   Mustard
Steamed Rice
Chinese Vegetables*
Fresh-Fruit Bowl
Macaroons
Tea

SWEET-AND-SOUR MEATBALLS

- ¾ cup fine dry bread crumbs
- 1 tablespoon instant minced onion
- 2 teaspoons salt
- ½ teaspoon pepper
- Water
- 3 pounds ground beef
- 1 pound bulk pork sausage meat
- 3 eggs, slightly beaten
- Cooking oil
- 1 bouillon cube
- 4 carrots
- 3 green peppers
- ¾ cup cider vinegar
- 1 cup firmly packed light brown sugar
- ¼ cup soy sauce
- ⅓ cup cornstarch

Add bread crumbs, onion, salt, and pepper to 1½ cups water; let stand a few minutes. Add to ground beef and pork with eggs and mix well. Shape into 36 balls. Brown in small amount of oil in skillet. Remove to roasting pan. Pour off fat in skillet; add 1½ cups water and bouillon cube; heat, strain, and pour over meatballs. Cover and bake in preheated moderate oven (350°F.) for about 50 minutes. Cut carrots into strips and cook until almost tender; cut green pepper into wedges and cook for a few minutes. Make sauce by combining 4 cups water, vinegar, sugar, and soy sauce. Bring to boil; thicken with cornstarch mixed with a little cold water; cook until thick and clear. Pour liquid off meatballs and discard. Add carrots and green peppers to meatballs. Pour sauce over all and heat gently. Makes 12 servings.

CHINESE VEGETABLES

- 1 medium head of Chinese cabbage
- 2 celery stalks
- 3 green onions
- 2 tablespoons cooking oil
- ¼ cup water
- 1 package (10 ounces) frozen snow-pea pods
- 3 tablespoons soy sauce
- 2 pimientos, chopped

Slice cabbage, celery, and onions diagonally. Put vegetables in a large saucepan and add oil and water. Cover and steam for 5 minutes. Add pea pods and soy sauce. Cover and steam for a few minutes longer, or until all are tender but still crisp. Season with salt, if desired. Add pimientos. Makes 12 servings.

CHAFING-DISH BUFFET
Menu with recipes for twelve servings

Beef Balls Stroganoff*
Cheese Toast Cups*
Carrot Rice*
Asparagus or Broccoli Vinaigrette
Fresh Strawberries With
Kirsch or Cream
Nut Butter Cookies*
Coffee

BEEF BALLS STROGANOFF

- 2 eggs
- 1½ cups milk
- ¾ cup fine dry bread crumbs
- 1 tablespoon salt
- 1 teaspoon pepper
- 3 tablespoons chopped parsley
- 3 pounds ground beef chuck
- ½ cup butter or margarine
- 1½ cups chopped onion
- 1½ pounds fresh mushrooms, sliced
- 2 teaspoons paprika
- 6 tablespoons all-purpose flour
- 3 cups beef stock, bouillon, or consommé
- 1 tablespoon Worcestershire
- Salt and pepper
- ¾ cup dairy sour cream

Beat eggs; add milk, bread crumbs, salt, and pepper. Let stand for a few minutes. Add parsley and beef; mix thoroughly. Shape into 1-inch balls and brown in ¼ cup butter for about 10 minutes. Remove from pan. In same pan melt remaining ¼ cup butter; add onions, mushrooms, and paprika and brown slightly. Stir in flour to coat vegetables and brown for 2 to 3 minutes more. Gradually add beef stock, stirring constantly. Add Worcestershire and salt and pepper to taste. Return beef balls to sauce. Cover and cook slowly for 20 minutes. Add sour cream to sauce just before serving, or spoon sour cream on meatballs in serving dish to be stirred into sauce at the table. Makes 12 servings.

CHEESE TOAST CUPS

Cut crusts from slices of cheese bread. Melt butter and brush lavishly on slices. Press bread into muffin-pan cups and brown in preheated moderate oven (375°F.) for 10 to 15 minutes, or until crisped and browned. (Can be made ahead and reheated.)

Note: If cheese bread is not available, plain toast cups can be made with white bread.

BUFFET

Oriental Buffet

CARROT RICE

Prepare either instant rice or raw rice according to package directions to make 12 servings. Add ¾ cup coarsely shredded raw carrots to rice.

NUT BUTTER COOKIES

- ⅔ cup soft butter
- 6 tablespoons confectioners' sugar
- 1 teaspoon vanilla extract
- 2 cups sifted all-purpose flour
- ¼ teaspoon salt
- ½ teaspoon almond extract
- 1 cup chopped nuts

Cream butter; add remaining ingredients gradually and mix well. Press into finger-shape rolls 2 inches long. Squeeze each roll in the palm and fingers of one hand to obtain irregular shape. Place on ungreased cookie sheet and bake in preheated slow oven (325°F.) for 15 to 20 minutes. Makes about 3½ dozen.

BUN—This is a small, sweetened or unsweetened, round or oval cake or roll, and a very old form of baked food. Usually it is made with yeast. The best known buns are Bath buns, named after an English resort city; hot cross buns, marked with a sugar cross (originally baked for Good Friday, although now baked throughout Lent); and Swedish saffron buns, served on St. Lucia Day (December 13). Young Swedish girls, dressed in white and wearing crowns with lighted candles, serve the saffron buns to their parents early in the morning. This custom inaugurates the Christmas season.

ENGLISH BATH BUNS

- ½ cup warm water*
- 2 packages active dry yeast or 2 cakes compressed yeast
- ½ cup milk
- 1½ cups sugar
- 1 teaspoon salt
- ¾ cup butter or margarine
- 4 egg yolks
- 4 whole eggs
- 4½ cups sifted all-purpose flour
- ½ teaspoon lemon extract
- ½ cup chopped candied fruit
- ½ cup sliced blanched almonds
- ½ cup milk

*Use very warm water (105°F. to 115°F.) for dry yeast; use lukewarm (80°F. to 90°F.) for compressed. Sprinkle dry yeast or crumble cakes into water in large bowl and let stand for a few minutes; stir to dissolve. Scald milk and add ½ cup sugar, salt, and butter; cool to lukewarm. Combine milk mixture, egg yolks, 3 whole eggs, flour, lemon extract, and yeast mixture. Beat until smooth, about 5 minutes. Cover and let rise until doubled, about 1¼ hours. Stir down, cover well, and chill in refrigerator overnight. Divide into small pieces; shape into balls and put on greased cookie sheets. Cover and let rise until doubled, about 50 minutes. Press fruit and almonds into the tops. Beat together remaining whole egg and milk. Brush buns with mixture. Sprinkle remaining 1 cup sugar over the tops. Bake in preheated moderate oven (350°F.) for 15 to 20 minutes. Serve warm. Makes about 24.

HOT CROSS BUNS

- ¼ cup water*
- 1 package active dry yeast or 1 cake compressed yeast
- 1 cup milk, scalded
- 1 teaspoon salt
- ½ cup sugar
- ½ cup shortening
- 4½ cups sifted all-purpose flour
- 3 egg yolks, slightly beaten
- ½ teaspoon ground cinnamon
- ½ cup dry currants
- Melted butter

*Use very warm water (105°F. to 115°F.) for dry yeast; use lukewarm (80°F. to 90°F.) for compressed. Sprinkle dry yeast or crumble cake into water. Let stand for a few minutes, then stir until dissolved. Pour hot milk over salt, sugar, and shortening and cool to lukewarm. Add yeast and 2 cups flour, beat well, and let rise until light. Add egg yolks, then remaining 2½ cups flour mixed with cinnamon. Add currants. Knead; put in large greased bowl. Brush top of dough with melted butter. Cover, and let rise until doubled in bulk. Shape into small round buns and place close together in greased pan. Let rise until doubled in bulk. With a very sharp knife cut a cross just through the top surface of each bun. Bake in preheated hot oven (400°F.) for 15 minutes, brush with melted butter, and continue to bake for 5 minutes more. Cool on a rack. If desired, brush each bun with a simple frosting made of confectioners' sugar moistened with water. Makes 1½ to 2 dozen.

SWEDISH SAFFRON BUNS

- ¾ cup milk
- ⅓ cup sugar
- 1 teaspoon salt
- ¼ cup butter or margarine
- 1 teaspoon powdered saffron
- 2 tablespoons boiling water
- ½ cup water*
- 2 packages active dry yeast or 2 cakes compressed yeast
- 1 egg, beaten
- 4 cups sifted all-purpose flour (about)
- ¼ cup dry currants or seedless raisins

Scald milk; stir in sugar, salt, and butter; cool to lukewarm. Meanwhile add saffron to boiling water; let stand. Measure warm water into a large bowl. *Use very warm water (105°F. to 115°F.) for dry yeast; use lukewarm (80°F. to 90°F.) for compressed. Sprinkle or crumble in the yeast. Let stand for a few minutes; then stir until dissolved. Stir in lukewarm milk mixture, beaten egg, saffron water, and

Oriental Buffet

BURGUNDY

2 cups flour; beat until smooth. Stir in currants, then enough remaining flour to make a soft dough. Turn out on floured surface; knead until smooth and elastic, about 8 minutes. Place in a greased bowl, turning to grease all sides. Cover; let rise in warm place, free from draft, until doubled in bulk, about 1 hour. Punch down. Turn out on floured board, cover, and let rest for 10 minutes. Cut off a piece of dough about 2 inches in diameter. Divide remaining dough into 16 equal pieces. Shape each piece into a ball; place in a well-greased small brioche mold or muffin cup. Divide the 2-inch piece of dough into 16 pieces; shape each into a small ball. Make a deep indentation in each bun; press a small ball into each indentation. Cover; let rise in a warm place, free from draft, until doubled in bulk, about 30 minutes. Bake in preheated moderate oven (375°F.) for about 15 minutes. Makes 16.

BURGUNDY—The name of a region of France which produces some of the greatest wines in the world. Outside of France, Burgundy is usually thought of as a red wine, but there are also superb dry white Burgundies, of which the best known is called Chablis. Good Burgundy is a rich, mellow wine, rather on the hearty side.

Burgundy as a region is also the home of some of the most glorious of all French cooking, famed throughout the world for the lusciousness of its foods and the care taken in their preparation. Especially well known are: the mustard from Dijon, made there since the days of the Romans; the sugar-coated Jordan almonds, still sold in the shop where they were first made nearly three and a half centuries ago; and the king of all beef stews, *boeuf bourguignon.*

BOEUF BOURGUIGNON

- ¼ cup finely diced salt pork or bacon
- 2 pounds boneless lean stewing beef, cut into 1½-inch cubes
- 2 tablespoons brandy
- 1 teaspoon all-purpose flour
- 1 teaspoon salt
- ¼ teaspoon pepper
- 1½ cups dry red wine
- 1 tablespoon butter
- 2 medium onions, coarsely chopped
- 1 medium carrot, cut into pieces
- 1 garlic clove, minced or pressed
- 1 bouquet garni
  Water or beef bouillon
- ½ pound mushrooms, sliced

In heavy skillet cook salt pork or bacon until crisp. Brown meat in hot fat; the meat must be dark brown. Transfer meat to greased casserole. Heat brandy, pour over meat, and flame. When flame has died down, stir flour into meat. Season with salt and pepper and add red wine. Add butter to fat in skillet and brown onions. To meat in casserole, add onions, carrot, garlic, *bouquet garni,* and enough water or bouillon to cover meat. Simmer, covered, over lowest possible heat, or in preheated moderate oven (350°F.), about 3 hours, or until meat is very tender and sauce dark brown. About 30 minutes before serving time, add mushrooms. Remove *bouquet garni* when dish is ready. Serve with boiled potatoes or buttered noodles. Makes 4 to 6 servings.

Note: This dish can be made ahead of time and refrigerated. Reheat slowly.

BUSY DAY DINNERS

Menus and Recipes to Serve Six

Creamy Chicken Bake with Easy Buttered Noodles*
Pickled-beet and Chinese-cabbage Salad
Apricot-Mandarin Ambrosia*
Crisp Gingersnaps

CREAMY CHICKEN BAKE WITH EASY BUTTERED NOODLES

- ½ cup chopped dried beef
- 12 chicken thighs, skinned
- 6 slices bacon, precooked and drained
- 1 package (3 ounces) cream cheese, softened
- 2 cans (10½ ounces each) condensed cream of mushroom soup
- 1½ cups dairy sour cream
  Chopped parsley
  Easy Buttered Noodles

Sprinkle dried beef into 3-quart casserole. Arrange chicken thighs, rounded side up, in casserole. Top each with ½ slice bacon. Combine next 3 ingredients and beat until blended. Pour over chicken. Cover tightly with lid or foil and bake in preheated moderate oven (325°F.) 2 hours. Remove lid and bake uncovered 20 minutes. Sprinkle with parsley and serve on noodles. Makes 6 servings.

Easy Buttered Noodles. In large saucepan, bring 3 to 4 quarts water and 1 tablespoon salt to rapid boil. Stir in 12 ounces noodles. Cover, remove from heat and let stand 15 to 20 minutes. Drain and toss with melted butter.

APRICOT-MANDARIN AMBROSIA

Drain 1 can (30 ounces) whole peeled apricots, reserving ¾ cup syrup (save remaining syrup for later use). Add to glass serving dish with 1 can (11 ounces) mandarin-orange wedges, drained. Flavor reserved syrup with 1 teaspoon grated lemon rind. Pour over fruits and sprinkle with ½ to 1 cup flaked or shredded coconut. Chill.

BUSY DAY DINNERS

Beef in Wine Sauce*
Heated French or Sourdough Bread
(spread with chive butter)
Bought Coleslaw or Shredded Red and
Green Cabbage with bottled
Coleslaw Dressing
Special Frosted Brownies*

BEEF IN WINE SAUCE

- 4 pounds boneless beef chuck, cut in 1½ inch to 2 inch cubes
  Garlic powder
- 2 cans (10½ ounces each) condensed mushroom soup
- 1 envelope (1⅜ ounces) onion-soup mix
- ¾ cup dry sherry
- 1 can (8 ounces) sliced mushrooms, drained
- 1 bag (20 ounces) frozen sliced carrots

Sprinkle meat lightly with garlic powder. Put in heavy casserole or Dutch oven. Mix together remaining ingredients, except carrots, and pour over meat. Mix well, cover and bake in preheated moderate oven (350°F.) 2 hours, or until meat is very tender, adding carrots during last 20 minutes of baking. Makes 6 to 8 servings.

SPECIAL FROSTED BROWNIES

- 1 package (13 ounces) frozen frosted brownies, thawed
- 6 tablespoons orange-flavor liqueur
  Vanilla ice cream

Cut brownies in 6 serving pieces. Poke a few holes in top. Pour 1 tablespoon liqueur over each piece. Let stand a few minutes, then top with ice cream.

Mixed-up-Meat Loaf*
Baked Rice and Spinach*
Canned Chinese Mixed Vegetables
Canned Plums (with grated
orange rind added to syrup)
Almond Cookies
Tea

MIXED-UP-MEAT LOAF

- 2 pounds meat-loaf mix (beef, veal and pork)
- 1 tablespoon instant minced onion
- ½ cup soy sauce
  Canned brown gravy with onions, heated

Mix together all ingredients, except gravy, and press into 9 x 5 x 3 inch loaf pan. Bake in preheated moderate oven (350°F.) about 1 hour. Let stand 15 minutes before slicing. Serve with gravy. Makes 6 servings.

BAKED RICE AND SPINACH

- 1 cup long-grain rice
- 1 package (10 ounces) frozen chopped spinach
- 2 chicken bouillon cubes
- 2 cups boiling water

Put rice and spinach in buttered 2-quart casserole. Dissolve bouillon cubes in 2 cups boiling water and pour over rice and spinach. Cover and bake in preheated moderate oven (350°F.) about 45 minutes. Makes 6 servings.

Glazed Smoked Picnic Shoulder*
Mixed Sweet Pickles
Mushroom-Barley Casserole*
Banana-Pineapple Salad with
Sour-Cream Dressing*
Toasted Pound Cake

GLAZED SMOKED PICNIC SHOULDER

- 1 smoked picnic shoulder, 5 to 7 pounds
- 1 carrot
- 1 onion
- 1 celery stalk
- 1 bay leaf
  Orange-marmalade Glaze

Put meat, fat side up, in large kettle and cover with cold water. Bring to boil and add next 4 ingredients. Cover and simmer 2½ to 3 hours. Remove meat from broth, take off rind and set meat, fat side up, on rack in shallow roasting pan. Score fat in diamonds or other shapes and spread with Glaze. Bake in preheated moderate oven (350°F.) about 20 minutes. Makes more than 6 servings. Use remaining meat for later meal.
Orange-marmalade Glaze. Mix ¼ cup each firmly-packed light-brown sugar and orange marmalade and 1 teaspoon dry mustard.

BANANA-PINEAPPLE SALAD WITH SOUR CREAM DRESSING

- 1 can (13¼ ounces) pineapple chunks, chilled and drained
- 2 bananas, sliced
- 1 can (8 ounces) jellied cranberry sauce, cut in ¼ inch cubes
  Lettuce cups
  Sour cream Dressing

Mix first 3 ingredients lightly. Serve in lettuce cups with dressing. Makes 6 servings.
Sour Cream Dressing. Mix well ¼ cup each dairy sour cream and mayonnaise, ¼ teaspoon dry mustard and ½ teaspoon lemon juice. Makes ½ cup.

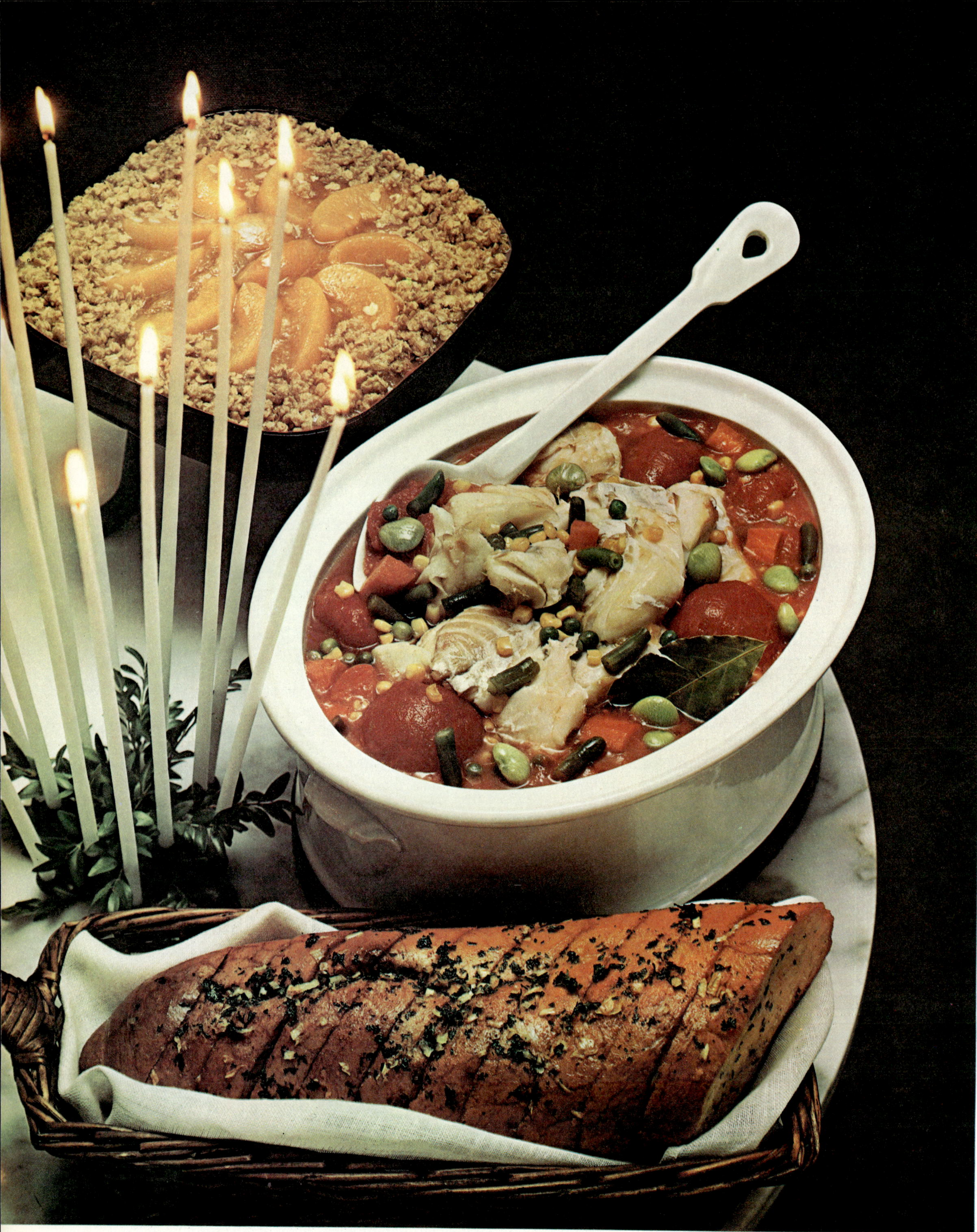

BUSY DAY DINNERS

Quick Fish Chowder*
Hot Onion Bread*
Deep-Dish Fruit Pie*

QUICK FISH CHOWDER

- 1 can (1 pound) tomatoes
- 2 packages (10 ounces each) frozen mixed vegetables
- 2 teaspoons salt
- ½ teaspoon pepper
- 1 bay leaf
- 2 tablespoons margarine
- 2 cups water
- ½ cup dry instant mashed potatoes
- 2 packages (12 ounces each) frozen cod fillets, partially thawed

Preheat oven to hot (400°F.). Put first 7 ingredients in saucepan, and bring to boil. Remove from heat, add instant potatoes; stir until smooth and slightly thickened. Put fish fillets in greased 3- to 4-quart casserole and pour mixture over top. Cover and bake 25 to 30 minutes, or until fish is white and firm and flakes easily. Makes 6 servings.

HOT ONION BREAD

- 1 tablespoon instant minced onion
- ½ teaspoon onion salt
- ½ cup soft margarine
- 1 loaf (11 ounces) French or Italian bread, sliced diagonally almost through
  Paprika
  Parsley flakes

Mix first 3 ingredients and spread between bread slices and on top. Sprinkle bread with paprika and parsley flakes and wrap in foil. Bake in preheated hot oven (400°F.) 20 minutes. Makes 6 servings.

DEEP DISH FRUIT PIE

- 1 can (20 ounces) pie-sliced apples
- 1 tablespoon lemon juice
- ¾ cup firmly packed brown sugar
- 1 can (21 ounces) peach pie filling
- 1½ cups regular rolled oats
- ¼ cup all-purpose flour
- ¾ teaspoon ground cinnamon
- ⅓ cup margarine
  Light cream (optional)

Put apples in greased shallow 9 inch square baking dish. Sprinkle with lemon juice and ½ cup brown sugar. Add peach pie filling. Mix remaining ½ cup brown sugar and next 3 ingredients. Cut in margarine to form a crumb mixture and sprinkle on pie filling, leaving center uncovered. Bake in preheated hot oven (400°F.) 25 to 30 minutes, or until top is browned and crisp. Serve warm, with cream, if desired. Makes 6 servings.

Curried Oven Pot Roast*
Buttered Noodles
Frozen Broccoli
Pear Cake Hélène*

CURRIED OVEN POT ROAST

- 1 can (10½ ounces) mushroom gravy
- 2 pounds chuck steak, bone in
- 2 teaspoons curry powder
- 1 teaspoon salt

Preheat oven to slow (300°F.). Pour gravy into Dutch oven and add steak. Sprinkle with curry powder and salt. Cover and bake about 2 hours. Cut meat in serving pieces and pour gravy over top. Makes 6 servings.

PEAR CAKE HÉLÉNE

- 1 bought sponge cake layer (one half 11 ounce package)
- 1 can (1 pound) sliced pears, drain and reserve half the liquid
  Vanilla ice cream
  Canned chocolate syrup

Put cake layer on serving plate and moisten with reserved pear syrup. Cover with pear slices and chill. Serve with vanilla ice cream and syrup heated by letting can stand in hot water. Makes 6 servings.

Tuna-Potato Casserole*
Cucumber-Iceberg Salad*
Fruit-filled Cake Ring*

TUNA POTATO CASSEROLE

- 8 medium potatoes, cooked and peeled
  Salt and pepper
- 2 cans (6 ounces each) flaked tuna, drained
- 2 eggs
- 2 cups milk
- 2 tablespoons grated Parmesan cheese
- 1 tablespoon seasoned fine dry bread crumbs

Preheat oven to moderate (350°F.). Cut potatoes in ¼-inch slices and put half in greased shallow 2-quart baking dish. Sprinkle lightly with salt and pepper. Cover with tuna, then with remaining potato slices. Beat eggs, milk and cheese together and pour over potatoes. Sprinkle with crumbs. Bake 45 minutes, or until custard is just set and potatoes are golden brown. Makes 6 servings.

BUTTER

CUCUMBER ICEBERG SALAD

    3 tablespoons each red-wine vinegar and salad oil
    2 tablespoons sugar
    ¼ teaspoon each pepper and dillweed
    ½ teaspoon salt
    1 large cucumber, peeled and cut in ½ inch cubes
    3 cups shredded iceberg lettuce

Mix all ingredients, except last 2, in salad bowl. Add remaining ingredients and toss lightly. Serve at once. Makes 6 servings.

FRUIT-FILLED CAKE RING

    1⅓ cups buttermilk baking mix
    ¾ cup sugar
    3 tablespoons shortening
    1 teaspoon each vanilla and almond extracts
    ¾ cup milk
    1 egg, slightly beaten
    1 can (1 pound) purple plums
    1 can (8 ounces) sliced pineapple

Preheat oven to moderate (350°F.). Grease and flour a 5-cup ring mold. Combine biscuit mix, sugar, shortening, flavorings and milk into mixing bowl; beat in egg. Pour into ring mold and bake 35 minutes, or until done. Unmold on serving plate. Drain fruits; combine and reserve syrups. Put cake back in mold, prick with cake tester or skewer and drizzle about ½ cup of reserved syrup on cake to moisten. Turn out on serving plate and arrange fruit in center. Serve with remaining syrup. Makes 6 servings.

Rosemary Lamb Stew*
Banana-Blueberry Fantasy*

ROSEMARY LAMB STEW

    1 can (1 pound) whole onions, drained
    3 large, unpeeled, raw potatoes, halved
    1 can (1 pound) sliced carrots, drain and reserve liquid
    2½ pounds lamb breast
    2 teaspoons instant chicken bouillon
    1 teaspoon dried rosemary leaves
    1 teaspoon seasoned salt
    ½ teaspoon seasoned pepper
    2 tablespoons soy sauce
      Celery tops and leaves (optional)

Preheat oven to moderate (350°F.). Put onions and potatoes (cut side up) in 4-quart Dutch oven. Add reserved liquid drained from carrots. Trim excess fat from lamb; cut meat in servings. Put on top of vegetables. Mix seasonings and sprinkle on lamb. Add celery and leaves, if desired. Cover and bake 2 to 2½ hours, or until meat is tender. Push meat aside and stir in carrots. Makes 6 servings.

BANANA-BLUEBERRY FANTASY

    3 large ripe bananas
      Lemon juice
    1 can (21 ounces) blueberry pie filling
      Frozen whipped topping

Put 6 dessert dishes on tray. Slice bananas into dishes and sprinkle with lemon juice. Spoon pie filling into dishes. Garnish with whipped topping. Makes 6 servings.

BUTTER—An edible animal fat, obtained from milk and cream which have been made solid by churning. Butter can be made from fresh or slightly acid milk (this affects the taste and spreading consistency); it can be salted or it can be sweet, that is, non-salted (Europeans prefer the latter). Good butter is the product of first-rate milk and cream, painstaking cleanliness, and skillful churning.

Butter has been a basic food since men began wandering to seek pasture for their animals: cattle, goats, sheep, asses, horses, and even camels. Probably butter originated spontaneously when the milk of these animals, carried in food containers, churned itself during the nomads' travels.

Butter was known to the ancient world as a symbol of goodness and plenty. The Bible is full of allusions to it: Judges 5:25, Job 29:6, Psalms 55:21, Proverbs 30:33, and Isaiah 7:15-22. The thought of butter and butter-making calls up charming visions of rural life in English butteries, where apple-cheeked lasses sat churning thick and satiny cream; or of the Swiss Alps, where the deep crocks of golden butter were cooled by crystal-clear glacier streams; or of the comfortable French farm kitchens ruled by bustling, aproned women.

The equipment used for making butter is often a fine token of the folk arts. It includes carved churns, painted cream containers, and carved butter molds and paddles.

Yet butter is not a universal product. In southern European countries oil, not butter, was used for fat since their climate made dairying impossible in less scientific days. In fact, European cooking can be classified in two broad ways: butter cookery and olive-oil cookery. The Chinese and Japanese do not use butter, but for the Tibetans and Indians it is a basic fat.

Perhaps the pleasure Western man takes in butter is not only a culinary one, but also one of nostalgia. Butter, basically a simple food, makes us feel that we still have a link with nature.

Availability—Salted and unsalted butter is sold packaged in ¼-pound sticks and 1-pound blocks. Whipped butter, salted, and unsalted, is sold in 8- to 12-ounce round cartons. Whipped salted butter is also sold in bars, 6 to a 1-pound package.

Butter is also sold in combinations such as honey butter.

BUTTER

Purchasing Guide—Butter is graded on flavor, color, body, texture, and salt. Each category is rated a certain number of points to achieve the following scores:

    U.S. Grade AA   (U.S. 93 Score)
    U.S. Grade A   (U.S. 92 Score)
    U.S. Grade B   (U.S. 90 Score)
    U.S. Grade C   (U.S. 89 Score)
    U.S. Grade GG   (U.S. 89 or lower Score)
      (or cooking grade)

According to federal law, butter must contain not less than 80% milk fat; coloring may be added.
2 sticks = ½ pound = 1 cup butter
1 stick = ½ cup = 8 tablespoons
⅓ cup butter = 5⅓ tablespoons

Storage—Keep in refrigerator, tightly wrapped to prevent absorption of odors. Take out only as much as you need for one meal to prevent deterioration of flavor due to exposure to light and warmth.
Refrigerator shelf: 2 weeks
Refrigerator frozen-food compartment, wrapped for freezing: 1 month
Freezer, wrapped for freezing: 1 year

Nutritive Food Values—High in fat with moderate amounts of vitamins A and D. Whipped butter contains ⅓ less calories than regular butter.
Sweet or salted, 1 tablespoon = 100 calories. (One pat about 1 teaspoon) = 35 calories

Basic Preparation—Should be used at low heat during sautéing because it smokes and browns if temperature is too high.

Not suitable for deep frying because of its low smoking point.

To Make Decorative Butter—Butter paddles, curlers, and molds can be bought in houseware stores. They can also be used for margarine.

Butter Curls—Begin at the far side of a 1-pound block of cold butter and draw a butter curler lightly and quickly toward you, making a thin shaving of butter which curls into a cylinder. Dip the curler into hot water each time.

Butter Balls—Scald and chill a pair of wooden butter paddles. Measure firm, but not cold, butter by measuring teaspoonfuls so that balls will be the same size. Roll lightly between paddles to shape into balls. Put on a chilled plate and store in refrigerator or drop into a bowl of ice water.

Butter Pats—Cut neat squares from a stick of cold butter with a sharp knife dipped into cold water or wrapped in wax paper. To add decoration, dip a fork in hot water and draw it diagonally across each square. Or garnish each square with a tiny parsley sprig.

Butter Molds—Use a special wooden butter mold and dip into ice water. Press firm butter into mold. Push to release butter. Chill until ready to serve.

To Clarify Butter—This is often done when sautéing chicken, veal, and fish because it doesn't burn as easily as whole butter. It also adds richness to cakes. Put any quantity of sweet butter in a deep saucepan. Melt butter over low heat and continue to heat until foam disappears from top and there is a light-brown sediment in bottom of pan. The liquid butter should remain golden. When perfectly clear, remove from heat and skim any brown crust from top. Pour off the clear butter, discarding sediment in pan. If a large amount of butter is being prepared, cool and strain through cheesecloth. Chill until ready to use.

BLACK BUTTER

Stir ⅓ cup butter over low heat until melted and dark brown. Add 1 teaspoon lemon juice or mild vinegar and salt and pepper. For Almond Black Butter, add ⅓ cup slivered blanched almonds when butter is beginning to brown. Serve on fish or meat.

LEMON BUTTER

Cream butter until very light and fluffy. Add a few drops of lemon juice to taste.

BUTTERMILK

MAÎTRE D'HÔTEL BUTTER

- ½ cup butter
- ½ teaspoon salt
- ⅛ teaspoon white pepper
- 2 tablespoons minced parsley
- 1 tablespoon lemon juice

Cream butter until fluffy. Beat in next 3 ingredients. Add lemon juice drop by drop. Makes about ½ cup.

HERB BUTTER

To Maître d'Hôtel Butter add 1 teaspoon ground thyme or marjoram and 1 teaspoon dried basil. Or use fresh herbs to taste. If desired, add ¼ teaspoon garlic salt. Good on broiled lamb chops, broiled steak, broiled fish.

BUTTER SPREADS FOR HOT BREADS

To ½ cup soft butter, add:

1 cup grated Parmesan cheese, ⅓ cup mayonnaise, ⅓ cup minced green onion.

¾ cup minced stuffed green olives, ½ cup ready-grated American cheese, 1 teaspoon scraped onion.

½ cup honey, ¼ cup chunk-style peanut butter. Sprinkle spread slices with cinnamon.

BUTTERMILK—This is the milk that is left over after butter has been churned. It contains very little fat, since the fat has gone into the butter.

Real buttermilk is a thin liquid with little fat globules, whereas commercial buttermilk is a smooth, homogenized product which is far more appetizing to drink than the original product.

Buttermilk varies, depending on whether the milk and cream used for butter were fresh or slightly soured. Most of today's buttermilk is made from freshly skimmed milk that has been pasteurized, cooled, inoculated with a special culture, and allowed to ferment under controlled conditions. The concentration of butterfat and other milk solids is the same as for skimmed milk. Salt is sometimes added to accentuate the flavor.

Purchasing Guide—Available in 1-quart containers.

Storage—Store, covered, in refrigerator to preserve flavor. Since buttermilk acidity increases during storage, use as soon as possible after purchase.

Nutritive Food Values—A good source of protein, calcium, and riboflavin.
1 cup = 90 calories

Basic Preparation—Buttermilk is used in recipes for beverages, sherbets, baked products, and salad dressings. When buttermilk is substituted for fresh milk in a recipe, baking soda must be used instead of baking powder for leavening. The proportions to use are:

¼ teaspoon baking soda + ½ cup buttermilk = 1 teaspoon baking powder + ½ cup fresh milk.

BUTTERMILK MERINGUE PIE

- 1 cup sugar
- ¼ cup all-purpose flour
- ½ teaspoon salt
- 1 whole egg
- 3 egg yolks
- 2 cups buttermilk
- 1 tablespoon butter
- 1 tablespoon lemon juice
- 1 baked 9-inch pastry shell
- Meringue

In top part of double boiler, mix sugar with flour and salt. Beat together whole egg, egg yolks, and buttermilk. Gradually stir into first mixture. Cook over boiling water until smooth and thickened. Add butter. Cool slightly and add lemon juice. Pour into cooled pie shell. Top with Meringue and bake in preheated hot oven (400°F.) for 5 minutes, or until slightly browned. Cool before serving. Makes 6 to 8 servings.

MERINGUE

Beat 3 egg whites with ¼ teaspoon salt until frothy. Gradually beat in 6 tablespoons sugar and beat until stiff and glossy. Pile lightly on pie, being sure to cover filling completely.

LOW-CALORIE BUTTERMILK SALAD DRESSING

- 3 tablespoons lemon juice
- 1¼ teaspoons seasoned salt
- ¼ teaspoon dry mustard
- 1 cup buttermilk
- Sugar

Combine all ingredients except sugar and blend well. Add sugar to taste. Good on lettuce-and-tomato or cottage-cheese salad. Makes 1 cup.

DANISH BUTTERMILK SOUP

- 2 eggs, well beaten
- 1 lemon, grated rind and juice
- ¼ cup sugar
- 1 teaspoon vanilla extract
- 4 cups buttermilk
- 1 cup heavy cream, whipped

Beat eggs with lemon rind, lemon juice, sugar, and vanilla. Whip buttermilk until frothy. Beat into egg mixture, a little at a time. Chill until frosty. Top with whipped cream. Serve with stewed fruit or preserves. A refreshing dessert for a hot weather meal. Serve with crisp cookies. Makes 4 servings.

BUTTERMILK SPOON BREAD

2 cups yellow cornmeal
1½ cups cold water
1 cup boiling water
2 tablespoons butter or margarine
2 teaspoons salt
2 eggs, beaten
1 teaspoon baking soda
1½ cups buttermilk

Stir cornmeal into cold water. Add boiling water and stir vigorously. Add remaining ingredients and mix well. Pour into buttered 2-quart casserole. Bake in preheated moderate oven (375°F.) for 45 minutes, or until firm and browned. Serve at once. Makes 6 to 8 servings.

BUTTERNUT SQUASH

MAPLE BUTTERNUT CAKE

½ cup butter or margarine
½ cup sugar
1 cup maple sugar
2 eggs, well beaten
2½ cups sifted all-purpose flour
2 teaspoons baking powder
½ teaspoon baking soda
½ teaspoon ground ginger
½ cup hot water
½ cup chopped butternuts
Maple Sugar Frosting

Cream butter until light. Gradually add sugars, blend thoroughly. Beat in eggs. Sift together flour, baking powder, baking soda, and ginger. Add to batter alternately with hot water, beating well after each addition. Stir in nuts. Pour into well-greased loaf pan 9¼ x 5¼ x 2¾ inches. Bake in preheated moderate oven (350°F.) for 45 minutes. Cool and frost with Maple Sugar Frosting.

MAPLE SUGAR FROSTING

2 cups maple sugar
¼ teaspoon salt
1 cup light cream
½ cup chopped butternut

Boil together maple sugar, salt, and cream until a little of the mixture dropped into cold water forms a soft ball (approximately 238°F. on a candy thermometer). Add nuts, cool slightly. Beat until creamy. Spread immediately since frosting will turn to fudge very quickly.

BUTTERNUT—This native North American nut, also known as a white walnut, is used primarily in cakes and cookies. Butternuts are very difficult to shell, but do not need blanching. They grow in small clusters inside spongy, hair-covered husks. In colonial days in America, before the advent of commercial dyes, the husks were used to color homespun wools and cottons.

The ripe nuts are used in cooking as you would other nuts.

Availability—These nuts are not shipped commercially, but are available in the areas where they are grown. Butternuts are grown from New Brunswick to Georgia and westward to the Dakotas and Arkansas.

Storage—Store as you would other nuts: covered, in a cool, dry place.
   Refrigerator shelf, unshelled: 1 year
   Refrigerator shelf, shelled: 3 to 6 months

Nutritive Food Values—They contain some protein and iron and are high in fat.
   3½ ounces = 629 calories
   6 or 7 nuts = 140 calories

BUTTERNUT SQUASH—A winter squash, smooth and hard-shelled, long and bulbous, with seeds contained in a small hollow in the base. The squash gets its name from its color which, for most of the year, is light brown or dark yellow. The flesh is almost orange. Its flavor is sweet, it mashes smoothly, and is comparatively quick-cooking.

Availability—August to March, with peak season October through December.

Storage—Keep in refrigerator or a cool place until ready to use.
   Refrigerator shelf, raw: 4 to 6 weeks
   Refrigerator shelf, cooked and covered: 1 to 4 days
   Refrigerator frozen-food compartment, prepared for freezing: 1 month
   Freezer, prepared for freezing: 1 year

Purchasing Guide—Weighs about 1 to 3 pounds. Look for squashes that seem heavy for their size, smooth-skinned with hard, tough rinds.

BUTTERSCOTCH

Nutritive Food Values—Butternut squash is an excellent source of vitamin A and also provides fair amounts of vitamin C, iron, and riboflavin.

3½ ounces, raw = 171 calories
1 cup, baked and mashed = 130 calories

Basic Preparation—Wash, then peel with vegetable parer. Cut off the underlayer of green along with the skin. Cut into halves and scoop out seeds and stringy portion. Slice or cut into cubes.

To Steam—Put cubes of squash in saucepan in about 1 inch of boiling salted water. Cover pan and cook for 20 to 30 minutes, or until tender. (A few slices of onion may be cooked with squash for additional flavor.)

Drain thoroughly, season; add a little butter or margarine. Return pan to heat and shake gently for about 1 minute to distribute seasonings and evaporate remaining liquid.

If squash is to be served mashed, follow directions above, then mash and serve.

To use leftover mashed butternut squash: melt a little butter in skillet; add 1 small onion, sliced, and fry until almost tender. Then stir in 2 to 3 tablespoons dark brown sugar. Add squash and blend well. Form squash into cakes and fry until brown on both sides.

To Bake—Cut squash into halves; scoop out seeds. Place in a shallow baking pan, skin side down. Brush with melted butter or margarine and sprinkle with salt and pepper. If desired, sprinkle with a little brown sugar or molasses. Bake, covered, in preheated moderate oven (350°F.) for 30 minutes; uncover and bake for 20 to 30 minutes longer, or until squash is tender. Serve in the shell or mash as above.

To Freeze—Bake or steam squash as above until tender. Cool; mash pulp. Package, allowing ½-inch headspace.

ANISE BUTTERNUT SQUASH

4 cups mashed cooked butternut or other yellow winter squash
⅓ cup sugar
¼ cup butter or margarine
1½ teaspoons aniseed, crushed
½ teaspoon salt

Combine all ingredients. Turn into a buttered 1-quart casserole. Bake in preheated moderate oven (375°F.) for 45 minutes, or until top is well flecked with brown. Serve hot with pork, poultry, or ham. Makes 6 to 8 servings.

BUTTERSCOTCH—This popular flavor is obtained by combining butter and sugar, usually brown sugar, and by cooking the two together in a number of different ways.

Foods flavored with butterscotch, such as cakes, cookies, frostings, puddings, and sauces, take the name, and become butterscotch cake, butterscotch frosting, butterscotch pudding, etc.

Butterscotch is also a hard candy.

BUTTERSCOTCH CREAM PIE

½ cup granulated sugar
⅓ cup hot water
2 cups milk
¼ cup butter or margarine
6 tablespoons all-purpose flour
¾ cup firmly-packed dark brown sugar
½ teaspoon salt
2 eggs
1 baked 9-inch pastry shell
1 cup heavy cream, whipped
Toasted slivered almonds

Place granulated sugar in small heavy saucepan or skillet. Cook over low heat without stirring until sugar melts and becomes golden brown. Remove from heat. Add water slowly. Cook without stirring until sugar dissolves. Add milk. Heat to almost boiling. Melt butter in top part of double boiler. Remove from heat. Add flour, brown sugar, and salt. Beat in eggs and milk mixture. Cook over boiling water, stirring constantly, until thickened. Cover and cook for 10 minutes, stirring occasionally. Cool to room temperature. Pour into baked shell. Chill for several hours. Top with whipped cream and sprinkle with almonds. Makes 6 to 8 servings.

BUTTERSCOTCH SAUCE

2 cups firmly packed light brown sugar
½ cup undiluted evaporated milk
¼ teaspoon salt
⅓ cup light corn syrup
⅓ cup butter or margarine

Combine all ingredients in a saucepan; bring to boil and cook for 3 minutes, 220°F. on a candy thermometer. Makes 2 cups.
Note: This sauce can be made a day ahead. Do not refrigerate.

BUTTERSCOTCH FILLING

3 tablespoons butter or margarine
½ cup firmly packed dark brown sugar
1½ cups milk
¼ cup all-purpose flour
½ teaspoon salt
1 egg, beaten
½ teaspoon vanilla extract

Melt butter in top part of double boiler. Add sugar and cook for 2 minutes over direct heat. Add 1 cup milk and heat over boiling water. Mix flour, remaining ½ cup milk, and salt until smooth. Gradually stir into hot mixture. Cook for 5 minutes, stirring constantly. Cover; cook for 10 minutes longer, stirring occasionally. Add mixture gradually to egg; return to double boiler and cook for 2 minutes. Cool; add vanilla. Use as filling in layer cake. Makes about 2 cups.

CABBAGE—*Brassica* is the Latin name of this leafy vegetable, which may be called man's best friend in the vegetable world. The word "cabbage" itself is an Anglicized version of the colloquial French word *caboche,* which means "head."

Cabbage comes in many varieties, some with loose heads, some with firm ones, and others with flat, conical, or egg-shape heads. Some cabbages are white, some green, some red; some have plain leaves and some curly ones. It grows in a large range of latitudes. Learned scholars have argued over its origin, which is both obscure and ancient. At least 4,000 years ago men were eating the leafy wild cabbage found on the coasts of Europe and northern Africa, and it appears that they also ate cabbage in China several thousand years ago. Egyptians, Greeks, and Romans adored cabbage, and Marcus Porcius Cato, the great Roman statesman, wrote five pages on it, anticipating the American taste for coleslaw: "It surpasses all other vegetables. It may be eaten either cooked or raw. If you eat it raw dip it into vinegar. . . . It promotes digestion marvelously."

The Celts, too, thought so highly of cabbage that they brought it into northern Europe. In Great Britain it became known through the centuries as the national flower of England.

Cabbage came to the North American continent via Jacques Cartier, who planted it in Canada on his third voyage in 1541-42. Though the early American colonists must have planted cabbage, if for nothing else but to feed their stock, there is no written record of it until 1669.

Cabbage is eaten in one form or another in most countries of the world. It is a favorite food of the Slavic and the Germanic peoples, and an important part of their daily diet.

The universality of cabbage is perhaps best illustrated by the number of legends that have sprung up around it. Babies were found in the cabbage patch, and in Scotland young women guessed at the figure and the size of their future husbands by drawing cabbages, blindfolded, on Halloween. To dream of cabbages meant sickness to loved ones and loss of money. And we are apt to forget that the man on the moon was sent there because he stole a cabbage from his neighbor on December 24. A child in white surprised him in this evil deed, and said: "Since you will steal on this holy night, let you and your cabbage go to the moon."

Sauerkraut is said to have originated in Asia, as a convenient way of preserving an essential food when no other food-preserving methods were available. All in all, it is certain that man would find it hard to live without cabbage.

CABBAGE

Availability—Available all year round in different varieties.

Danish—This is a compact, solid-headed, late-maturing cabbage. The leaves are tight and smooth around the top, and the heads are round and somewhat flattened or oval.

Domestic—The heads, somewhat angular in outline, are usually less compact than Danish, and the leaf tissues are more tender and brittle. The leaves are a little crumpled or curled and do not overlap as far at the crown as the Danish. They are largely an early or midseason crop.

Pointed (called "green" or "new" cabbage)—Smaller head than Danish and Domestic. Greener color.

Red—The leaves are relatively loose. Several varieties of this reddish-purple cabbage are common, especially in the New York area and in Wisconsin.

Savoy—It is readily identified by crinkled leaves that shade from dark to pale green, and heads that are loosely formed. This cabbage, a favorite with people of Latin descent, is becoming increasingly popular here. The flavor is a little mellower than that of other green cabbage.

Celery or Chinese (Pe-Tsai) Cabbage—Although it is called cabbage, this vegetable is a more distant member of the cabbage family. The long, firm tapering "stalks" (about 4 inches thick and 10 to 16 inches long) resemble a cross between oversize romaine lettuce and celery. Its tightly closed broad leaves are crisp, the color pale green to white. It is used mainly in salads, but many interesting cooked dishes can be made with it.

Purchasing Guide—A head of cabbage should be solid and heavy for its size. New cabbage, which comes from southern areas during the winter, is usually not as solid as winter (stored) cabbage but is greener. Avoid heads showing injury, decay, or yellow leaves. If the base of some of the outer leaves is separated from the stem, the cabbage may be strong in flavor or coarse in texture when cooked. Celery cabbage should be firm, oval shape, and well blanched.
1 pound = about 4 cups raw = 2 cups cooked

Storage—Remove any discolored leaves from head of cabbage. Place in a covered container or moistureproof bag, or wrap in foil or wax paper, and keep in the refrigerator.
Refrigerator shelf or vegetable compartment, raw: 3 to 8 days
Refrigerator shelf, cooked: 1 to 4 days
Refrigerator frozen-food compartment, prepared for freezing: 2 to 3 months
Freezer, prepared for freezing: 1 year

Nutritive Food Values—Raw cabbage is a very good source of vitamin C and some vitamin A; celery cabbage has a smaller amount. During the cooking process, however, there may be some vitamin loss.
1 cup finely shredded raw = 20 calories
1 cup cooked = 30 calories
1 cup sliced celery cabbage, raw = 10 calories

Basic Preparation—Wash head well. Cut according to way it is to be used. If cabbage is old, cut round heads into wedges and remove center core; or shred it. *Never overcook cabbage.*

To Boil, Wedges—Put about 1 inch of water in a saucepan; add about ½ teaspoon salt per pound of cabbage, and the wedges. Cook rapidly, uncovered, for 2 to 3 minutes; then cover pan, lower heat, and cook for 10 to 12 minutes more, or until tender but still crisp. Drain, season to taste, and add butter or margarine if desired.

To Boil, Shredded—Follow same method as for wedges, but use only ½ inch of water and cook for only 5 to 8 minutes. Drain, season, and serve at once.

To Braise—In a skillet melt enough butter, margarine, or bacon fat to cover the bottom of the pan. Add cabbage wedges or shreds; cook gently for 2 to 3 minutes, turning until the vegetable is coated with fat. Then cover tightly and let steam until tender, about 15 minutes for wedges, 8 to 10 for shreds.

Cook red cabbage by any of the methods above, but add a little vinegar or lemon juice or a few apple slices to help hold the color.

To Prepare Uncooked Cabbage—Two methods are used to slice or shred cabbage for coleslaw and the many other ways of serving cabbage raw.

1. Coarse shredding or grating on a regular grater is preferred if the juice is to be drawn from cabbage, as in a coleslaw which is dressed with vinegar and seasonings only. Dressings also soak into grated cabbage more rapidly.

2. Slicing, paper-thin, is preferred when longer, drier shreds are desired. This is done with a slicing knife on a board or with a mechanical vegetable shredder. The resulting slaw or salad pieces have more form and the cabbage stays crisper.

To Freeze—Use solid green and white heads. Trim all bruised pieces. Remove core and cut cabbage into pieces. Blanch in boiling water for 3 to 4 minutes, depending on size. Cool in ice water. Pack tightly to prevent air spaces, and allow ½-inch headspace.

Prepare celery cabbage in the same way, blanching pieces for only 70 seconds.

Cabbage Rolls with Sauerkraut and Pork

CABBAGE

CABBAGE ROLLS WITH SAUERKRAUT AND PORK

- 6 to 8 large cabbage leaves
- 2 cups cooked rice
- ½ pound sausage meat
- 2 tablespoons finely chopped onion
- Salt and pepper
- 2 cups (1-pound can) sauerkraut
- 1 smoked pork hock
- Water
- Paprika
- Dairy sour cream

Cook cabbage leaves in small amount of boiling salted water for 3 to 4 minutes. Drain and dry on paper towels. Mix rice, sausage meat, onion, salt, and pepper. Fill and roll the cabbage leaves. Secure with toothpicks or poultry skewers. Place half of sauerkraut in a skillet. Top with cabbage rolls and pork hock. Cover with remaining sauerkraut. Add enough water to cover and simmer for 2 hours, adding more water when needed. Sprinkle with paprika and serve with sour cream. Makes 6 to 8 servings.

FRENCH CABBAGE SOUP

- 3 cups chopped raw potatoes
- 1 pound lean bacon or ham, in one piece
- 3 quarts water
- 2 pounds cabbage, coarsely sliced
- 6 peppercorns, crushed
- 6 parsley sprigs
- 1 bay leaf
- ½ teaspoon each of ground thyme and marjoram
- 2 garlic cloves, mashed
- 2 onions
- 2 carrots, quartered
- 2 celery stalks, sliced
- 2 turnips, peeled and chopped (optional)
- 1½ cups drained canned red or white beans
- Salt

Place potatoes and bacon in deep kettle. Add water. Bring to boil. Add all other ingredients except beans and salt. Simmer, covered, 2 hours, or until meat is tender. Remove meat; slice into serving pieces. Skim off excess fat from soup. Return meat to soup. Add beans. Season to taste with salt. Heat thoroughly. Makes 8 servings.

CABBAGE

CABBAGE SOUP
[Japanese Style]

- 3 cups beef broth (or 3 cups water and 3 bouillon cubes)
- 1 tablespoon soy sauce
- 1 teaspoon monosodium glutamate
- ¼ teaspoon black pepper
- 1 pound lean pork steak, sliced very thin cross-grain
- ¾ head cabbage, cut in 3 wedges and sliced lengthwise in ⅛-inch strips
- 3 stalks celery, thinly sliced
- 3 green onions, white part thinly sliced, tops finely chopped
- 1 tablespoon butter

In large saucepan, combine first 4 ingredients. Bring to boil, add meat and boil 5 minutes. Stir in cabbage. Bring to a boil, add celery and white part of onion. Boil 1 minute, then stir in butter. Season with additional soy sauce, if desired, and sprinkle with green-onion tops. Makes 4 large servings. **Note:** If a heartier soup is desired, serve soup on ½ pound cooked vermicelli seasoned with soy sauce to taste.

CABBAGE ALMOND SOUP

- 2 cups finely chopped cabbage
- ½ cup chopped blanched almonds
- ½ cup water
- 2 tablespoons butter
- 1 teaspoon caraway seeds
- 2 teaspoons salt
- ¼ teaspoon paprika
- 1 egg, well beaten
- 4 cups milk
- ¼ cup grated sharp Cheddar cheese

Cook cabbage and almonds in water for 10 minutes; add butter, caraway seeds, salt, and paprika. Mix egg with milk, add to cabbage mixture, and heat just to boiling, stirring occasionally. Top with cheese. Makes 4 servings.

RED CABBAGE WITH APPLES

- 1 head red cabbage about 2½ pounds
- ¾ cup boiling water
- 3 large cooking apples, peeled, cored and sliced
- Dash of pepper
- 3 tablespoons butter or margarine, melted
- ¼ cup cider vinegar
- 1½ teaspoons all-purpose flour
- ¼ cup firmly packed brown sugar
- 2 teaspoons salt

Wash and shred cabbage very fine. Discard core and tough ribs. Add boiling water and cook 12 to 15 minutes. Just before cabbage is done, add apples and simmer 10 minutes longer. Then add remaining ingredients. Toss lightly with fork to blend. Heat gently and serve. Makes 6 servings.

DOLMAS

- 1 cabbage, about 2 pounds
- 2 cups chopped onion
- ¼ cup olive oil
- ½ cup raw rice
- ½ cup chopped parsley
- ¼ cup raisins
- ¼ to ½ teaspoon ground allspice
- ¼ to ½ teaspoon ground cinnamon
- ¾ teaspoon salt
- 1 can (8 ounces) tomato sauce

Prepare cabbage as in general directions, reserving liquid and setting aside 8 outer leaves. Chop remaining cabbage and put in 9 or 10-inch skillet. Sauté onion in the olive oil until golden. Add 1 cup boiling hot cabbage liquid and rice; cover and simmer 15 minutes. Add parsley, raisins, spices, salt and ¼ cup tomato sauce and simmer 5 minutes longer. Divide mixture into leaves and make packages, folding in sides. Arrange on chopped cabbage. Mix remaining ¾ cup tomato sauce with ½ cup cabbage liquid and pour on top of rolls. Cover and simmer 45 minutes, or until cabbage is tender, adding more liquid if necessary. Makes 4 servings.

CABBAGE IN CREAM

- 2 quarts shredded green cabbage
- Salt
- ½ cup light cream
- 3 tablespoons butter
- Dash of ground nutmeg
- Pepper

Cook cabbage in ½ inch of boiling salted water for 5 to 8 minutes, or until tender. Drain. Add cream and butter; heat slowly, stirring gently with a fork. Add nutmeg, and salt and pepper to taste. If cheese sauce is desired, stir ¼ pound sharp Cheddar cheese, shredded, into the sauce and stir until cheese is melted. Crisply fried bacon may be crumbled over the cabbage and sauce. Makes 4 to 6 servings.

CABBAGE, TOMATOES, AND GREEN PEPPER

- 3 onions, sliced
- 2 tablespoons butter
- 1 green pepper, cut into 1-inch pieces
- 2 large tomatoes
- ½ medium head green cabbage
- Salt and pepper

Cook onions in butter for 3 minutes. Add green pepper; cover and cook for 5 minutes. Cut tomatoes into halves and cabbage into 4 wedges; add to onion and green pepper. Season to taste, cover, and simmer for about 15 minutes. Makes 4 servings.

CABBAGE

WILTED CABBAGE

- 4 slices bacon
- ½ cup cider vinegar
- 2 tablespoons sugar
- 1 teaspoon salt
- ⅛ teaspoon pepper
- ½ cup water
- 3 cups finely shredded red cabbage
- 3 cups finely shredded green cabbage

Fry bacon in skillet until crisp; remove and reserve. To fat in skillet, add vinegar, sugar, salt, pepper, and water and bring to boil. Divide mixture, adding half to red and half to green cabbage. Cook cabbages separately, about 5 minutes for green cabbage, and 8 to 10 minutes for red cabbage. Serve in 2-sectioned dish; crumble crisp bacon over top. Makes 4 servings.

SWEET-AND-SOUR RED CABBAGE

- 1 onion, chopped
- 3 tablespoons butter or margarine
- 9 cups shredded red cabbage
- 1 large tart apple, diced
- 3 tablespoons cider vinegar
- 1 cup water
- 3 tablespoons brown sugar
- 1 tablespoon caraway seeds
- 1¼ teaspoons salt
- ¼ teaspoon pepper
- ⅓ cup seedless raisins

Cook onion in butter for 5 minutes. Add cabbage; cover and cook for 5 minutes longer. Add remaining ingredients, cover, and simmer for about 10 minutes. Makes 6 servings.

BROWNED SAUERKRAUT

- 1 onion, chopped
- 2 tablespoons shortening, melted
- 1 quart sauerkraut, drained
- 1 medium potato, peeled and grated
- 1 teaspoon caraway seeds
- Boiling water

Cook onion in shortening until golden brown. Add sauerkraut. Cook over medium heat, stirring frequently, for 10 minutes. Add potato, caraway seeds, and boiling water to cover. Simmer, uncovered, over low heat for 30 minutes. Cover and simmer for 20 minutes longer. Makes 6 servings.

CURRIED CABBAGE IN BEER

- 3 tablespoons butter or margarine
- 2 teaspoons curry powder
- ½ teaspoon salt
- ⅔ cup beer
- 6 cups shredded cabbage

Melt butter in large skillet. Stir in curry powder, salt, beer and cabbage. Cover and cook, stirring once or twice, 10 minutes, or until cabbage is tender. Makes 4 servings.

STUFFED WHOLE CABBAGE WITH BÉCHAMEL SAUCE

- 1 small whole green cabbage
- 1 pound ground beef chuck
- ¼ cup chopped onion
- 1 tablespoon butter or margarine
- 1 teaspoon salt
- ⅛ teaspoon pepper
- Pinch of garlic powder
- 2 cups beef bouillon or 2 bouillon cubes dissolved in 2 cups boiling water
- Béchamel Sauce

Trim coarse outside leaves from cabbage. Cut out the middle of cabbage (save cut portion for coleslaw). Brown meat with onion in butter. Add salt, pepper, and garlic powder. Spoon into cavity of cabbage. Tie cabbage in cheesecloth. Bring bouillon to a boil, drop in cabbage. Cover and cook for 20 minutes, or until cabbage is tender. Serve hot with Béchamel Sauce. Makes 4 to 6 servings.

PANNED CHINESE CABBAGE

- 2 tablespoons butter
- 1 quart shredded Chinese cabbage
- Salt and pepper

Heat butter in skillet. Add cabbage, cover, and cook for about 3 minutes, stirring twice. Season with salt and pepper. Makes 4 servings.

WESTERN PERFECTION SALAD

- 1 box (3 ounces) lemon-flavored gelatin
- 1 cup hot water
- 1 cup cold water
- 2 tablespoons wine vinegar
- 1½ teaspoons salt
- ¾ cup shredded or finely chopped carrots
- ¾ cup shredded or chopped green cabbage
- ¾ cup diced celery
- Salad greens
- Sour cream or other dressing, as desired

Dissolve gelatin in hot water. Stir in cold water, vinegar and salt. Chill until thickened to the consistency of unbeaten egg whites. Fold in vegetables and pour into pan 8 x 8 x 2 inches. Chill until firm. Cut into 6 servings and put on greens. Serve with dressing. Makes 6 servings.

Cabbage

SAVOY CABBAGE, POLONAISE

- 1 medium head savoy cabbage
- 1 teaspoon sugar
- 1 teaspoon salt
- 3 tablespoons butter or margarine
- 1 cup soft bread crumbs

Remove core. Shred cabbage medium fine. Cook in ½ inch of boiling water with sugar and salt in a covered saucepan for 6 to 8 minutes. Drain and turn into greased 1-quart baking dish. Melt butter, add bread crumbs, and mix well. Sprinkle on cabbage. Bake in preheated moderate oven (350°F.) for 20 minutes, or until crumbs are brown. Makes 4 to 6 servings.

CABBAGE SLAWS

A collection of recipes that prove how successfully shredded cabbage combines with many different foods and flavorings.

COUNTRY-STYLE COLESLAW

- 1 tablespoon cornstarch
- 1½ teaspoons salt
- Dash of cayenne
- 1 teaspoon powdered mustard
- 1½ tablespoon sugar
- ¼ teaspoon paprika
- 2 eggs
- ⅓ cup cider vinegar
- 1 cup milk
- 3 cups coarsely shredded green cabbage
- Parsley

In top part of double boiler, combine first 7 ingredients; beat well. Add vinegar and milk and mix well. Cook over boiling water, stirring constantly, until thickened. Cool and refrigerate. At serving time mix enough dressing with cabbage to just moisten; sprinkle with parsley. Makes 4 servings.

DILLY CARROT SLAW

- 3 cups shredded cabbage
- 1 teaspoon salt
- 1 turnip, shredded
- 1 small carrot, shredded
- 1 green pepper, finely diced
- ¼ teaspoon dill seed
- Mayonnaise-Sour Cream Dressing

Cover cabbage with salt and let stand 45 minutes. Squeeze free of water. Mix with next 4 ingredients and add Dressing to moisten. Makes 4 to 6 servings.

Mayonnaise-Sour Cream Dressing

Mix well juice of 1 lemon, ¼ cup dairy sour cream, ½ cup mayonnaise, ¼ teaspoon pepper, 1 tablespoon sugar, pinch of thyme and a dash of paprika.

RED CABBAGE SLAW

Toss 3 cups shredded red cabbage with plain French dressing. Season to taste with salt and pepper. Top with slices of white onion. Makes 4 servings.

CURRIED PEAR SLAW

Combine ½ cup mayonnaise with 1 tablespoon curry powder and 1 tablespoon chutney. Mix with 3 cups shredded green cabbage, and season with salt and pepper. Top with slices of pear, sprinkled with lemon juice. Makes 4 servings.

SOY GINGER SLAW

Mix ¾ cup mayonnaise with 2 tablespoons soy sauce and ¼ teaspoon ginger. Combine 3 cups shredded green cabbage with slivers of green pepper and 2 chopped green onions. Add enough dressing to moisten. Top with remaining dressing and pieces of chutney if desired. Makes 4 servings.

BUTTERMILK HERB SLAW

Mix ¾ cup buttermilk with 1 tablespoon cider vinegar, 1 tablespoon sugar, ½ teaspoon salt, and 2 teaspoons chopped fresh dill or marjoram (or ½ teaspoon dried). Mix with 3 cups chopped green cabbage. Top with slices of radish. Makes 4 servings.

HOT BACON SLAW

Fry 4 slices of bacon until crisp. Remove from pan and crumble. Remove all but 2 tablespoons fat; add 3 tablespoons cider vinegar, 2 tablespoons water, ½ teaspoon powdered mustard, and a dash each of sugar, salt, pepper, and cayenne. Bring to boil; add 3 cups shredded green cabbage, toss, and heat for about 1 minute. Makes 4 servings.

DILL MUSTARD SLAW

Combine ½ mayonnaise with 1 tablespoon dill-pickle juice and 2 tablespoons prepared mustard. Mix with 3 cups shredded green cabbage. Top with pickle and radish slices. Makes 4 servings.

EVERYDAY SLAW

Combine 3 cups shredded green cabbage with slices of green onion and pieces of pimiento. Moisten with mayonnaise, vinegar, and salt and pepper to taste. Makes 4 servings.

CABBAGE RELISH

- 4 cups finely chopped green cabbage
- 1 medium onion, chopped
- ½ green pepper, chopped
- 2 pimientos, chopped
- 1 tablespoon salt
- ½ cup cider vinegar
- ⅓ cup sugar
- ½ teaspoon celery seeds
- ¼ teaspoon mustard seeds
- Dash of cayenne

Combine vegetables with salt. Let stand for about 1 hour. Add remaining ingredients and mix well. Good with baked beans, fish, frankfurters, or hamburgers. Makes about 1 quart.

BUTTERMILK OR YOGURT DRESSING

- 1 cup buttermilk or yogurt
- ¼ teaspoon salt
- ⅛ teaspoon pepper
- ¼ teaspoon dry mustard
- 1 teaspoon Worcestershire
- Dash cayenne
- 1 tablespoon malt vinegar
- 1 garlic clove

Combine all ingredients except garlic. Peel garlic clove; cut in half; put on toothpick; stand it upright in dressing. Chill. Remove garlic before serving. Makes 1 cup.

CABBAGE PALM

The name is given to several kinds of palm trees, with edible "hearts." One of these is *Oreodoxa oleracea*. It can grow to more than 100 feet in height, but is usually cut down for food when about three years old. The parts eaten are the tender central leaves, used as greens, and especially the terminal bud and the tender inside of its thick stem, the "hearts of palm." The taste of these is bland and delicate.

Fresh cabbage palm is available only in southern Florida and in the tropics. Canned hearts of palm are sold in specialty food stores.

HEARTS OF PALM WITH BUTTER SAUCE

- 2 cans (14 ounces each) hearts of palm
- 6 tablespoons butter
- ½ teaspoon fresh lemon juice
- Chopped parsley

Place hearts of palm and liquid in saucepan. If hearts are very thick, split lengthwise. Add 1 tablespoon butter. Simmer for 15 minutes. Meanwhile, melt remaining 5 tablespoons butter in a small saucepan; continue to heat until butter is lightly browned. Add lemon sauce and ½ teaspoon parsley. Drain hearts of palm and serve with butter sauce and additional parsley. Makes 6 servings.

HEARTS OF PALM SALAD

- 1 large head lettuce, torn into bite-size pieces
- 1 small avocado, peeled and diced
- 1 can (14 ounces) hearts of palm, drained
- ⅓ cup French dressing
- Salt and pepper

Toss lettuce and avocado in a large salad bowl. Cut hearts of palm into ¼-inch slices; add to bowl. Lightly mix in French dressing and seasonings to taste. Makes 4 to 6 servings.

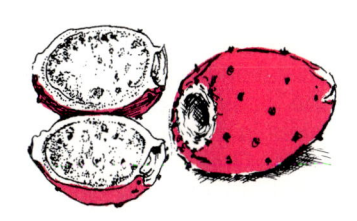

CACTUS PEAR

Prickly pear is another name for this fruit of one of a group of plants known as succulents, which grow in arid hot climates, both in the Old and the New World. In the United States, they are indigenous to the Southwest. There are a number of edible varieties, with a water content that averages eighty-five per cent and a high sugar content. The two most common ones are the *Fiscus-indica* and the *Tuna*. The *Fiscus-indica* has an oval fruit about one and a half to three inches in diameter, with a yellowish skin and pink or reddish pulp. The fruit of the *Tuna* is pear-shape or roundish, and measures about one to one and a half inches in diameter.

Since the fruits are high in water content, thirsty animals (and people) often turn to them as lifesavers in drought times. The fruits grow the prickles to protect themselves against the onslaughts of animals so that they can mature their seeds in peace.

Cactus pears have a mild, sweet flavor and they are usually eaten raw.

Availability—The fruit is available from October to January.

Purchasing Guide—When buying cactus pears, select fruit that is bright in color, firm but not hard, with a thin skin and the fewest number of spines.

Storage—The fruit keeps best at moderate temperatures; it should not be refrigerated.

Nutritive Food Value—3½ ounces, raw = 42 calories

Basic Preparation—Cacti are served peeled, which is best done by slitting the skin lengthwise so that it will come off easily. Slice them and remove the seeds. Chill and serve with lemon juice and sugar, or with cream. Cacti can also be made into bland preserves or candies.

CAKE COOKBOOK

CAKE—However inspired, no written definition of the word cake could approximate the glories of sweetened dough, baked, filled, frosted, and made ravishing with edible decorations. Such creations can bring happiness to both our childhood and mature years, for few, if any, people are immune to their charm.

The word "cake" comes to us from Middle English, and may have had earlier origins in Old Norse. From the earliest days of civilization, man has always considered cake a food for the gods as well as for himself. The Egyptians made cakes in animal, bird, and human forms for their various gods; Greeks offered honey cakes to their gods; and in the North honey cakes were offered to Thor at the winter solstice to ensure a fruitful year to come.

Few pleasures are greater than turning out a perfect cake. And perfect cakes can be achieved by any cook who is careful and who is willing to follow recipe directions. Cake-making is an exact process; the ingredients and their relation to each other are balanced like a chemical formula; in fact, during the baking, a chemical process takes place, transforming the raw ingredients into a delicious new entity.

There are two main classifications of cake in American fare, those made with fat and those made without.

CAKES MADE WITH SHORTENING

They are often called butter or shortened cakes and all of them can be filled and frosted. There are three types:

Standard cake—A layer, loaf, or cupcake, which is made with shortening, sugar, flour, and a chemical leavening agent. These cakes are baked in layer-cake, springform, loaf, or muffin pans. They include white, yellow or golden; chocolate, spice, and fruitcakes; and some tortes. A torte is a cake flatter and richer than an American layer cake.

Poundcake—As the name suggests, traditionally a poundcake contains a pound of sugar (2¼ cups), a pound of butter (2 cups), a pound of eggs (2 cups, about 8 large eggs), a pound of all-purpose flour (4 cups), a flavoring such as vanilla and/or mace, and no chemical leavening agent. Through the years this has been modified by varying the amounts of the ingredients and even adding chemical leavening and some liquid.

Chiffon cake—This is a relative newcomer to the world of cakes and it always contains some leavening agent such as baking powder. The distinguishing characteristic of the chiffon cake is that an oil instead of a solid fat is always used. This cake has a firmer texture than a conventional cake, and looks like a spongecake. It keeps well.

MIXING CAKES MADE WITH SHORTENING—There is more than one method for mixing these cakes. The four most popular follow:

Conventional Method—Butter or shortening is creamed until light and fluffy. The sugar is beaten into the creamed mixture. Eggs are separated and the yolks are beaten in this mixture, one at a time, followed by the flavorings. Then the dry ingredients, such as flour, baking powder, and salt, are sifted together and added to the batter alternately with the liquid ingredients, starting and ending with dry ingredients. Nuts and fruits, if any, are added next. Finally, the egg whites are beaten stiff and folded gently into the batter for additional leavening power.

Modified Conventional Method—This differs from the method described above inasmuch as the eggs are kept whole and are beaten into the creamed shortening. Proper long beating insures a fine texture. Poundcakes are made by this method.

Quick or One-Bowl Method—Recipes follow two patterns. In the Quick Method, dry ingredients are sifted into a bowl, then all the shortening, liquid (or part of it), and flavorings are added. This is beaten for a specified time. In a last step, the eggs (with any remaining liquid) are added, and the whole again beaten for a specified time. Occasionally this method is varied by creaming the shortening first because soft shortening is essential to the success of this method: one has to be able to combine completely by beating.

In the one-bowl method, all of the ingredients are put into a mixing bowl and beaten for a specified time. Again, as above, the shortening must be soft; in fact, all ingredients should be at room temperature before starting. This is the method used in most modern cake mixes. Electric mixers are great aids in this method.

Chiffon Cake Method—All the dry ingredients are sifted into a bowl. A well is made in the center and oil, egg yolks, liquid, and flavorings are added. This is beaten for a specified time. In turn this mixture is folded into very stiffly whipped egg whites.

CAKES MADE WITHOUT SHORTENING

These include the angel foods and spongecakes. They use little or no chemical leavening; the air beaten into the egg whites acts as the principal leavening agent. In order to achieve their characteristic fine and tender texture, they should be prepared with special care. Since these cakes are delicate, it is better to use a thin glaze or a soft whipped frosting.

Angel-Food Cake—This is made by first sifting together cake flour and part of the sugar. Since so much depends on the beating of the egg whites, there is a specific procedure for this. First, the whites are beaten until they are just foamy, then an acid such as cream of tartar is added to hold the whites firm and increase the whiteness of the finished cake. Then the beating continues, with the rest of the sugar being added gradually, until the whites are stiff and will stand in sharply pointed peaks. The time at which sugar is added will vary according to the recipe. Generally, if an electric mixer is used, sugar is added earlier than when a whisk or hand beater is used. Finally, the first mixture of cake flour and sugar is slowly folded into the whites by sifting it over the whites while folding continues. As soon as the flour has disappeared into the whites, stop. An ungreased tube pan is always used for baking because the presence of any form of fat will prevent these cakes from reaching maximum

CAKE

height. After baking, the pan is turned upside down on a rack, on its own legs, or over a funnel, until the cake is absolutely cool. At this point if it has not pulled away from the pan slightly, it can be loosened with a knife.

Spongecake—The procedure is the same as in angel-food cakes, except that egg yolks are added. First, the egg whites are beaten until stiff. The egg yolks are beaten until light and lemon-colored. Next, the sugar is beaten into yolks gradually, followed by the flavorings. Then, the egg-yolk mixture is beaten into the beaten egg whites. Finally, the flour is sifted over the batter and folded in carefully, until it has disappeared.

CAKE MIXES

Cake mixes are an important part of the cake picture and are available in an increasingly large number of varieties. Since they eliminate a large part of the work involved in cake-making, the home-maker can introduce her own imaginative, personal touches by adding spices, flavorings, finely chopped nuts and fruits, peels, coconut, grated chocolate, maraschino cherries; by using interesting frostings and fillings; and by cutting or baking the cake into unusual shapes. To get the lightest cake possible, sift the mix before beating with liquid.

CAKE FROSTINGS, FILLINGS, GLAZES

These are sweet decorative coatings placed between layers or over the tops and sides of the cake to add to the flavor and appearance.

Frosting—Frosting or icing means the same thing. Frostings are both cooked and uncooked.

Cooked frostings, such as White Mountain Frosting, are made by beating a hot sugar syrup into beaten egg whites. Another method is to cook sugar, butter, and liquid into a candylike frosting such as in Fudge Frosting.

Uncooked frostings, such as Butter Frosting, are made by beating together butter, some liquid, flavoring, and confectioners' sugar. Decorators' Frosting is made by beating egg whites with confectioners' sugar.

Filling—Cooked fillings include liquid or fruit thickened with cornstarch, egg, or flour, such as Cream Filling or Pineapple Filling.

Uncooked fillings include those made with whipped cream, chopped fruit, jelly, or instant pudding.

Glaze—A glaze is a thin glossy coating with a firm consistency. It can be cooked or uncooked. Some are baked or broiled onto cakes, others are spread on hot cakes.

FROSTING A CAKE—Before frosting a cake, it must be thoroughly cooled. Brush off all loose crumbs. Place strips of wax paper on a platter. Place cake on top. Spread layer with cooled filling or frosting. Top with second layer. Frost sides of cake thinly with a small spatula. Allow to dry for a few minutes. Spread sides of cake again thickly with frosting. Spread top of cake decoratively with remaining frosting. Carefully pull out wax paper from under the cake, leaving the platter clean.

HINTS FOR SUCCESSFUL CAKE-MAKING

Use Accurate Equipment—Use nested aluminum measuring cups without dents. Use nested aluminum measuring spoons. Avoid fancy measuring spoons since they may be inaccurate.

Have the Necessary Accessories—Have both a rubber and a straight-blade spatula handy; a timer is also desirable.

Read Recipe Completely—Assemble all ingredients and equipment and put on kitchen table or counter. Let shortenings, eggs, and milk reach room temperature. Sift flour *before* measuring. Unless specified differently, the flour used in these recipes is all-purpose flour.

Measure Precisely—Do not make any substitutions or guesses when measuring. Level off each measurement to be completely even. Use the sharp end of a spatula or knife.

Preheat Oven for 10 to 15 Minutes—The importance of this cannot be sufficiently stressed. Many cakes have been ruined by being placed in a barely warm oven. This caused them to fall before they can rise. Conversely, too hot an oven will cause cakes to rise in irregular peaks.

Place the Cake Correctly—Bake the cake on the middle shelf of the oven. Layer-cake pans should be arranged so as not to touch each other or the sides of the oven. If layers are baked on two shelves, stagger them so that one does not sit directly under the other. To bake properly, the heat must circulate evenly around the pans.

Check Your Oven—Ovens sometimes do not hold the desired indicated temperature. Double-check yours with a portable oven thermometer. If you have any doubts, have the oven checked by a service man.

About Baking Pans and Cooling Racks—For best results, it is essential to use baking pans of the size specified in the recipe and to fill them no more than two-thirds full. Pans are measured across the top. Glass, enamel, or dark metal pans absorb and hold more heat than shiny pans. If either of these is used, oven temperature should be lowered by 25°.

Layer-cake pans come in standard sizes, with stationary or loose bottoms. The latter make all cake removing easier, especially when the cake is a spongecake. The standard sizes of round layer-cake pans are 8 x 1¼ inches, 9 x 1¼ inches, and 10 x 1¼ inches. Some come 1½ inches high, but there is hardly any difference in the finished product.

There are also loaf, rectangular, and square cake pans in various sizes. If storage space is limited, two loaf pans measuring 9 x 5 x 3 inches, one rectangular pan measuring 13 x 9 inches, and two square cake pans measuring 8 or 9 inches should be chosen.

Tube pans are needed for angel foods. Spring pans which have removable sides are very useful for baking large cakes and removing them easily. The best all-purpose spring pan measures 9 inches in diameter and 3 inches deep. A tube pan 10 x 4 inches is necessary for angel food, sponge-, and chiffon cakes.

Cake-cooling racks are made from heavy wire, set on little legs. They allow a cake to cool uniformly on all sides.

About the Phrases Used in Recipes—Since many recipes are written in condensed form, some reading between the lines may be helpful to the novice or unsuccessful cake maker. Here are explanations of some of the phrases used:

"Cream shortening and sugar until light and fluffy." The

CAKE

shortening specified may be butter, margarine, vegetable shortening, or lard. Let the fat soften to room temperature, then cream until it is fluffy, using the back of a spoon, your hand, or an electric mixer. Creamed shortening should have no lumps; it may change in color, becoming lighter. Now begin to add sugar; do it gradually, making sure the sugar is being absorbed. Give it plenty of fast beating at this stage, so that the whole looks very light and fluffy. You are now beginning to entrap, or incorporate, air, which gives lightness to the cake as well as the smooth, even texture called "fine-grained."

Much of a cake's success depends on proper creaming. This step should not be confused with mixing, which it definitely is not. When shortening and sugar are creamed together properly, the grainy appearance of the sugar has changed. Under-creaming produce a batter which results in a tough cake.

"Add flavorings, then egg yolks, one at a time, beating well after each addition."
The latest theory is that flavoring that is creamed into the fat will be carried and held better throughout the batter. (Directions, however, may add this to liquid or at the end.) Again, as above, spend time and energy beating or creaming well after each egg yolk is dropped in and after all are added; the go-easy period comes later. (Follow same procedure if whole egg is added now.) Here, too, the importance of proper beating or creaming cannot be sufficiently stressed. This should produce a mixture that is smooth, fluffy, and satiny, and it should be done *before* the next step, the addition of the dry ingredients and liquid.

"Sift dry ingredients together and add to creamed mixture altenately with liquid, beginning and ending with dry ingredients. The batter is beaten until smooth after each addition." Always sift the flour before measuring (unless using an instantized flour). Spoon the flour lightly into a measuring cup; level off the excess with a straight-edge knife or spatula. Do not knock or tap the cup; it will cause the flour to pack. Put flour in a sifter along with level measures of salt, baking bowder, baking soda, and other dry ingredients specified, such as spices. The flour mixture is usually sifted into batter by thirds, the liquid poured in by halves; thus mixing will start and end with flour. Beat after each addition until smooth, with no lumps, and again at the end, but only until batter is well combined. Extensive beating here may toughen a cake, and an all-purpose flour batter is beaten less than cake-flour batter. In the modified conventional method, the mixing ends here.

"Fold in stiffly beaten egg whites." Egg whites should stand at room temperature until warmed. Beat egg whites until they are just stiff, with sharp, pointed peaks. Insufficiently beaten whites do not hold as much air, yet overbeating is a worse mistake. If small white flecks or clots form, it means the whites have passed beyond their capacity to hold air and are beginning to break down. Slide the whites from the bowl onto the top of the batter, when with a spatula or spoon gently fold them over and over from the center of the batter to edge of bowl, turning bowl as you do this, until all the egg whites have been absorbed.

"Grease and flour pans" or *"Line pans with wax paper"* or *"Line pans with paper and grease"* or *"Grease pans"* or *"Do not grease pans."* All these phrases for the preparation of the baking pans are found in recipes. Sometimes the kind of cake being baked determines the method; at other times the method may be a matter of personal preference. Pans that are greased and floured usually produce a thin brown crust on the layer or loaf. If this is not desirable, as may be the case for an all-white layer cake, one of the two paper methods may be preferable. A little of the crust always pulls off with the paper. A word about the pans: Use the size recommended, and do not fill it more than two-thirds full of batter.

As for greasing pans, it is not necessary to grease the sides; layer cakes rise better in pans with ungreased sides. The flouring is done by placing a small quantity of flour on the bottom of a *greased* pan and swirling it around to coat the bottom evenly. Many cooks find that it is easier to remove the cake when the pan is heavily greased and floured. However, if you are using a standard layer-cake pan (which has no loose bottom), you may find that a wax-paper lining in the ungreased pan makes cake removal easier. In this case, be sure to grease the wax paper lightly on both sides.

Springforms can be treated like layer-cake pans. They present no problem since the sides come off anyway, leaving the cake loose. Fruitcake, which bakes for a long time, requires extra insulation at the bottom and sides of the cake or loaf pan in which it is to be baked. Line the bottom and sides of the pan with heavy, unglazed brown paper, and grease the paper on both sides. Angel foods and spongecakes are baked in totally ungreased and unfloured pans.

How to Tell When Cake Is Done—Press the middle of the cake lightly; if no imprint remains, and if cake pulls away a little from the side of the pan, the cake is done. Or stick a cake tester into the center; if it comes out clean, the cake is done.

About Removing Cakes from Pans—When removing cakes made with fat from the pans, let the cakes stand on the rack for a few minutes after baking before trying to remove them. A little steam will form during this period which will help to push the cake out. Then put a cake rack over the top, invert the cake, still in the pan, and remove the pan. Cool cake thoroughly on a rack away from drafts before frosting or decorating. Cakes baked in ungreased pans should be cooled in the pan upside down on a rack. When cake is thoroughly cooled, cut it out of pan with a sharp knife.

About Cake Portions—The number of portions in cakes varies, depending on the kind of cake and the use it is put to: if it is to end a meal or to be served with a beverage, for example. The following table gives an approximate number of portions in cakes of a given size.
13 x 9 x 2 makes twenty-four 2-inch squares
13 x 9 x 2 makes twelve 3-inch squares
8-inch square loaf cake makes 6 servings
9-inch square loaf makes 6 to 8 servings
8-inch round layer cake makes 8 servings
9-inch round layer cake makes 8 to 10 servings
10-inch torte makes 10 to 12 servings

STANDARD CAKES

DELICATE WHITE CAKE

⅔ cup soft butter
1½ cups sugar
1 teaspoon vanilla extract
½ teaspoon almond extract
2½ cups sifted cake flour
2½ teaspoons baking powder
⅔ cup milk
4 egg whites
½ teaspoon salt
½ teaspoon cream of tartar

Cream butter until light and fluffy. Add sugar gradually, beating until light and fluffy. Add extracts. Sift together flour and baking powder and add to creamed mixture alternately with milk, beating until smooth, beginning and ending with dry ingredients. Beat egg whites until foamy; add salt and cream of tartar. Beat until stiff but not dry. Fold into first mixture. Pour into two 9-inch layer pans lined on the bottom with greased wax paper. Bake in preheated moderate oven (375°F.) for 20 to 25 minutes. Cool for 5 minutes. Turn out on rack; peel off paper. Cool, and frost as desired.

RAINBOW CAKE

Make Delicate White Cake. Divide batter into 3 parts. Leave one part plain, color one part pink and one green. Alternate 3 parts in layer pans and bake as directed. Make Fluffy White Frosting. Divide into 3 parts. Color ½ pink, ¼ yellow, and remaining ¼ green. Reserve half of pink for sides of cake. Alternate colors on bottom layer of cake and run a knife through colors to get a rainbow effect. Add top layer and repeat frostings. Spread pink frosting on sides, and decorate top with crushed peppermint candy.

FLUFFY WHITE [SEVEN-MINUTE] FROSTING

2 egg whites
1½ cups sugar
⅛ teaspoon salt
⅓ cup water
2 teaspoons light corn syrup
1 teaspoon vanilla extract

In top part of double boiler combine egg whites, sugar, salt, water, and syrup. Put over boiling water and beat with rotary beater or electric mixer for 7 minutes, or until mixture will stand in stiff peaks. Blend in vanilla.

STRAWBERRY CREAM CAKE

Make Delicate White Cake. Substitute ½ cup quick strawberry-flavored drink mix for ½ cup of the sugar. Spread sweetened whipped cream on one layer and top with sliced fresh strawberries; add more cream. Cover with other cake layer and top with cream and strawberries.

TWO-EGG CAKE

½ cup shortening
1 cup sugar
½ teaspoon vanilla extract
2 eggs, separated
1¾ cups sifted cake flour
2 teaspoons baking powder
½ teaspoon salt
½ cup milk

Cream shortening; gradually add sugar and beat until light and fluffy. Add vanilla and egg yolks, one at a time, beating well after each. Sift together dry ingredients and add to creamed mixture alternately with milk, beginning and ending with dry ingredients. Beat egg whites until stiff but not dry and carefully fold into batter. Pour into two 8-inch layer pans lined on the bottom with greased wax paper. Bake in preheated moderate oven (375°F.) about 25 minutes; cool on rack for 5 minutes; remove from pan. Remove paper, cool and frost as desired.

GOLD BUTTER CAKE

½ cup butter
1 cup sugar
½ teaspoon lemon extract
1½ cups sifted cake flour
1½ teaspoons baking powder
½ teaspoon salt
Pinch of ground mace
4 eggs, well beaten
Orange-Lemon Glaze or other glaze

Cream butter until light and fluffy. Add sugar gradually, beating until light and fluffy. Add lemon extract. Sift together dry ingredients and add to creamed mixture alternately with eggs, beating well after each addition, beginning and ending with dry ingredients. Turn into greased and floured 8-inch tube pan, or greased and floured loaf pan 9 x 5 x 3 inches. Bake in preheated oven (350°F.) for 50 minutes. Cool for 5 minutes. Turn out on cake rack. Cool, and cover with Orange-Lemon Glaze. When glaze has set, cake can be stored in tightly covered container.

Orange-Lemon Glaze

1¼ cups sifted confectioners' sugar
Grated rind of 1 orange
Grated rind of ½ lemon
2 tablespoons fresh orange juice
1 teaspoon fresh lemon juice

Combine sugar, fruit rinds, and juices. Stir until well blended. Spread over top and sides of cake. Let stand to set before cutting cake.

CAKE

Orange-Honey Glaze

Combine grated rind of ½ orange, ⅓ cup fresh orange juice, and ⅓ cup honey. Mix well. Spread over top and sides of cake while it is still warm.

Apricot Glaze

Measure 1 cup drained canned or stewed apricots and press through sieve. Put in a saucepan with 1¼ cups sugar. Heat to boiling point, stirring constantly until sugar is thoroughly dissolved. Spread this, while still warm, over top and sides of cake.

ORANGE COCONUT CAKE

- 1 cup butter
- 2 cups sugar
- ½ teaspoon almond extract
- 4 eggs, separated
- 3 cups sifted cake flour (see step 6)
- 2¼ teaspoons baking powder
- ¼ teaspoon salt
- 1 cup milk

Orange Filling

- 2 tablespoons butter or margarine
- ⅔ cup sugar
- ⅓ cup cornstarch
- 1 can (6 ounces) frozen orange-juice concentrate
- Grated rind of ½ lemon
- 1 tablespoon lemon juice
- 1 cup water
- 2 egg yolks, slightly beaten

Coconut Frosting

- 1½ cups sugar
- ½ teaspoon cream of tartar
- ⅛ teaspoon salt
- ½ cup hot water
- ½ cup egg whites (4 large eggs)
- ¼ teaspoon almond extract
- 2 cups grated fresh or packaged flaked coconut (see to Prepare Fresh Coconut)

With pastry brush and softened butter or margarine (not from the 1 cup), grease bottom and sides of 3 round 9 inch layer-cake pans 1½ inches deep. Line bottoms with waxed paper cut to fit. Have top oven rack in center of oven. Put second rack about 2 inches below. Turn on oven; set at 350°F. With electric mixer or large spoon, beat butter until fluffy. Gradually add sugar and beat after each addition until light and well blended. Add flavoring and half the egg yolks and beat well. Then add remaining egg yolks and beat well. Sift, then lightly spoon flour into measuring cup for dry ingredients and fill heaping full. Do not shake down or pack with spoon. Level off with metal spatula. Put measured flour into sifter with baking powder and salt and sift into bowl. Add dry ingredients and milk alternately to butter mixture in small amounts, blending after each addition until smooth. (Use lowest speed of electric mixer, or wooden spoon.) Thoroughly wash and dry electric mixer or rotary beater and bowl. (Even a speck of butter on beater or in bowl will prevent egg whites from becoming stiff.) Beat egg whites until they stand in soft, glossy points, but not until dry. With large spoon or rubber spatula, gently fold whites into batter. To do this, drop beaten whites on top of batter. With sides of spoon, cut down through batter to bottom of bowl. Turn spoon and bring it up side of bowl, folding some batter over whites. Do not press down on whites. Continue until whites are evenly distributed. Divide batter equally among pans, spread evenly to sides with spatula. Put pans on oven racks so that one pan is not directly beneath another. Bake 20 to 25 minutes, or until done. Cake is done when it shrinks from sides of pan and surface springs back when pressed lightly with finger. Let pans stand on cake racks 3 to 5 minutes. Carefully loosen around edges with spatula. Turn layers upside down on racks. Slowly peel off paper, then turn right side up. Cool thoroughly.

TO MAKE FILLING—Melt butter in top part of double boiler. Mix sugar and cornstarch and stir into butter. Add next 4 ingredients and mix until well blended. Put over boiling water and cook, stirring, until thickened. Cover and cook 5 minutes. Slowly stir in egg yolks and mix well. Cool and chill.

TO MAKE FROSTING—Mix first 4 ingredients in saucepan. Bring to boil, stirring until sugar is dissolved. Cover and boil about 1 minute to wash down any sugar crystals that may have formed on sides of saucepan. Uncover, insert candy thermometer and cook without stirring to 240°F. When thermometer reaches 236°F., beat egg whites until stiff but not dry. With electric mixer at high speed, add sugar syrup slowly to egg whites. Add flavoring and beat 5 to 8 minutes, or until frosting is cool and holds its shape.

TO FILL AND FROST CAKE—Spread filling between layers of cake, then spread frosting generously on top and sides. Sprinkle with coconut, pressing gently into frosting on sides of cake.

TO STORE CAKE—After serving cake first day, cover with cake cover or lightly with foil or plastic wrap, tucking it in tightly under plate. Store in refrigerator. Remove from refrigerator ½ hour before serving. Cake will keep well several days. (Do not freeze.)

Orange Coconut Cake

CAKE

ORANGE RUM CAKE

- 1 cup butter or margarine
- Granulated sugar
- Grated rind of 2 large oranges and 1 lemon
- 2 eggs
- 2½ cups sifted all-purpose flour
- 2 teaspoons baking powder
- 1 teaspoon baking soda
- ½ teaspoon salt
- 1 cup buttermilk
- 1 cup finely chopped walnuts
- Juice of 2 large oranges
- Juice of 1 lemon
- 2 tablespoons rum
- ¼ cup confectioners' sugar
- Walnut halves and citron pieces

With pastry brush and softened butter or margarine (not from the 1 cup), grease bottom and sides of 9- or 10-inch tube pan. (If using a fluted or other fancy pan, be sure it holds at least 2½ quarts when measured to the brim with water.) Turn on oven; set at 350°F. With electic mixer or large spoon, beat butter until fluffy. Gradually add 1 cup granulated sugar and beat after each addition until light and well blended. Add grated rinds. Add eggs one at a time, beating after each until very light. Sift, then lightly spoon flour into measuring cup for dry ingredients and fill heaping full. Do not shake down or pack with spoon. Level off with metal spatula. Put measured flour into sifter with baking powder, soda and salt and sift into bowl. Add dry ingredients and buttermilk alternately to butter mixture in small amounts, blending after each addition until smooth. (Use lowest speed of electric mixer, or wooden spoon.) Fold in chopped walnuts and spread batter evenly in pan. Bake about 1 hour. Cake is done when it shrinks from sides of pan and surface springs back when pressed lightly with finger. Meanwhile, strain juices into saucepan. Add 1 cup granulated sugar and the rum. When cake is done, remove from oven. Bring mixture in saucepan to boil and pour slowly over cake in pan. If cake does not absorb all of mixture as it is poured, reserve remainder; spoon on later. Let cake stand a day or two before serving. Remove cake from pan to cake plate; sprinkle lightly with granulated sugar, if desired. Mix confectioners' sugar with enough water to make of spreading consistency. Spread on nut halves and let stand until firm. Press nuts on top of cake and decorate with citron pieces.

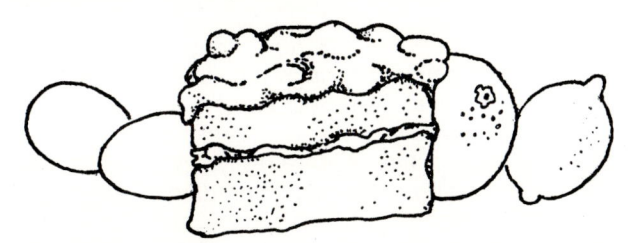

TO STORE CAKE—Cover with cake cover or loosely with foil or plastic wrap, tucking it in tightly under plate. Store in cool place. Stored this way, cake will keep several weeks. To keep almost indefinitely wrap in freezer paper or foil and freeze.

CREAM-FILLED CHOCOLATE CAKE

- 2¼ cups sugar
- 3 tablespoons water
- 2 ounces (2 squares) unsweetened chocolate, melted
- ¾ cup butter
- 1 teaspoon vanilla extract
- 4 eggs, separated
- 2¼ cups sifted cake flour
- 1 teaspoon cream of tartar
- ½ teaspoon baking soda
- ½ teaspoon salt
- 1 cup milk
- Cream Filling
- Chocolate Cream-Cheese Frosting

Combine ¼ cup sugar, water and chocolate. Cream butter; add remaining 2 cups sugar gradually, beating until light and fluffy. Add vanilla, then egg yolks, one at a time, beating well after each. Add chocolate mixture and blend thoroughly. Sift together dry ingredients and add to first mixture alternately with milk, beating until smooth, beginning and ending with dry ingredients. Fold in egg whites, beaten until stiff but not dry. Pour into three 9-inch layer pans lined on the bottom with greased wax paper. Bake in preheated moderate oven (350°F.) for about 50 minutes. Cool for 5 minutes. Turn out on racks and peel off paper. Cool, and put layers together with Cream Filling; spread top and sides of cake with Chocolate Cream Cheese Frosting.

Cream Filling

- ½ cup sugar
- 3 tablespoons all-purpose flour
- ⅛ teaspoon salt
- 1½ cups milk
- 2 eggs, beaten
- ½ teaspoon vanilla extract

In top part of double boiler mix ¼ cup sugar, flour, and salt. Add ½ cup milk and stir until smooth. Pour in remaining milk and cook over boiling water, stirring constantly, for 10 minutes, or until smooth and thickened. Mix remaining ¼ cup sugar and eggs. Add hot mixture slowly, stirring constantly. Return to double boiler and cook for 5 minutes longer, or until very thick, stirring constantly. Cool, and add vanilla.

DEVIL'S FOOD CAKE

- 1½ cups (9 ounces) semisweet chocolate pieces
- ⅓ cup butter or margarine, softened
- 1½ cups firmly packed light brown sugar
- 1½ teaspoons vanilla extract
- 2 eggs
- 1¾ cups sifted all-purpose flour
- 1¼ teaspoons baking soda
- 1 teaspoon salt
- ½ cup buttermilk
- ¾ cup boiling water

CAKE

Devils Food Cake

Melt chocolate pieces in top part of double boiler over hot, not boiling, water; cool. Cream butter; add sugar gradually, beating until light and fluffy. Add vanilla. Add eggs, one at a time, beating well after each addition. Stir in chocolate. Sift together dry ingredients, and add alternately with buttermilk, beating until smooth. Stir in water. Pour onto two 9-inch layer pans, lined on the bottom with wax paper. Bake in preheated moderate oven (375°F.) about 25 minutes. Turn out on racks, and peel off paper. Cool, and frost with desired chocolate frosting.

Chocolate Cream-Cheese Frosting

- ¼ cup butter or margarine
- 1 package (8 ounces) cream cheese
- 3 ounces (3 squares) unsweetened chocolate, melted
  Dash of salt
- 3 cups sifted confectioners' sugar
- ⅓ cup light cream
- 1 teaspoon vanilla extract

Cream butter. Add cheese, chocolate, and salt; blend. Add sugar alternately with cream, beating thoroughly after each addition. Add vanilla.

LORD BALTIMORE CAKE

- ½ cup soft butter or other shortening
- 1 cup sugar
- 1 teaspoon vanilla extract
- 3 egg yolks
- 2 cups sifted cake flour
- 2 teaspoons baking powder
- ½ teaspoon salt
- ⅔ cup milk
  Fluffy White Frosting (above)
- ½ cup almond-macaroon crumbs
- ¼ cup chopped walnuts
- ¼ teaspoon almond extract
- ¼ cup chopped blanched almonds
- 12 quartered candied cherries
- 2 teaspoons fresh lemon juice
- 1 tablespoon sherry
  Whole candied cherries
  Angelica

Cream butter and sugar until light. Add vanilla. Add egg yolks, one at a time, beating well after each. Add sifted flour, baking powder, and salt alternately with milk, beating until smooth. Pour into two 8-inch layer-cake pans, lined on the bottom with wax paper. Bake in preheated moderate oven (375°F.) for 25 minutes. Make frosting. To one third of frosting stir in almond-macaroon crumbs, walnuts, almond extract, blanched almonds, cherries, lemon juice, and sherry. Spread between cooled layers. Use remaining frosting for top and sides of cake. Decorate top with whole candied cherries and strips of angelica.

HONEY SPICE CAKE

- ½ cup soft butter
- 1 teaspoon grated lemon rind
- ¾ cup honey
- 2 cups sifted cake flour
- 2 teaspoons baking powder
- ¾ teaspoon salt
- 1 teaspoon ground cinnamon
- ¼ teaspoon each of ground nutmeg and cloves
- 2 eggs, separated
- ½ cup milk
- ⅔ cup raisins
- ¾ cup chopped filberts
  Butterscotch Frosting

Cream butter and lemon rind until light. Gradually beat in honey. Sift together dry ingredients. Add about one fourth to first mixture; beat until smooth. Add egg yolks, one at a time, beating well after each. Add remaining dry ingredients and milk alternately to first mixture, beginning and ending with dry ingredients. Beat until smooth. Stir in raisins and ½ cup nuts, and fold in stiffly beaten egg whites. Pour into two 8-inch layer pans lined on the bottom with greased wax paper. Bake in preheated moderate oven (375°F.) for about 25 minutes. Cool for 5 minutes. Turn out on rack and peel off paper. Cool, and frost with Butterscotch Frosting. Sprinkle with remaining ¼ cup nuts.

Butterscotch Frosting

- 1 package (6 ounces) butterscotch pieces
- 2 tablespoons water
- 1 package (8 ounces) cream cheese
- ⅛ teaspoon salt
- 1 tablespoon light cream
- 1 teaspoon vanilla extract
- 1 cup heavy cream, whipped

Melt butterscotch pieces in top part of double boiler over hot, not boiling, water. Stir in 2 tablespoons water and remove from heat; cool to lukewarm. Beat until fluffy the cream cheese, salt, and light cream. Blend in first mixture and vanilla. Fold in whipped cream.

OLD-FASHIONED SPICE CAKE

- ½ cup vegetable shortening
- 1 cup granulated sugar
- 3 eggs
- 1⅓ cups all-purpose flour
- 1 teaspoon soda
- ½ teaspoon salt
- 2 teaspoons cinnamon
- 1 teaspoon each ground ginger and cloves
- 1 teaspoon crushed cardamom seed (optional)
- 1 cup dairy sour cream
  - Fine dry bread crumbs
  - Confectioners' sugar (optional

Cream shortening; gradually add granulated sugar and beat well. Add eggs one at a time, beating thoroughly after each. Add sifted dry ingredients, except cardamom, alternately with sour cream, blending well. Add cardamom, if desired. Grease well a 2-quart fluted tube pan, sprinkle with crumbs and shake out excess. Pour batter into pan and bake in prehated slow oven (325°F.) about 50 minutes. Let cool in pan on rack 10 minutes before turning out. Cool and sprinkle with confectioners' sugar.

FROSTED MARBLE CAKE

- ½ cup shortening
- 1½ cups sugar
- 1¼ teaspoons vanilla extract
- 2 cups sifted cake flour
- ¾ teaspoon salt
- 2 teaspoons baking powder
- ½ cup milk
- ½ cup egg whites (about 4)
- 2¼ ounces (2¼ squares) unsweetened chocolate, melted
- 3 tablespoons water
  - Chocolate Frosting
- ¼ cup chopped pecans

Cream shortening; add 1¼ cups of the sugar gradually, beating until light and fluffy. Add vanilla. Sift together dry ingredients and add alternately to creamed mixture with milk, beating until smooth, beginning and ending with dry ingredients. Fold in stiffly beaten egg whites. Divide batter into halves. Add remaining ¼ cup sugar to chocolate and water; heat and stir until blended and thick. Cool, and blend into half of batter. Alternate light and dark layers in greased, wax-paper-lined loaf pan, 9 x 5 x 3 inches. Cut through with knife to improve marbling. Bake in preheated moderate oven (350°F.) for about 1 hour. Turn out on rack, remove paper, and cool. Frost with Chocolate Frosting and sprinkle with chopped nuts.

Chocolate Frosting

Melt 1 package (12 ounces) semisweet chocolate pieces and 3 tablespoons butter over hot water. Remove from heat; stir in ½ cup sifted confectioners' sugar, ½ cup undiluted evaporated milk, 1 teaspoon vanilla, ¼ teaspoon salt. Beat until smooth.

BLITZ TORTE

- 4 egg whites
- 2 cups plus 2 tablespoons sugar
- ½ cup soft butter or margarine
- 1¾ cups sifted cake flour
- 2¼ teaspoons baking powder
- ¾ teaspoon salt
- ½ cup plus 2 tablespoons milk
- 1 teaspoon vanilla extract
- 2 eggs
- ¼ cup slivered blanched almonds
  - Pneapple Filling
  - Whipped cream or whipped topping

Beat egg whites until foamy. Gradually add 1 cup sugar, beating until stiff. Set meringue aside. Cream butter lightly. Sift in remaining 1 cup plus 2 tablespoons sugar, flour, baking powder, and salt. Add milk and vanilla; mix until flour is dampened. Then beat for 2 minutes at low speed of electric mixer. Add eggs and beat for 1 minute longer. Pour into two 9-inch layer pans lined on the bottom with greased wax paper. (If convenient, use loose-bottomed pans.) Spread meringue on batter and sprinkle with nuts. Bake in preheated moderate oven (350°F.) for about 35 minutes. Cool for about 5 minutes. Cut around edge with a sharp knife. Turn out on a rack and remove wax paper. Quickly use another rack to turn meringue side up again. Cool, put layers together with Pineapple Filling and spread whipped cream on sides.

Pineapple Filling

- ¼ cup sugar
- 1 tablespoon all-purpose flour
- Dash of salt
- 2 egg yolks, beaten
- ½ cup milk
- 1 tablespoon butter
- 1 cup (9-ounce can) crushed pineapple, drained

In top part of double boiler mix sugar, flour, and salt. Stir in egg yolks and milk. Cook and stir over boiling water until thick. Stir in butter and pineapple.

ANNIVERSARY CAKE

- 1½ cups butter
- 3 cups sugar
- 5¼ cups sifted cake flour
- 5¼ teaspoons baking powder
- 1¼ teaspoons salt
- 1½ cups milk
- 1 tablespoon grated lemon rind
- 1½ cups grated fresh coconut or canned flaked coconut
- 9 egg whites
- Orange Filling
- Lemon-Orange Butter-Cream Fosting

Cream butter until light and fluffy. Add 2¼ cups sugar gradually, beating until light and fluffy. Sift together next 3 dry ingredients; add to creamed mixture alternately with milk, beating until smooth, beginning and ending with dry ingredients. Stir in lemon rind and coconut. Beat egg whites until foamy; gradually add remaining ¾ cup sugar and beat until stiff but not dry. Fold into batter. Pour into six 9-inch layer pans lined on the bottom with greased wax paper. Bake in preheated moderate oven (375°F.) for 15 to 20 minutes. Cool for 5 minutes. Turn out on racks and peel off paper. (If oven is not large enough, or you do not have enough pans, make as many cakes as you can, and while first cakes are cooling, repeat the baking procedure.) When all layers are baked and cooled, make a 6-inch cardboard circle and cut around 3 of the layers, thus making 6-inch layers. Use scraps for pudding or other desserts. Prepare Orange Filling and Lemon-Orange Butter-Cream Frosting.

To Fill and Frost Cake—Put one 9-inch layer on cake plate; spread with one third of filling. Add second 9-inch layer; spread with one third more of filling. Add last 9-inch layer and spread with frosting. Add 3 small layers, spreading remaining filling between. Frost top and sides of cake. Decorate with frosting, using pastry tube.

To Serve—Cut top tier into 6 wedge-shape pieces and put on serving plates. Then cut bottom tier into 10 to 12 servings.

Orange Filling

- ¾ cup cake flour
- 1½ cups sugar
- ¼ teaspoon salt
- 6 tablespoons water
- 3 tablespoons grated orange rind
- Grated rinds of 1½ lemons
- 2¼ cups fresh orange juice
- 6 tablespoons fresh lemon juice
- 4 egg yolks, beaten

In heavy saucepan mix first four ingredients and blend until smooth. Add rinds and juices. Cook, stirring, until mixture thickens and becomes almost translucent. Stir a small amount of hot mixture into slightly beaten egg yolks. Stir into mixture in saucepan and cook, stirring, for a few minutes longer. Cool.

Lemon-Orange Butter-Cream Frosting

You need 1½ times this recipe. Do not make all at once.

Prepare one recipe as below. Then make again, halving the amount of each ingredient listed and use this batch for final decorating.

- 1 cup sugar
- ⅛ teaspoon cream of tartar
- ⅛ teaspoon salt
- ¼ cup water
- 2 egg whites
- 1 teaspoon grated lemon rind
- ⅔ cup soft butter
- ¼ cup orange juice

In small saucepan mix sugar, cream of tartar, salt, and water. Cook until 240°F. registers on candy thermometer, or until a small amount of the syrup dropped into cold water forms a soft ball that holds its shape. Beat egg whites with rotary beater or electric beater until stiff but not dry. Add syrup very slowly to egg whites, beating constantly. Add grated lemon rind and cool thoroughly. Cream butter until light. Add egg-white mixture to butter, 2 to 3 tablespoons at a time, beating well after each addition. Beat in orange juice.

KENTUCKY JAM CAKE

- 1 cup soft butter or margarine
- 2 cups sugar
- 5 eggs
- 1 cup seedless blackberry jam
- 3 cups sifted all-purpose flour
- 1 teaspoon baking soda
- ½ teaspoon salt
- ½ teaspoon each of ground cloves and allspice
- 1 cup buttermilk
- 1 cup chopped nuts
- 1 cup chopped dates or raisins
- Caramel Frosting

Cream butter and sugar until light. Add eggs, one at a time, beating well after each addition. Add jam and beat well. Add sifted dry ingredients alternately with buttermilk, beating until smooth, beginning and ending with dry ingredients. Stir in nuts and dates. Pour into four 8-inch layer pans lined on the bottom with greased wax paper. Bake in preheated slow oven (325°F.) for about 35 minutes. Cool; spread Caramel Frosting between layers and on top of cake.

Caramel Frosting

- 2 cups firmly packed light brown sugar
- 1 cup granulated sugar
- 2 tablespoons light corn syrup
- 3 tablespoons butter
- Dash of salt
- ⅔ cup cream
- 1 teaspoon vanilla extract

Place all ingredients in a saucepan. Bring to a boil, cover, and cook for 3 minutes. Uncover and cook until a small amount of mixture forms a soft ball when dropped into cold water (236°F. on a candy thermometer). Cool for 5 minutes, then beat until thick. If too stiff, add a little hot water.

APRICOT-COCONUT TORTE

- 2 dozen coconut cookies
- 4 cups dried apricots
- Water
- 2 envelopes unflavored gelatin
- 1½ cups unsalted butter
- 3 cups confectioners' sugar
- 6 eggs, separated
- Grated rind of 1 orange
- Grated rind and juice of 1 lemon
- ⅛ teaspoon salt
- ½ cup granulated sugar
- 1 cup heavy cream, whipped
- 1 can (17 ounces) unpeeled apricot halves, well drained
- chopped pistachio nuts

Crumble coconut cookies and sprinkle ½ cup on the bottom of deep 9-inch spring-form pan. Cook apricots in 3 cups water until tender and water is absorbed. Force through sieve or ricer, or purée in blender. Cool. Soften gelatin in ½ cup cold water. Dissolve over hot water or very low heat. Stir into apricots. Cream butter, add confectioners' sugar, and beat until blended. Beat in egg yolks, one at a time. Then beat in apricots, orange and lemon rinds, and lemon juice. Add salt to egg whites and beat until foamy. Gradually add granulated sugar and beat until stiff, but not dry. Fold into apricot mixture. Pour about one fourth of mixture into pan. Add a layer of crumbled cookies and continue alternating ingredients until all are used. Chill overnight. Remove to a serving plate, leaving cake on pan base, if preferred. Garnish with whipped cream, apricot halves and chopped nuts. Makes 12 servings.

CHOCOLATE CHARLOTTE RUSSE

- 4 ounces (4 squares) unsweetened chocolate
- ¾ cup granulated sugar
- ⅓ cup milk
- 6 eggs, separated
- 1½ cups unsalted butter
- 1½ cups confectioners' sugar
- ⅛ teaspoon salt
- 1½ teaspoons vanilla extract
- 3 dozen ladyfingers split
- 1 cup heavy cream, whipped
- Shaved unsweetened chocolate

Melt chocolate squares in top part of double boiler over hot water. Mix granulated sugar, milk, and egg yolks. Add to chocolate, and cook until smooth and thickened, stirring constantly. Cool. Cream butter well. Add ¾ cup confectioners' sugar, and cream thoroughly. Add chocolate mixture, and beat well. Beat egg whites with salt until stiff; gradually beat in remaining ¾ cup confectioners' sugar. Fold into chocolate mixture. Add vanilla. Line deep 9-inch springform or loose-bottomed pan with split ladyfingers. Put in alternate layers of one third of mixture and remaining ladyfingers. Chill overnight. Remove to cake plate. Garnish with whipped cream and shaved chocolate.

CAKE

POUNDCAKES

LOAF POUNDCAKE

Use standard measuring cups and spoons. Make no substitutions in ingredients, read recipe through before starting and give it your undivided attention when making cake. One hour before preparing cake, remove butter and eggs from refrigerator and let stand at room temperature. Butter should be soft but not soupy. Put butter in large bowl of electric mixer or bowl to be used.

  About 5 large eggs
  Lemon rind
1¾ cups regular all-purpose flour (not self-rising, instant, unbleached or cake flour)
½ pound (1 cup) butter (do not use unsalted or whipped)
 1 teaspoon vanilla extract
1¼ cups granulated sugar
  Confectioners' sugar

Butter bottom and sides of 2-quart loaf pan about 9 x 5 x 3 inches. Preheat oven to slow (325°F. for aluminum pan, 300°F. for glass pan). Break 4 large eggs into small bowl and beat with fork just enough to combine yolks and whites. Pour into liquid measuring cup. If not full, beat another egg slightly and add enough to make 1 cup. Other size eggs can be used as long as they measure 1 cup. (Reserve remaining egg, covered, in refrigerator to be used for French toast, scrambled eggs, omelet, etc.) Grate yellow part of lemon rind onto piece of waxed paper, measure 1 teaspoon and wrap in same paper to avoid drying out. Spoon unsifted flour lightly into measuring cup for dry ingredients and fill heaping full. Do not shake down or pack with spoon. Level off with metal spatula. Put in small bowl. Measure remaining ¾ cup, using ½-cup and ¼-cup measures. Turn electric mixer to medium, or proper setting for creaming, and cream butter with lemon rind and vanilla until fluffy, scraping down sides of bowl once or twice with rubber spatula. Gradually add granulated sugar, creaming until very well blended, scraping sides of bowl several times. Add eggs, about ¼ cup at a time, beating well after each addition; do not overbeat. Don't worry if mixture appears a little curdled after last addition. Turn mixer to lowest speed and add flour all at once, mixing until smooth and well blended and flour disappears. Do not overmix. Scrape bowl frequently. Pour into prepared pan, smoothing top with spatula. Put pan in center of preheated oven and bake cake in aluminum pan 1 hour, cake in glass pan 1 hour and 10 minutes. To test, pull rack gently toward you and insert testing wire in cake to bottom of pan. If no crumbs cling to wire, cake is done. Remove from oven; let stand on rack 5 minutes. Invert pan on rack; when cake drops out, gently and quickly turn right side up. Let stand on rack until thoroughly cooled. Sprinkle top with confectioners' sugar just before serving. Store airtight in cake saver or wrap in plastic, foil or waxed paper and store in cool place. Do not refrigerate.

To make cake by hand, cream butter and flavorings well with spoon. Gradually add sugar, creaming well after each addition. Add eggs, ¼ cup at a time, beating well after each addition. Add flour all at once and mix until smooth. Do not overmix. Bake as above.

STRAWBERRY DREAM TORTE

 3 packages (8 ounces each) poundcake
 4 envelopes unflavored gelatin
  Cold water
 3 boxes (1 pound each) frozen sliced strawberries, thawed
 ⅛ teaspoon salt
 3 cups heavy cream, whipped
 1 quart fresh strawberries
 ¾ cup sugar
1½ tablespoons cornstarch
  Red food coloring

Cut cake in ¼-inch slices about 1½ inches wide and 4 inches long. (Have about 20 strips this size for sides of pan. Scraps can be used for layers.) Butter lightly a deep 9-inch springform or loose-bottomed pan. Line bottom and sides of pan with cake strips. Meanwhile, soften gelatin in ¾ cup cold water; dissolve over hot water or very low heat. Stir quickly into strawberries. Add salt, and fold in cream. Pour about one fourth of mixture on cake in pan. Add another layer of cake, and continue alternating ingredients until all are used. Chill overnight. Add glaze a few hours before serving. To make: Wash, and hull berries. Crush enough small uneven ones to make 1 cup. Keep remainder whole. Mix sugar and cornstarch in small saucepan. Add crushed berries and ¼ cup cold water; mix well. Cook, stirring, until thickened. Cool. Add a few drops red coloring. Arrange berries on cake and spoon glaze over fruit. Chill. Remove to serving plate, leaving cake on pan base, if preferred.

CHOCOLATE POUNDCAKE

 1 cup soft butter or margarine
1¼ cups sugar
 1 teaspoon vanilla extract
 5 eggs, separated
 2 ounces (2 squares) unsweetened chocolate, melted
 2 cups sifted all-purpose flour
 ½ teaspoon baking powder
 ½ teaspoon salt

Cream butter until light and fluffy. Add 1 cup sugar gradually, beating until light and fluffy. Add vanilla, then egg yolks, one at a time, beating well after each. Blend in cooled chocolate. Add sifted flour, baking powder, and salt; beat until smooth. Beat egg whites until stiff but not dry. Gradually beat in remaining ¼ cup sugar. Fold into first mixture. Pour into loaf pan, 9 x 5 x 3 inches lined on bottom with greased wax paper. Bake in preheated slow oven (300°F.) about 1¾ hours. Cool for 5 minutes. Turn out on rack and peel off paper. When cool, sift confectioners' sugar over top, if desired.

CAKE

BUNDT POUNDCAKE

- 1½ cups butter
- 2⅔ cups sifted all-purpose flour
- ¼ teaspoon baking soda
- ½ teaspoon ground mace
- 2¼ cups granulated sugar
- 2 tablespoons lemon juice
- 2 teaspoons vanilla extract
- 8 eggs, separated
- ¼ teaspoon salt
- ¾ teaspoon cream of tartar
- Confectioners' sugar (optional)

With pastry brush and softened butter from the 1½ cups, grease bottom and sides of 3½-quart cast-iron *bundt* pan with nonstick coating or 10 x 4-inch aluminum tube pan. Dust pan with flour (not from the 2⅔ cups), turn pan upside down and shake to remove excess. Turn on oven; set at 300°F. Sift flour into bowl, then spoon lightly into measuring cup for dry ingredients and fill heaping full. Do not shake down or pack with spoon. Level off with metal spatula. Put flour in sifter with soda, mace and 1¼ cups granulated sugar. Sift into bowl containing butter and blend well with fingers. Stir lemon juice and vanilla into unbeaten egg yolks. Add a small amount at a time to butter mixture, blending well with fingers after each addition. With electric mixer or rotary beater, beat egg whites with the salt until whites stand in soft glossy points, but not until dry. Gradually add remaining 1 cup granulated sugar, beating after each addition until blended. With spoon or rubber spatula, gently fold in cream of tartar. With spoon or hands, gently fold whites into batter until whites are distributed evenly throughout. Spoon into pan, smoothing top with back of spoon. Set pan down hard on counter to remove any air bubbles. Bake about 2 hours. Cake is done when it shrinks from sides of pan and surface springs back when pressed lightly with finger. Turn off heat and leave cake in oven 30 minutes. Remove from oven and let stand in pan on cake rack 30 minutes. Loosen sides with spatula, turn cake out on rack and let stand until completely cold. Put cake on serving plate; sprinkle with confectioners' sugar, if desired.

TO STORE CAKE—Cover with cake cover or loosely with foil or plastic wrap, tucking it in tightly under plate. Store in cool place. Stored this way, cake will keep several weeks. If frozen, then wrapped well and stored in freezer, cake will keep almost indefinitely.

APRICOT BRANDY POUNDCAKE

- 1 cup butter or margarine, softened
- 2½ cups sugar
- 6 eggs
- 1 teaspoon each vanilla, orange and rum extracts
- ½ teaspoon lemon extract
- 3 cups sifted cake flour
- ¼ teaspoon baking soda
- ½ teaspoon salt
- 1 cup dairy sour cream
- ½ cup apricot brandy

Cream butter; gradually add sugar and beat until light. Add eggs one at a time, beating thoroughly after each. Add flavorings, then sifted dry ingredients alternately with sour cream and brandy. Blend well. Pour into greased 3-quart *bundt* pan and bake in preheated slow oven (325°F.) about 1 hour and 15 minutes. Cool in pan on rack.

HALF-A-POUNDCAKE

- 1 cup soft butter
- Sifted all-purpose flour
- ¼ teaspoon baking soda
- 1½ cups sugar
- 1½ tablespoons fresh lemon juice
- 1½ teaspoons vanilla extract
- 5 large eggs, separated
- ⅛ teaspoon salt
- 1 teaspoon cream of tartar

Grease a 9-inch tube pan or loaf pan, 9 x 5 x 3 inches with 1 tablespoon butter. Dust with flour and tap to remove excess. Sift 1½ cups flour, soda, and ¾ cup of the sugar into bowl. Add remaining butter and mix in well with fingers. Add lemon juice and vanilla, then egg yolks, one at a time, mixing with fingers until well blended. Beat egg whites with salt until stiff but not dry. Gradually beat in remaining ¾ cup sugar; fold in cream of tartar. Add to first mixture and fold in with hands or a rubber spatula until whites are thoroughly mixed in. Spoon into pan and spread evenly with back of spoon. Jolt pan on table to remove air bubbles. Bake in preheated slow oven (325°F.) for 1 hour, or until done. Then turn off heat and let stand in oven for 10 to 15 minutes longer. Loosen with spatula and turn out on wax-paper-covered rack; cool. Dust with confectioners' sugar, if desired. Store in an airtight container.

HOLIDAY POUNDCAKE

Follow Half-A-Poundcake recipe. Spread top of cooled cake with Glaze, allowing some to run down sides. Decorate with marzipan. **Glaze:** Mix 2 cups sifted confectioners' sugar, ½ teaspoon vanilla extract and enough milk to make glaze of spreading consistency.

Whitby Nun's Cake

Follow Half-A-Poundcake recipe, omitting vanilla. Add 1 tablespoon caraway seeds, 1 teaspoon ground cinnamon, 1 teaspoon rose water, and ½ teaspoon ground coriander (optional).

Antebellum Spice Cake

Follow Half-A-Poundcake recipe, adding the following spices: 1½ teaspoons ground cinnamon, ½ teaspoon ground allspice, ¾ teaspoon ground cloves, ¼ teaspoon ground nutmeg. If desired, frost with Seafoam Frosting.

CAKE

Seafoam Frosting

In top part of double boiler combine 2 unbeaten eggs, 1½ cups firmly packed light brown sugar, dash of salt, and ⅓ cup water. Beat for 1 minute with rotary or electric beater. Put over boiling water and beat constantly for 7 minutes, or until frosting will stand in stiff peaks. Remove from boiling water, add 1 teaspoon vanilla, and beat for 1 minute.

Canadian Orange-and-Lemon Poundcake

Follow Half-A-Poundcake recipe, adding grated rinds of 1 medium orange and ½ lemon. Omit vanilla and use 1½ tablespoons fresh orange juice; reduce lemon juice to 1½ teaspoons.

Nut Poundcake

Fold 1 cup coarsely chopped nuts into cake batter made from Half-A-Poundcake recipe. If desired, use 1 teaspoon almond extract and ½ teaspoon vanilla extract instead of the vanilla.

Traditional English Poundcake

Follow Half-A-Poundcake recipe, omitting lemon juice and vanilla and substituting 2 tablespoons brandy, ½ teaspoon ground nutmeg, and ¼ teaspoon ground mace.

Colonial Ginger Poundcake

Follow Half-A-Poundcake recipe, omitting lemon juice and vanilla and substituting 2 tablespoons brandy, ½ teaspoon ground nutmeg, ¼ teaspoon ground mace, and 2 teaspoons ground ginger.

Holiday Poundcake

CAKE

CHIFFON CAKE

ORANGE CHIFFON CAKE

- 2 cups all-purpose flour
- 1½ cups sugar
- 3 teaspoons baking powder
- 1 teaspoon salt
- ½ cup vegetable oil
- 7 egg yolks
- ¾ cup cold water
- 2 tablespoons grated orange rind
- 1 cup egg whites (7 or 8)
- ½ teaspoon cream of tartar

In large bowl, stir together first 4 ingredients. Make a well in center and add in order: oil, egg yolks, cold water and the orange rind. Stir until smooth. Put egg whites and cream of tartar in large mixing bowl. Beat with mixer or rotary beater until *very stiff peaks* are formed. Gradually pour egg-yolk mixture over beaten whites, folding gently *just* until blended. Pour into ungreased 10 x 4-inch tube pan. Bake in preheated slow oven (325°F.) 65 to 75 minutes, or until top springs back when touched lightly with finger. Invert pan on funnel and let hang until cake is completely cool. To remove from pan, loosen first by moving spatula up and down against side of pan. Next, hit edge of pan against counter top and then gently shake cake out onto cake plate. Leave cake bottom side up and frost or decorate as indicated in individual recipe.

Orange Chiffon Cake

Raspberry Petal Cake

CAKE

TO STORE CAKE—Bake cake the day before frosting and decorating. Put cold cake in large plastic bag or cake saver. Store all frosted cakes in refrigerator. For longer storage, cake can be wrapped and frozen up to 3 months.

LEMON CHIFFON CAKE

Follow above recipe, omitting orange rind. Add 2 teaspoons grated lemon rind, and 2 teaspoons vanilla with the water.

RASPBERRY PETAL CAKE

- 1 package (10 ounces) frozen raspberries, thawed
- 3 tablespoons cornstarch
- ½ cup water
- ½ cup butter, softened
- 1 cup sifted confectioners' sugar
- 2 eggs, separated
- Grated rind of 1 lemon
- 1 tablespoon lemon juice
- 3 tablespoons granulated sugar
- 1 Lemon Chiffon Cake
- Frosting
- Tea roses (optional)

To make filling, whirl raspberries in blender or force through ricer or seive. Mix cornstarch with water and put in small saucepan with berries. Bring to boil, stirring, and cook until clear and thickened. Cool, stirring occasionally. Cream butter, add confectioners' sugar and beat until light. Add egg yolks one at a time, beating well after each. Beat in raspberry mixture, lemon rind and juice. Beat egg whites until stiff. Gradually add granulated sugar and beat until sugar is dissolved. Fold into mixture and chill while cutting cake. Put cake, bottom side up, on serving plate. With sharp thin-bladed knife, cut layer 1 inch thick from top of cake and set aside. Cut down into cake 1 inch from outer edge and 1 inch from center hole, leaving a wall of cake about 1 inch thick. Remove center with curved knife or spoon, being careful to leave base of cake at bottom 1 inch thick. Fill cavity with chilled filling, pressing filling gently but firmly to eliminate holes. Replace top of cake and press down gently. Refrigerate overnight. (If cake is filled in morning, chill all day and frost just before serving.) To frost, put about 1 teaspoon Frosting on tip of small flexible spatula. Beginning at base of cake, form small petals by pressing spatula with Frosting against side of cake. Repeat to form petals in rows around cake, overlapping slightly. If desired, arrange a few roses in center. Makes 16 servings.

Frosting

In small bowl of electric mixer, stir together 1 package (6½ ounces) fluffy white-frosting mix and 1½ cups heavy cream. Chill 1 hour, then blend and beat until stiff peaks are formed. Add a few drops of red food coloring and mix lightly to form a two-toned frosting or mix completely for a solid pink.

Marble Chiffon Cake

MARBLE CHIFFON CAKE

- ¼ cup boiling water
- Sugar
- 2 envelopes no-melt chocolate
- 2¼ cups sifted cake flour
- 2 teaspoons baking powder
- 1 teaspoon salt
- ½ cup vegetable oil
- 7 eggs, separated
- ¾ cup cold water
- 1 teaspoon vanilla extract
- ½ teaspoon cream of tartar
- Fluffy Chocolate Butter Frosting
- 2 ounces unsweetened chocolate, melted, and cooled

Blend boiling water, 2 tablespoons sugar and no-melt chocolate. Set aside. Sift flour, 1½ cups sugar, baking powder and salt. Make a well in center of dry ingredients and add oil, then egg yolks, cold water and vanilla. Beat until well blended and smooth. In large bowl, beat egg whites with cream of tartar until very stiff peaks form. Pour egg-yolk mixture in thin stream over entire surface of egg whites, gently folding to blend. Remove one third of batter to separate bowl and gently fold in reserved chocolate mixture. Spoon half of light batter into ungreased 10-inch tube pan. Top with half the chocolate batter. Repeat layers with remaining batters. With narrow spatula, swirl gently through batters to form a marbled pattern. Bake in preheated slow oven (325°F.) 55 minutes. Raise temperature to 350°F. and bake 10 minutes, or until done. Invert cake in pan on rack until cold. Remove from pan and spread top and sides with frosting. Dribble chocolate over top.

Note—Two kinds of chocolate are necessary in this recipe. However, melted chocolate on top of cake can be omitted.

Fluffy Chocolate Butter Frosting

- 6 tablespoons butter, softened
- ¼ teaspoon salt
- 1 teaspoon vanilla extract
- 1 pound (about 4 cups) sifted confectioners' sugar
- 2 egg whites
- 3 envelopes no-melt unsweetened chocolate or 3 ounces unsweetened chocolate, melted and cooled
- 2 to 3 tablespoons milk

Cream butter, salt and vanilla. Add sugar alternately with egg whites, beating well after each addition. Add chocolate and enough milk to make frosting of spreading consistency.

STRAWBERRY RHAPSODY

- 1 Lemon Chiffon Cake
- 1 package (6 ounces) strawberry-flavor gelatin
  Water
- 2 cups heavy cream, whipped
- ¼ cup sugar
- 1 package (1 pound) frozen sliced strawberries, thawed, drained and syrup reserved
- 1 tablespoon cornstarch
  Flaked coconut
  Fresh strawberries

Remove light-brown crust from cake and break cake in bite-size pieces. Set aside on jelly-roll pan. Dissolve gelatin in 1 cup boiling water, add ½ cup cold water and set bowl in ice water. Stir constantly until mixture begins to set, or reaches consistency of unbeaten egg whites. Whip until fluffy. Whip cream with sugar until soft peaks form. Fold into gelatin mixture with berries. Spoon a layer of gelatin mixture into loose-bottomed 10-inch x 4-inch tube pan, using about one fourth of mixture. Then add one third of cake bits. Alternate layers, beginning and ending with gelatin mixture; chill overnight. Loosen around edges and around center with flexible spatula. Lift up cake, holding center tube. Loosen around bottom and invert on serving plate. (Even off top if pieces have stuck to pan.) To reserved strawberry syrup, add cornstarch dissolved in small amount of cold water. Cook, stirring, until clear and thickened. Cool, stirring. Glaze top and sides of cake with mixture. Sprinkle sides of cake with coconut and fill center with fresh strawberries. Makes 16 servings.

CHOCOLATE CUSTARD CAKE

- 1 Orange (or Lemon) Chiffon Cake
- 1 container (1 pound 1½ ounces) frozen vanilla-flavor pudding, thawed
- 1 cup frozen dark-chocolate-flavor pudding, thawed
- 12 ounces semisweet chocolate squares, melted
- 2 cups dairy sour cream
- 2 teaspoons vanilla extract
  Toasted sliced almonds
  Fresh-mint sprigs (optional)

Using sharp thin-bladed knife, slice cake in 4 crosswise layers. Stir puddings until smooth. Set largest layer of cake on serving plate and spread with 1 cup vanilla pudding. Top with second layer and spread with chocolate pudding. Add third layer and spread with remaining vanilla pudding (1 cup). Top with fourth layer and chill while making frosting. (Or chill overnight, if preferred.) Melt chocolate in top of double boiler over hot water. Beat in sour cream and vanilla extract until smooth. Frost top and sides of cake, making swirls with a small flexible spatula. Decorate with almonds, and fresh mint, if desired. Makes 16 servings.
Note—This frosting loses its gloss when refrigerated.

ANGEL FOOD AND SPONGECAKES

CHERRY ANGEL-FOOD CAKE

- 1 cup sifted cake flour
- 1½ cups sugar
- 1½ cups egg whites (about 12)
- 1½ teaspoons cream of tartar
- ½ teaspoon salt
- 1 teaspoon vanilla or almond extract
- ⅓ cup well-drained finely minced maraschino cherries
  Pink Fluffy Frosting

Sift flour and ¾ cup sugar together. Beat egg whites until foamy; add cream of tartar, salt, and vanilla, and beat until mixture begins to hold its shape. Gradually add remaining ¾ cup sugar and beat until mixture is very stiff and glossy. Sift flour mixture onto egg whites, a little at a time, and carefully fold in until well blended. Fold in finely minced cherries. Spoon into ungreased 10-inch tube pan and run knife through mixture to break up any large air holes. Bake in preheated slow oven (325°F.) for about 1 hour. Invert pan on cake rack until cold. Remove from pan and frost.

Pink Fluffy Frosting

- 1 cup sugar
- 10 tablespoons water
- 2 egg whites
- ¼ teaspoon cream of tartar
  Dash of salt
- ¼ teaspoon almond extract
- ½ teaspoon vanilla extract
- ½ teaspoon fresh lemon juice
  Red food coloring

Boil sugar and 5 tablespoons water until 232°F. registers on candy thermometer, or until syrup forms 2-inch threads (see Candy). Beat egg whites, cream of tartar, salt, and remaining 5 tablespoons water until stiff enough to form peaks. Add hot syrup gradually, beating constantly. Add extracts and lemon juice; continue to beat until mixture is thick enough to spread. Tint delicate pink with a few drops of red food coloring. Frost center, top, and sides of cake. Make peaks on frosting with tip of spatula.

CAKE

SPONGECAKE

- 1½ cups egg whites (about 12)
- 1 teaspoon cream of tartar
- ½ teaspoon salt
- 1⅓ cups granulated sugar
- 1⅓ cups sifted cake flour
- ⅔ cup egg yolks (8 or 9 yolks)
- Grated rind of 1 orange or 1 teaspoon orange extract
- Confectioners' sugar

Beat egg whites until foamy. Add cream of tartar and salt and beat until whites begin to hold their shape. Gradually add sugar and beat until mixture is very stiff and glossy. Carefully fold sifted flour into whites. Combine egg yolks and orange rind and beat until thick and lemon-colored. Gradually fold into first mixture. Pour into ungreased 10-inch tube pan and bake in preheated slow oven (325°F.) for 1¼ hours. Invert on rack until cold. Remove cake and dust with confectioners' sugar.

DAFFODIL SPONGECAKE

- 1 cup egg whites (7 to 9)
- 1 teaspoon cream of tartar
- ½ teaspoon salt
- 1 teaspoon vanilla extract
- 1 cup sugar
- 1 cup sifted cake flour
- 4 egg yolks
- Grated rind of ½ orange
- Yellow Jacket Frosting

Beat egg whites until frothy. Add cream of tartar, salt, and vanilla and beat until whites begin to hold their shape. Gradually add sugar and beat until very stiff and glossy. Fold in flour in thirds. Beat egg yolks until thick and lemon-colored. Divide batter and fold egg yolks and rind into half. Put by tablespoons into ungreased 9- or 10-inch tube pan, alternating yellow and white mixtures. Bake in preheated slow oven (300°F.) for about 1 hour. Invert on rack to cool. Remove from pan. Spread top and sides with Yellow Jacket Frosting.

Yellow Jacket Frosting

- 1⅔ cups sugar
- 3 tablespoons light corn syrup
- ½ cup water
- 3 egg yolks
- ¼ teaspoon salt
- Grated rind of ½ orange
- Grated rind of ½ lemon
- 1 teaspoon fresh lemon juice

In saucepan mix sugar, corn syrup, and water. Cook without stirring until 250°F. registers on candy thermometer, or until a small amount of mixture dropped into cold water forms a hard ball. Beat egg yolks with salt until thick and lemon-colored. Gradually add hot syrup and beat until thick and of spreading consistency. Stir in grated rinds and juice.

Chocolate Custard Cake

HOLIDAY CAKES

What makes a holiday cake? Something a little special, something festive. It may be a subtle flavoring not used on ordinary days, a sprinkling of nuts and candied fruits, a decorative touch to celebrate the season, unusual size or shape. Holiday cakes are show-off cakes, a little richer, more elaborate than usual.

FRUITCAKE TIPS

Preparation—Different combinations of fruits and nuts can be used in any fruitcake, but the total amount should be the same as given in the recipe. Chop or slice the fruits and nuts a day or so before making the cake, if more convenient, and refrigerate.

Glazing and Decorating—Before serving or gift wrapping, cakes can be glazed and decorated. Melted tart jelly or equal parts of honey or corn syrup and water, boiled 2 minutes, can be brushed warm on cold cakes. Press on designs made of candied cherries and nuts; leaves cut from citron, angelica or green candied cherries; and slices of red or green candied pineapple into glaze. Brush again with glaze and put in preheated slow oven (300°F.) about 10 minutes to set. Glazed dried fruits such as prunes and apricots make attractive decorations. To prepare, cover fruits with water and simmer, covered, 10 minutes; drain. Bring to boil equal parts of honey, sugar and water. Add fruits and simmer about 15 minutes. Drain on cake rack. Remaining mixture can be used to glaze cake. Fruitcakes aren't usually frosted but the top can be spread with almond paste and a thin layer of confectioners'-sugar frosting. For the frosting, mix 1 cup sifted confectioners' sugar, 1 egg white and a few drops of almond extract. Melted semisweet chocolate is a good substitute for the frosting on white fruitcakes.

Storage—Dark fruitcakes keep better than light ones since the larger proportion of fruit to batter adds moisture. Both types keep better if refrigerated. They can also be frozen. When refrigerated, they should be wrapped in foil, waxed paper or plastic and, if possible, put in a tight container. Dark cakes can be wrapped first with a cloth soaked in brandy, wine or bourbon. Liquor should not be put on white fruitcakes since it may make them soggy. Wrapped and refrigerated, dark cakes will keep several months, light ones about 2 weeks. Dark cakes will, of course, ship better.

Serving—Fruitcakes, especially dark ones, are better if allowed to age a week or two before eating. Chilled cakes usually cut best. Slice thin with a serrated knife, if available. If not, use a thin sharp knife.

BOURBON PECAN FRUITCAKE

- ½ cup butter, softened
- 1 cup plus 2 tablespoons sugar
- 3 eggs, separated
- 2 teaspoons freshly grated nutmeg
- ½ cup bourbon
- 1½ cups all-purpose flour
- 1 teaspoon baking powder
- 1 pound (4¼ cups) shelled pecans, coarsely chopped
- 1¼ cups seeded raisins, coarsely chopped

Cream butter; gradually add sugar and beat until light. Add egg yolks one at a time, beating thoroughly after each. Mix nutmeg and bourbon and add alternately to mixture with 1 cup flour sifted with the baking powder; blend thoroughly. Dredge nuts and raisins with remaining ½ cup flour, add to batter and mix well to distribute evenly. Fold in stiffly beaten egg whites. Put in 10-inch tube pan lined on the bottom with waxed paper, then greased. Let stand in pan 10 minutes. Bake in preheated slow oven (325°F.) about 1 hour and 15 minutes. Cool in pan on rack, then turn out on plate and peel off paper. Invert right side up on another plate (handle carefully since cake crumbles easily).

Note—If desired, pour ½ cup bourbon over cake before wrapping.

CANDIED FRUITCAKE

- 3 packages (8 ounces each) imported pitted dates
- 1 pound candied pineapple (half green, half yellow), plus some green for decoration
- 1 pound whole candied cherries, plus some for decoration
- 2 cups all-purpose flour
- 2 teaspoons baking powder
- ½ teaspoon salt
- 4 eggs
- 1 cup sugar
- 2 pounds (8 cups) pecan halves, plus some for decoration
- Light corn syrup

Use two 9-inch x 3¼-inch loose-bottomed tube pans or two 9-inch x 5-inch x 3-inch loaf pans; or use one of each. With pastry brush, grease pans well with softened butter or margarine. Set pan on piece of brown paper and trace around edge and inside of tube. Then cut out tracing and fit in pan. Cut a strip the right length and width and fit around side of pan. For loaf pan, cut bottom and all side sections separately. Turn on oven; set at 275°F. Using shears dipped occasionally in cold water, cut dates in half crosswise. Cut 1 pound pineapple in coarse pieces. Put fruits in large bowl with 1 pound cherries. Spoon flour lightly into measuring cup for dry ingredients and fill heaping full. Do not shake down or pack with spoon. Level off with metal spatula. Put in sifter with baking powder and salt and sift onto fruits. Mix fruits and dry ingredients well with fingers, separating pieces of fruit so that all are well coated with dry ingredients. With electric mixer or rotary beater, beat eggs until frothy. Gradually beat in sugar. Add to fruit mixture and mix well with large spoon. Add 2 pounds pecan halves and mix with hands until nuts are evenly distributed and coated with batter. Pack into pans, pressing down with palms of hands. If necessary, rearrange pieces of fruit and nuts to distribute them evenly. Decorate tops with rows of whole red candied cherries, thin slices of green pineapple and pecan halves. Bake tube cakes about 1¼ hours; loaf cakes, 1½ hours. (Tops of cakes should look dry but will not be brown. If there is any doubt, leave cakes in oven a few minutes longer since a little extra baking does no harm.) When tube cakes are done, let stand in pans on cake racks about 5 minutes. Then run spatula around edge, lift cake out of pan sides and carefully peel off paper

CAKE

around sides. Cool on cake racks, then invert on serving plate. Remove pan bottom and peel off paper. Turn cake right side up, brush with corn syrup and cool completely. Let cakes in loaf pans stand in pans on cake racks about 30 minutes before inverting on oblong cutting board. Peel off paper, turn right side up and brush with corn syrup; cool.

DARK CHOCOLATE FRUITCAKE

    1 package each seedless and seeded raisins
    ½ cup chopped mixed candied fruit
    1 cup hot black coffee
    1 cup grape juice
    2 teaspoons ground cinnamon
    1 teaspoon each ground nutmeg and cloves
    ¼ teaspoon ground ginger
    1 cup vegetable shortening
    2 ounces unsweetened chocolate
    ½ cup maraschino cherries with syrup
    1 cup chopped nuts
    4 eggs
    2 cups firmly packed dark-brown sugar
    4 cups all-purpose flour
    1 teaspoon salt
    2 teaspoons baking soda
      Sherry or brandy

Put raisins, candied fruit, liquids and spices in saucepan and bring to boil. Simmer 5 minutes, remove from heat and stir in shortening and chocolate; cool. Slice cherries and add with syrup and nuts to first mixture. Beat eggs slightly; gradually add sugar and beat until light and foamy. Add sifted dry ingredients alternately with fruit mixture, stirring until well blended. Pour into two 9-inch x 5-inch x 3-inch loaf pans lined on the bottom with waxed paper. Bake in preheated slow oven (300°F.) 1½ to 1¾ hours. Let stand in pans on rack until cold. Turn out and peel off paper. Wrap in cloths moistened with sherry and store at least 2 weeks before cutting. Remoisten cloths when necessary.

ECONOMY FRUITCAKE

    1 cup firmly packed brown sugar
    ¼ cup molasses
    ½ cup plus 1 tablespoon shortening
    2 cups seeded raisins, cut in pieces
    8 ounces dates, cut in pieces
    1 cup dry currants
    1 cup strong coffee
    1 egg
    2 cups all-purpose flour
    ½ teaspoon baking soda
    1 teaspoon baking powder
    1 teaspoon ground cinnamon
    ¼ teaspoon ground cloves
    ¼ teaspoon salt

Put first 7 ingredients in saucepan, bring to boil and boil 5 minutes; cool. Stir in egg and sifted dry ingredients. Pour into 9-inch x 5-inch x 3-inch loaf pan lined on the bottom with waxed paper. Bake in preheated slow oven (300°F.) about 1½ hours. Turn out and cool on rack.

Candied Fruitcake

CAKE

BÛCHE DE NOËL

  Granulated sugar
2 envelopes no-melt unsweetened chocolate
3 tablespoons cold water
  Vanilla extract
¼ teaspoon baking soda
4 eggs
½ cup sifted all-purpose flour
½ teaspoon each baking powder and salt
  Confectioners' sugar
1 cup heavy cream
¼ cup each chopped nuts and candied orange peel
  Flaked coconut
  Green food coloring
  Chocolate Frosting

Mix 2 tablespoons sugar, the chocolate, water, 1 teaspoon vanilla and the soda until thick and smooth; set aside. Beat eggs until foamy. Gradually add 1 cup granulated sugar and beat until very thick and lemon-colored. Fold in sifted flour, baking powder and salt. Then quickly fold in chocolate mixture and spread in 15 x 10 x 1-inch pan, greased and lined with waxed paper and greased again. Bake in moderate oven (375°F.) 15 to 18 minutes, or until tester comes out clean. (Do not overbake.) Loosen around edges and invert cake on towel sprinkled with confectioners' sugar. Remove paper and trim off crisp edges. Cool 5 minutes, then roll up in towel and put on cake rack. Cool thoroughly. Whip cream and fold in nuts, orange peel and ½ teaspoon vanilla. Unroll cake and spread with cream mixture, reroll, wrap in towel and chill. Tint coconut green with a little food coloring rubbed in with fingertips. Spread top, sides and ends of roll with frosting and sprinkle with coconut.

Chocolate Frosting

Cream ¼ cup softened butter or margarine with 2 envelopes no-melt unsweetened chocolate. Gradually blend in 3 cups confectioners' sugar alternately with about ⅓ cup milk, and add 1 teaspoon vanilla.

BRANDY YULE FRUITCAKE

1½ cups almonds
1½ cups walnuts
8 ounces pitted whole fresh dates
1 cup drained maraschino cherries
⅔ cup chopped candied orange peel
½ cup seedless raisins
¾ cup each all-purpose flour and sugar
½ teaspoon each baking powder and salt
3 eggs, beaten
  Brandy

Mix nuts and fruits in large bowl. Sift dry ingredients over nuts and fruits and mix well. Mix eggs and 1 tablespooon brandy; add to fruits and nuts; mix well. Grease a 9-inch x 5-inch x 3-inch loaf pan and line with waxed paper; grease paper. Press mixture into pan. Bake in preheated slow oven (300°F.) about 1 hour and 45 minutes. Cool in pan on rack 10 minutes, then turn out on rack and peel off paper. Cool thoroughly and wrap in several layers of cheesecloth moistened with brandy.

Brandy Yule Fruitcake
Bûche De Noel

Hungarian Coffeecake

CALORIE

CALORIE—Solids are measured in ounces, pounds, grams or kilograms; liquids in fluid ounces, pints, quarts, liters and milliliters. Food energy supplied by proteins, fats, and carbohydrates is measured in calories (more properly Kilocalories). Fats contain roughly twice as many calories per gram as do proteins or carbohydrates. How many calories should one ingest each day? That will depend on one's age, weight, and daily activity. If more calories are ingested than the body needs for energy, the body will store away the excess in the form of fat.

Many of the caloric values given for various foods in this Encyclopedia are based on a portion of 100 grams, about 3½ ounces. In some cases the caloric values are given in cup measurements for convenience.

WHEN A COOK GOES CAMPING

by LELIA CARSON COX

No matter how cleverly you plan, the problem of space in camp cookery, is the problem that will come nearest to defeating you. Always carry a rectangular folding aluminum table with you. If the campsite provides a table for dining, you have a kitchen counter when you place your camp stove in the center of the table you've brought. If the campsite doesn't provide a table, then eat off a tree stump or the tailgate rather than give up your cooking-table space. Commandeer any other flat uncluttered space available. For instance, overturn and utilize all empty boxes, lined up near the stove. Camp cooking is, unfortunately, less a matter of the right amount of basil than it is the wrong amount of pots and dishes and available surface to put them on.
Follow these rules:

(1) If at all possible, bring along *two* ice chests. Those inexpensive lightweight foam-plastic chests are very adequate, especially to serve as a second chest if your first one is insulated metal. (2) Always buy cracked ice, or buy a block and crack it yourself. Crushed ice melts twice as rapidly. (3) Use one ice chest for all your drinks (soft, beer, milk or otherwise); use the other for staples (meat, fruit, canned things you need chilled). If your camp runs like others, the constant opening of the drink box will deplete its ice supply three times as fast as that of the pantry chest. (4) If possible, replace the cold drink just taken with one from the supply you, with foresight, *always* keep beside the drink chest. (5) The last thing each night, think about the next day's menus and bury in ice the canned fruit juice you'll have for breakfast and the canned grapes, for instance, that you'll use for salad. Never use up precious ice by storing canned things permanently; plan to put them in ice only far enough ahead to allow time for chilling. (6) As for your camp stove, the rule is simple—avoid at all costs preparing more than two hot dishes (even if you have three burners).

The easiest way to pack supplies is in a series of smallish boxes—little things get lost easily in big boxes, and big boxes can't be stuffed into little crannies in the car trunk. Have one box for seasonings, spices and bottled ingredients. Have one or two more for canned goods and other staples.

Label each one on *all four sides* in big black printing and consider them your kitchen file cabinets. Get them ready long before camping season and leave them in the basement or in a pantry or anywhere away from other groceries. Buy canned goods all during the year with an eye to what you'll want in camp; take your time adding to the supply and wait for specials. When you see a "4 for $1" sale on canned peaches, for instance, buy them. When you go home, do *not*—whatever you do—put them on your regular grocery shelves. Put them in the right file box. By the time you're ready to camp, you'll probably have your grocery boxes filled with items you don't want to shop for, eliminating last-minute dashing around.

Work on your seasonings and staples boxes the same way. Save coffee cans with fitted plastic tops and use them for canisters—flour, sugar, a small one for brown sugar, salt, etc. Fill them, ready to go, with the amount you estimate you'll need for your camping season. Save little spice jars with tops as you empty them, and refill with the spices and seasonings you've decided you'll need.

Label each bottle and canister on top, as well as on one side. Use freezer tape and write on it with *indelible* pen. This is important, as you'll discover to your grief after the first rain drenches your supplies; dried oregano and tarragon look remarkably alike under glass, as do peanut oil and olive oil. Buy a supply of baby milk bottles with the ounces marked; they're great for transporting oil, vinegar, vinaigrette sauce, etc. Take an empty one, too, and use it in camp for making salad dressings. Then you don't soil another measuring cup or spoon, and the smallest unsoiled vessel in camp life is like caviar in the cupboard.

Now, what to take in the way of utensils. This is a very personal matter and every camp cook has his own rabid opinions on the subject. I feel very strongly that utensil makers have put something over on the great camping public. You don't *need* all those little pots that nestle into one another and then into a final big one—most of them are shaped for cooking asparagus upright or heating baby bottles, anyway. The one thing you *don't* want in a camp kitchen is extraneous baggage.

Here's what to take: (1) a big 8-quart aluminum pot with cover, for boiling lobster, corn on the cob and pasta; (2) a smaller pot, about a 2-quart size, with lid, for doing everything the larger pot doesn't; (3) a very large black cast-iron skillet with top—10 inches is a good size, and if you can find a *square* one with cover, buy that—it has more frying surface than a round one, and space is of the essence on a camp stove; (4) a black cast-iron Dutch oven 8 inches to 10 inches wide and about 6 inches deep, with cover—fried and nonbulky things get cooked in the skillet, including the bread; all the stews and soups and such get the Dutch-oven treatment; (5) a 4-cup measuring cup, or larger, which you use for mixing or measuring; (6) an aluminum measuring cup (increasingly difficult to find in the stores), which you can use directly on the stove for melting butter or heating small amounts of liquid as well as for measuring; (7) a large colander or strainer to fit over your 8-quart pot; (8) an unlimited supply of heavy-duty aluminum foil; (9) a pair of strong kitchen shears and a vegetable peeler.

And last, when you're actually one day from taking off for the woods and the waters, do some pre-camp cooking. The first day out is nothing if not chaotic, no matter how experienced one is. So try to plan at least the first day's food. Take along a salad, for instance, like the Firstday Bean Salad. I often take a small cooked roast beef or corned beef, which I serve cold for the first night's dinner with a hot vegetable and then finish up the next day in a salad or cold cuts for lunch.

Hard-cook eggs and boil potatoes and take them along. They'll keep at "room" temperature and, of course, even longer in your ice chest. Fry some of the potatoes for dinner and use the rest for a potato salad the next day.

And by all means make a giant supply of vinaigrette dressing to take. I make at least a quart, and sometimes more, to last the entire trip. It's the difference between salads and no salads in camp. Because of the difficulty in keeping greens, salads are a rarity in camp. Your trusty vinaigrette sauce makes delicious salads of the fresh, seasonal vegetables you are able to buy along the way. Use them to the utmost, cooked or raw—the lush ripe tomatoes and deep green cukes you find in rural areas, the little new potatoes, the baby peas and okra and opulent corn, and don't forget the fruit—strawberries, peaches, apples.

A classic vinaigrette sauce is always made with the same proportions—three parts oil to one part vinegar, seasoned to your taste quite liberally with salt and pepper. This is the classic French dressing. The oil may be peanut or olive (I prefer a mixture of both); the vinegar should be a good wine vinegar. Vary this basic sauce at serving time by adding herbs or other seasonings to the amount of sauce you intend to use at the time.

All recipes make 4 servings unless otherwise indicated.

PAN-FRIED TROUT WITH ANCHOVIES

- 6 small trout or other fish
- Salt and pepper
- ½ cup all-purpose flour
- 4 to 6 tablespoons olive oil
- ¼ cup butter
- 4 fillets (or more) canned anchovies
- 1 cup dry white wine
- 1 teaspoon chopped fresh mint (if there happens to be any growing on the banks)
- 1 tablespoon chopped parsley
- 3 tablespoons lemon juice

Clean fish, dry well on paper towel and score diagonally 3 times on both sides. Salt and pepper fish and coat with the flour. Heat the olive oil in iron skillet and fry fish slowly until browned on both sides, about 10 minutes in all, or until fish flakes easily. Remove fish to serving plate (warmed over hot skillet) and cover with foil. Melt butter in same skillet over low heat. Add anchovies cut in very small pieces and simmer gently about 5 minutes. Add wine, cover and simmer 1 minute. Add mint (if available) and parsley, simmer a few more minutes and add lemon juice. Return fish to sauce in skillet and heat through, about 3 minutes. Makes 6 servings.

Note—also good with butterfish, croakers, sunfish, porgies.

CHEESY BACON OMELET

- 6 slices bacon
- 4 eggs
- ¼ cup milk
- ⅛ teaspoon pepper
- ¾ cup shredded Cheddar or other sharp cheese

Using shears, cut bacon in small pieces and fry in skillet until crisp. Drain, reserving 2 tablespoons fat. Wipe skillet with paper towel and put fat back in skillet. Blend eggs, milk and pepper and pour into hot skillet. Lift edges of omelet as it cooks, letting runny part of omelet go underneath to cook. When eggs are beginning to set, sprinkle with bacon pieces and then the cheese. Cover skillet just until cheese melts; fold half the omelet over; serve. Makes 4 servings.

JUMBO SKILLET CHEESEBURGER

- 2 eggs, beaten
- 1 can (10½ ounces) condensed cream of mushroom soup
- ⅓ cup milk
- ½ teaspoon pepper
- 2 teaspoons poultry seasoning
- 2 slices day-old bread, crumbled
- 1½ pounds lean ground beef
- 1 tablespoon shortening
- 2 medium onions, sliced in rings
- 1 can (10½ ounces) condensed cheese soup

Mix first 7 ingredients, mixing well with fork until all ingredients are well blended. Melt shortening in skillet. Spread meat in it and top with sliced onion rings. Cover and cook over medium heat 20 minutes, or until meat is done to your liking. Stir cheese soup, spoon over meat, cover and heat just through, about 5 minutes. Cut in wedges. Makes 8 hefty servings.

BEAN AND FRANK POT

- 1 envelope (1⅜ ounces) onion-soup mix
- 2 cans (1 pound each) pork and beans
- ⅓ cup catsup
- 2 tablespoons firmly packed brown sugar
- 2 tablespoons prepared mustard
- 1 package (1 pound) franks, sliced
- ¼ cup water

Combine all ingredients in saucepan or Dutch oven. Cover and cook over very, very low heat 20 minutes. Stir occasionally; this sticks easily. Makes 6 to 8 servings. If there is any left over, leave in same pot. Next day heat gently; add enough water to stir into soup consistency. Add one or two bouillon cubes and simmer at least 15 minutes. Great soup.

CAMPING

GINGER PORK WITH PINEAPPLE DRUMSTICK RICE

- 2 pounds lean pork shoulder or fresh Boston butt
- Pineapple Drumstick Rice
- ⅓ cup cider vinegar
- 2 teaspoons ground ginger
- Soy sauce
- Chopped green onion (if available)

If pork shoulder or Boston butt is sliced, cut along fatty veins in small pieces and trim well of fat. If meat is not sliced, trim off fat and cut meat into 1 inch dice. Drain all syrup from pineapple used in rice recipe into 2-quart saucepan, add vinegar and ginger and stir in pork pieces. Cover, heat to boiling point and reduce heat to low and simmer meat 1 hour, or slightly less if meat is tender and not at all pink (time depends on size of pork bits). Dip pork out with slotted spoon and serve with rice, soy sauce and onion. Makes six servings.

PINEAPPLE DRUMSTICK RICE

- 1 box (7 ounces) chicken-flavor rice mix
- 1 can (15¼ ounces) pineapple slices (reserve juice for simmering pork bits)
- 2 large stalks celery

Using ¼ cup less water than called for, prepare rice as directed on package. While it comes to boil, cut pineapple slices and celery in small chunks. Stir into rice, replace cover and proceed with rice as package directs.

CHICKEN WINGS CACCIATORE

- 4 pounds chicken wings
- ½ cup all-purpose flour
- Salt and pepper
- 6 tablespoons olive oil
- ½ teaspoon instant minced garlic
- 2 tablespoons instant minced onion
- 1 can (1 pound) tomatoes
- 1 can (4 ounces) mushroom stems and pieces, undrained
- 1 large green pepper
- Green Rice

Cut off third joint, or wing end, leaving 2 "drumsticks" connected. (At home you would use wing ends to make broth. At camp, do what you will—discard, or fry separately for crisp nibbles.) Combine flour, salt and plenty of pepper in paper or plastic bag. Add chicken and shake until thoroughly coated. Heat oil in large cast-iron skillet. Fry half the wings on both sides until golden, put aside (they needn't remain warm) and then fry the rest in same pan. You should not have to add more oil. Return all chicken to skillet, sprinkle with more salt and pepper, garlic and onion. Add tomatoes and mushrooms and tuck slices of seeded green pepper, cut lengthwise, between chicken pieces. Cover and simmer very, very slowly—just a bubble or two. Occasionally stir gravy up from bottom, coating all chicken pieces and shifting top pieces to bottom and bottom pieces to top. Cook slowly about ½ hour, or until chicken is tender and sauce thick. Serve hot with potatoes or rice. Makes 4 to 6 servings plus leftovers that are great to nibble cold.

CHUTNEY LAMB CHOPS

- ½ cup chutney, finely chopped
- 2 tablespoons lemon juice
- 1 teaspoon curry powder
- 1 teaspoon ground ginger
- ¼ cup butter or margarine
- 4 shoulder lamb chops, 1¼ inches thick
- ¼ cup hot water

In saucepan, combine first 5 ingredients. Cook slowly over low heat, stirring, for 5 to 10 minutes. Lightly grease bottom of large skillet; brown chops quickly on one side and turn. Spread half of chutney mixture on browned side of chops. Cook over low heat 10 minutes; turn chutney side down and spread chops with remaining half of chutney mixture. Cook very slowly 10 minutes longer or until desired doneness. Remove chops to serving plate and keep hot. Add water to pan and scrape up chutney mixture and browned bits; heat through and serve over chops. Makes 4 servings.

Note: Leftover chutney sauce is scrumptious on biscuits.

FIRST-DAY BEAN SALAD

- ¼ cup dairy sour cream
- 2 tablespoons wine vinegar
- 2 teaspoons prepared mustard
- ¼ teaspoon hot pepper sauce
- ½ teaspoon salt
- 1 can (1 pound) cut green beans, drained, or 2 cups cooked green beans
- 1 can (1 pound) red kidney beans, drained and rinsed
- 2 tablespoons finely chopped green pepper

In measuring cup, blend sour cream with next 4 ingredients. Combine beans, add green pepper and stir in sour-cream mixture. Let stand at least an hour to blend flavors. Take in plastic container with cover for lunch or dinner your first day out. Serve chilled, if you have room in your ice chest for the container, or at "room" temperature up to 6 hours after making. Good either way. Makes 4 to 6 servings.

SKILLET CORN BREAD

- 1 teaspoon sugar
- 1 teaspoon salt
- ½ teaspoon baking soda
- 1 teaspoon baking powder
- 1 cup water-ground cornmeal
- 1 egg
- ½ cup buttermilk
- 1 tablespoon bacon fat or other shortening

For this recipe, mix the sugar, salt, soda and baking powder at home. Put enough for 2 or 3 batches in individual plastic bags, put them in a jar and label. Mix dry ingredients in small bowl. Beat egg and buttermilk together in 4-cup measure and stir in dry ingredients. Heat bacon fat in iron skillet and pour in batter. Cover and "bake" over fairly low heat 10 minutes. Turn over onto cover and slide back into skillet. Cover and "bake" 10 minutes longer.

CANADIAN COOKERY

Emerald Lake, British Columbia

CANADIAN COOKERY

This great and wonderful country sweeps across thousands of miles, from Atlantic to Pacific and northward to the Arctic. It is a land of towering beauty and fascinating contrasts. In Quebec, you will find an old walled city which might have been imported, intact, from France, and on the other side of the continent in Victoria, a replica of an English seaside town. The rugged seacoast of the east with its picturesque fishing villages is as much part of Canada as are the great wheat and oil-rich plains and the endless forests and numberless lakes of the north. There are cities as modern and bustling as any in the United States. And there are small picturesque villages where only French is spoken. A Moslem mosque graces Edmonton, a Hindu temple, Vancouver. A new Trans-Canada Highway spans the country for 5,000 miles, opening new worlds of beauty for all who travel on it and its connecting road links. National parks and camp sites make it possible for visitors to enjoy the vacation of their hearts' desire: fishing, hunting, swimming, boating, and sailing; reliving history and learning about Canadian ways from a friendly, hospitable people.

Food is plentiful in Canada and there is a wide variety. The fish and seafood on the east coast are superb. Among the delicious local specialties are the fiddleheads, the fern fronds as they emerge from the ground, before they uncurl, which are served like asparagus boiled with butter; and the wild dike mushrooms from the Fundy shore of Nova Scotia.

In Quebec, there is an interesting French cuisine and among the best known dishes, for instance, are a delectable pea soup and *Tourtière,* a main dish made from minced pork.

In Ontario, where Germans, Dutch, Irish, Chinese, and Hungarians made their new homes, you'll find the various specialties of their homelands. You'll also find the cookery of England and Scotland, the homeland of so many of Ontario's early settlers.

The golden plains that sweep westward for thousands of miles toward the provinces of Manitoba, Saskatchewan, Alberta, and the Rockies were settled toward the end of the 19th century and new settlers arrive every year: northern Europeans from Scandinavia, Scotland, and Germany, ten thousand Icelanders, eastern Europeans from the Ukraine, Russia, and Poland. Here you will find the borsch, the cabbage dishes, and the dumplings of the Slavic countries, and the smörgåsbord and open sandwiches of the Scandinavians.

This is the home of wild rice and of saskatoons, small berries that resemble firm blueberries crossed with wild currants, which grow wild near the rivers. Buffalo meat is often on sale in the stores.

On the Pacific coast, bountiful British Columbia, larger than the states of Washington, Oregon, and California combined, offers matchless fish from its tumbling rivers and calm lakes, game from its deep forests, and beautiful fruit. In the capital of Victoria, you'll catch nostalgic glimpses of England in ravishing gardens, teashops, and cricket matches followed by cricket teas.

In the Yukon Territory, along the highway that leads to Alaska, you are in great fishing country—and all fishing is great in Canada. Here, too, you are in "sourdough" country, for the men and women of the Klondike gold rush in 1898 needed starchy foods to sustain them on the long trail. Necessity taught the prospectors the art of the "sourdough" starter for their breads; some sourings are kept to make sponge for the next day and some again for the next and so on.

In the Yukon, as in the Northwest Territories, where the scenery is on the grandest scale, the fish and the game match the surroundings. Moose, caribou, and bear (whose paws are said to be delicious); snow goose, ptarmigan, and other Arctic birds; trout, salmon; cloudberries (the yellow delicacy of the North) abound here, practically for the taking.

To the American observer, Canadian and American food habits appear quite similar. Three meals a day is the pattern, and as many people eat a hot dinner at noon as at night. Most Canadians tend to serve meat, poultry, or fish at the noon meal, and they eat more potatoes with their main meal than do Americans.

Canadians are also partial to cakes and cookies at noon and evening meals and they serve tea far more often than do Americans.

SCALLOP BISQUE

- 1 pound scallops
- 1 tablespoon finely chopped onion
- 3 tablespoons butter or other fat
- 2 tablespoons all-purpose flour
- 2 cups milk
- ¼ teaspoon salt
- ⅛ teaspoon pepper
  Spice bag with 6 peppercorns, 1 whole garlic clove, and 1 bay leaf

Rinse scallops to remove any grit and chop into ½-inch pieces. Cook onion in butter until tender. Blend in flour and gradually add milk. Cook and stir over low heat until slightly thickened. Add salt, pepper, spice bag, and scallops. Cook gently for 10 minutes. Remove spice bag and serve. Makes 4 servings.

FILET PIQUANT
[Spicy Fish Fillets]

- 2 pounds fish fillets
- ½ cup fine dry bread crumbs
- 1 tablespoon cider vinegar
- 1 tablespoon Worcestershire
- 1 tablespoon fresh lemon juice
- ½ cup melted butter or margarine
- 1 teaspoon prepared mustard
- 1 teaspoon salt
- ⅛ teaspoon white pepper
  Paprika

Wipe fish with damp cloth. Place fish in greased shallow baking dish, the bottom of which is covered with bread crumbs. Combine remaining ingredients except paprika and pour over fish. Garnish with paprika and baste several times. Bake in preheated hot oven (450°F. to 500°F.), allowing 10 minutes per inch thickness for fresh fish and about 20 minutes per inch thickness for frozen fish. Makes 6 servings.

CANADIAN COOKERY

BOEUF DU POITOU
[Poitou Beef]

  3 to 4 pounds beef bottom round or chuck
  3 onions, sliced thin
  3 carrots, each cut into 3 pieces
  1 bay leaf
½ teaspoon dried savory
  1 tablespoon salt
  1 teaspoon pepper
  1 tablespoon honey

Place all ingredients in an earthenware bean pot and cover with cold water. Bake in preheated slow oven (300°F.) for 4 hours. Do not remove cover during cooking period. Serve hot or cold. Makes 6 servings.

LE JAMBON DE CAMPAGNE
[Country Ham]

¼ cup ham fat
1 slice (1 to 1½ pounds) ham
2 pounds raw potatoes

Melt ham fat in a large iron skillet. Brown fairly thick slice of ham on both sides. While it is browning, slice potatoes as for French-fries. Remove ham from pan and keep it hot. Put potatoes in melted ham fat and cook over high heat, stirring them often until they begin to brown. Put ham slice on top of potatoes. Cover and cook over low heat until potatoes are thoroughly cooked, about 30 minutes. To serve, turn like a pancake. The bottom will be golden brown and crusty. Makes 6 servings.

CANADIAN RUM CAKE

  1 pound dates, pitted or ½ pound, pitted
  1 pound walnuts, shelled or ½ pound nutmeats
¾ cup butter
1½ cups firmly packed light brown sugar
  1 teaspoon baking soda
  1 cup boiling water
  3 eggs, well beaten
2¼ cups sifted all-purpose flour
¾ teaspoon salt
  2 tablespoons rum
    Rum Glaze (optional)

Chop dates and walnuts. Cream butter and sugar until well blended. Add dates and nuts. Mix soda with water and pour over first mixture. Add eggs. Stir in flour and salt, beating until smooth. Add rum and blend well. Turn into greased pan, 13 × 9 × 2 inches and bake in preheated slow oven (300°F.) for 1½ hours. Cool in pan on wire rack for 10 minutes, then remove from pan. May be frosted with Rum Glaze, if desired.

Rum Glaze

Mix ¾ cup confectioners' sugar with 2 teaspoons butter and 1 tablespoon rum. Frost cake while it is still warm.

Canadian Rum Cake   Halibut Paysanne

CANADIAN COOKERY

HABITANT PEA SOUP

2 cups dried yellow peas
2 quarts plus 1 cup cold water
½ pound salt pork, blanched and minced
1 onion, minced
½ cup minced celery
2 carrots, chopped
¼ cup minced parsley
   Salt and pepper
½ teaspoon ground allspice

Pick over peas and soak overnight or according to package directions. Boil for 10 minutes in water to cover. Drain; discard water. Place peas in deep kettle. Add cold water, salt pork, vegetables, salt and pepper to taste, and allspice. Simmer, covered, over lowest possible heat for 2 to 3 hours. Makes 6 to 8 servings.

TOURTIERÈ
[Pork Pie]

1 pound ground lean pork
1 teaspoon salt
½ teaspoon pepper
¼ teaspoon ground nutmeg
⅛ teaspoon ground mace
2 teaspoons cornstarch
1 cup water
   Pastry for 2-crust 8-inch pie, unbaked

Combine all ingredients except pastry. Blend thoroughly. Simmer, covered, for 30 minutes, stirring frequently. Roll out pastry and use half to line an ungreased 8-inch pie pan. Pour meat mixture into pan. Cover pie with remaining pastry and seal edge with water. Prick with a fork to allow steam to escape during baking. Bake in preheated hot oven (425°F.) for 10 minutes. Reduce heat to moderate (350°F.) and bake for 35 minutes longer, or until top is brown. Makes 6 servings. **Note:** Some people flavor their *Tourtière* with ¼ teaspoon each of ground cloves, cinnamon, and marjoram instead of the nutmeg and mace.

HALIBUT PAYSANNE
[Country Halibut]

2 pounds halibut steaks, 1 inch thick
½ teaspoon salt
¼ teaspoon white pepper
¼ cup catsup
1 can (6 ounces) sliced mushrooms
½ cup sliced green onions

Place steaks in greased baking dish and season with salt and pepper. Brush top of each steak with catsup. Top with mushrooms and sprinkle with green onions. Bake in preheated hot oven (450°F.), allowing 10 minutes cooking time per inch thickness for fresh fish and about 20 minutes per inch thickness if fish is frozen. Makes 6 servings.

Habitant Pea Soup   Tourtière

SALT COD CHOWDER

- 1 pound salt codfish
- ½ cup diced onion
- ½ cup diced celery
- 1 small green pepper, diced
- ¼ cup butter or margarine
- 2½ cups water
- 2 cups (one 1-pound can) tomatoes
- 1½ cups (one 12-ounce can) tomato juice
- 1 can (10 ounces) condensed tomato soup
- ¼ cup tomato catsup
- 2 tablespoons tomato paste
  Spice bag: 1 bay leaf, 2 whole cloves, 3 parsley sprigs, 2 garlic cloves, quartered, ½ teaspoon crumbled dried tarragon, and ¼ teaspoon crumbled dried thyme
- ¼ teaspoon paprika
- ½ teaspoon hot pepper sauce
- ½ tablespoon Worcestershire
- 1 cup cooked white rice

Soak cod overnight. Bring to a boil with fresh water 4 times, washing cod several times as water is being changed between boilings. Sauté onion, celery, and green pepper in butter for about 5 minutes. Add next 6 ingredients with spice bag and boil vigorously for 20 minutes. Add paprika, hot pepper sauce, Worcestershire, and cod which has been flaked. Cover and simmer for 15 minutes. Just before serving, remove spice bag and add cooked rice. Serve garnished with salted whipped cream and a sprinkling of chopped parsley, if desired. Makes 8 servings.

RAPPIE PIE

- 1 stewing chicken (about 5 pounds)
- 2 large onions, peeled
  Water
- 6 large raw potatoes
  Salt and pepper
- 2 tablespoons butter or margarine

Wash cleaned chicken and pat dry. Place in a deep pot with 1 onion and boiling salted water to cover. Simmer, covered, for 1½ to 2 hours, or until chicken is tender. Remove skin and bone from chicken and cut meat into slices. Boil stock down to make about 1½ cups. Peel potatoes and grate them. Place potatoes on a double thickness of cheese-cloth and squeeze out all the liquid. Chop the second onion coarsely. In shallow baking dish place layers of grated potato and chicken, sprinkling each with salt, pepper, and chopped onion, ending with a layer of potato. Pour in the reduced stock. Dot with butter. Bake in preheated moderate oven (350°F.) for about 1½ hours, or until potatoes are crisply brown on top. Makes 6 servings.

STUFFED BREASTS OF GROUSE

Bone the breasts of the bird with a sharp knife. Using your favorite stuffing, put boned breasts together in pairs, sandwich fashion. Wrap together with bacon strips; fasten with toothpicks or small skewers. Bake in preheated moderate oven (350°F.) for 45 minutes, basting frequently with orange juice. Serve with white dill sauce. (Add ⅓ cup minced dillweed to 2 cups medium white sauce.) Allow 1 bird for each serving.

ROAST SNOW GOOSE

- 1 goose (8 to 10 pounds)
- 3 to 4 cups cooked wild rice
  Salt and pepper
  All-purpose flour
- ½ teaspoon each of crumbled dried tarragon and thyme
- 3 to 4 strips of salt pork
- ½ cup dry red wine
- ½ cup beef bouillon
- 2 tablespoons melted butter

Wipe goose with a damp cloth. Stuff with rice and close opening. Rub goose with salt, pepper, flour, tarragon, and thyme. Place on a rack in a roasting pan. Lay pork slices over breast. Roast in preheated hot oven (400°F.) for 10 minutes. Reduce heat to slow (325°F.) and continue to roast for 1½ hours, or until tender (this will depend on the age of the goose). Baste several times with wine mixed with bouillon and butter. Makes 6 to 8 servings.

PAIN DE VEAU
[Veal Loaf]

- 2 tablespoons butter
- 1 onion, minced
- 2 pounds ground veal
- ½ pound ground salt pork
- 1 teaspoon salt
- ½ teaspoon pepper
- 1 tablespoon chopped parsley
- 1 tablespoon fresh lemon juice
- ½ cup dry bread crumbs
- 2 tablespoons tomato sauce
- ¼ cup milk
- 1 egg
  Bacon fat from 2 slices of bacon

Heat butter and sauté onion until golden brown. Combine onion with remaining ingredients except bacon fat, and blend well. Pack mixture into a loaf pan, 9 × 5 × 3 inches. Brush top with bacon fat. Bake in preheated moderate oven (350°F.) for about 1 hour. This loaf may be eaten cold or served hot with gravy or tomato sauce. Makes 4 to 6 servings.

CARIBOU STEW

- 2 pounds boneless moose or caribou or stewing beef, cubed
- 3 tablespoons fresh lemon juice
- 1 teaspoon salt
- 1 teaspoon chili powder
- ⅓ cup all-purpose flour
- 2 tablespoons shortening
  Hot water
- ½ cup chopped parsley

CANAPÉ

Sprinkle meat with lemon juice. Season with salt, and chili powder. Dredge with flour. Heat shortening and brown meat in it on all sides. Add hot water to cover. Simmer, covered, over low heat for about 2 hours, or until meat is tender. Remove cover 15 minutes before serving and cook down gravy to desired consistency. Add parsley. Serve with boiled potatoes, noodles, or rice. Makes 4 to 6 servings.

RAGOÛT DE PATTES
[Pork Hock Stew]

- 2 garlic cloves (optional)
- 3 pounds pork hocks
- 1 tablespoon salt
- ¼ teaspoon pepper
- ¼ teaspoon each of ground cloves, cinnamon, and nutmeg
- ¼ cup drippings or other fat
- 2 medium onions, chopped
- Water
- ¾ cup browned flour

If desired, poke a garlic sliver into each pork hock. Mix salt, pepper, and spices and sprinkle hocks with mixture, coating each well. Brown in fat. Add onions and water to cover. Cover pot and simmer for 2 to 3 hours, or until meat is *very* tender. Sprinkle browned flour over mixture and stir to blend. Cook for 20 minutes longer, stirring frequently. Makes 6 servings. **Note:** To brown flour spread it evenly on baking sheet and place in hot oven (400°F.) for about 10 minutes, or until brown; or place in skillet over low heat, stirring constantly, until brown.

RÔTI D'AGNEAU
[Roast Leg of Lamb]

- 1 leg of lamb (4 to 5 pounds)
- 1 garlic clove, slivered
- 2 tablespoons butter
- 1 onion, chopped
- ½ cup diced celery
- 5 carrots, sliced
- Parsley
- Salt and pepper
- ¾ cup dry white wine

Wash lamb and pat dry. Make several cuts through surface of meat and insert slivers of garlic. Coat lamb with butter. Sear on all sides over high heat. Add vegetables, season, and put in preheated moderate oven (350°F.) for 2½ to 3 hours, or until meat thermometer registers 175°F. for medium. For well done, roast for 3½ to 4 hours, or to 180°F. on meat thermometer. Baste frequently. Just before serving, remove meat, and add wine to pan drippings to make gravy. Serve very hot. Makes 6 to 8 servings.

BLUEBERRY COFFEE CAKE

- 1¾ cups all-purpose flour
- 1½ teaspoons baking powder
- ¼ teaspoon salt
- ⅔ cup sugar
- 1 egg, well beaten
- ⅓ cup vegetable oil
- ½ cup milk
- 1 cup fresh or thawed frozen blueberries
- Cinnamon Topping

Mix dry ingredients. Combine egg, oil and milk and add to first mixture. Beat well with spoon until smooth. Pour into oiled 9-inch square pan and sprinkle with berries, then with topping. Bake in preheated moderate oven (375°F.) about 40 minutes. Cut in squares and serve warm or cold.

CINNAMON TOPPING

Mix until crumbly ¼ cup flour, ⅓ cup sugar, ¾ teaspoon cinnamon and 2 tablespoons butter or margarine.

GRAND-PÈRES
[Maple Dumplings]

- 1½ cups all-purpose flour
- 2 teaspoons baking powder
- ½ cup sugar
- ½ teaspoon salt
- ¼ cup butter or margarine
- ⅔ cup milk
- 1½ cups maple syrup
- ¾ cup water
- Cream

Mix dry ingredients in bowl. Cut in butter to form fine crumbs. Add milk and mix with fork to form soft dough. Put syrup and water in 10-inch skillet and bring to boil. Drop in batter by tablespoonfuls. Cover and simmer 12 minutes, or until dumplings are done. Serve with cream. Makes 6 servings.

FRESH PEAR PIE

- Pastry for 2-crust 9-inch pie, unbaked
- 4 to 5 pears, peeled and cored
- ⅔ cup sugar
- ⅛ teaspoon salt
- ¼ teaspoon each of ground mace and ginger
- 1½ tablespoons quick-cooking tapioca
- 3 tablespoons fresh orange juice
- 1 teaspoon fresh lemon juice
- 1 tablespoon butter

Line 9-inch pie pan with pastry. Slice pears into pastry, heaping pears somewhat in center of pie. Combine sugar, salt, mace, ginger, and tapioca. Sprinkle over pears. Add orange and lemon juice. Dot with butter. Cover with top crust, cut vent, and flute rim. Bake in preheated oven (425°F.) for 40 to 50 minutes, or until pears are tender. Makes 6 to 8 servings.

RHUBARB FOOL

6 cups sliced rhubarb
½ teaspoon salt
¼ cup water (about)
1½ cups sugar
Heavy cream, whipped
½ teaspoon vanilla extract

Cook rhubarb with salt and just enough water to prevent scorching. Drain off excess liquid. Strain through food mill or whirl in blender. Stir in sugar to taste. Measure rhubarb and add equal amounts of whipped cream. Add vanilla; blend. Chill before serving. Makes 6 servings.

CANAPE—The literal translation for the French word *canapé* is "couch." As a culinary term, it is used for small pieces of bread, toast, crackers, or pastry, topped with a bit of tasty food. In other words, the topping sits on the bread or other base as if it were sitting on a couch.

Canapés can be plain pieces of bread spread with something as simple as a savory butter, or they can be ornate little shapes piled high with a filling. They can be either hot or cold, but they must be open-faced. They are served whenever a tidbit is needed: at cocktail parties, at coffee or teatime, or for midnight snacks. Ideally, canapés intrigue the appetite and the eye; they are not meant to still serious hunger.

CANAPÉ BUTTERS

Cream butter and add other ingredients.
Caraway or Poppy Seed—½ cup butter, ½ cup caraway or poppy seeds, ground.
Caviar—¼ cup butter, 2 tablespoons caviar, ¼ teaspoon grated onion, 1 teaspoon fresh lemon juice.
Caviar-Cream Cheese—Cream ¼ cup butter and 3 ounces cream cheese. Top with caviar and garnish.
Chive—½ cup butter, ¼ cup chopped chives, dash of Worcestershire.
Curry—½ cup butter, 2 finely chopped shallots sautéed in 1 tablespoon butter, 1 to 2 tablespoons curry powder, 1 teaspoon arrowroot, 2 tablespoons heavy cream. Force through a fine sieve.
Green Pepper—¼ cup butter, 2 tablespoons grated green pepper, well drained, a few drops of fresh lemon juice.
Honey—¼ cup butter, ¼ cup honey.
Horseradish—½ cup butter, ¼ cup grated horseradish.
Lemon—¼ cup butter, ½ teaspoon grated lemon rind, 1 tablespoon fresh lemon juice.
Mushroom—½ cup butter, 1 cup finely chopped raw mushrooms, ½ teaspoon salt, dash of pepper. Force through a fine sieve.
Mustard—½ cup butter, ¼ cup prepared mustard.
Olive—¼ cup butter, 2 tablespoons finely chopped green or stuffed olives, few drops of onion juice.
Paprika—¼ cup butter, 2 teaspoons paprika, a few drops of fresh lemon juice.

CANAPÉ

Pimiento—½ cup butter, ¼ cup mashed pimiento, 2 teaspoons drained pickle relish.
Piquant—½ cup butter, 1 tablespoon capers, 1 tablespoon chives, 2 small sweet gherkins, 1 anchovy fillet, 3 or 4 pickled onions, and a few leaves of fresh tarragon, chopped together. Force through a fine sieve.
Sardine—1 cup butter, 1 cup finely mashed skinless boneless sardines; juice of half or whole lemon. Force through a fine sieve.
Shrimp—1 cup butter, 1 cup minced cooked shrimps, ¼ teaspoon salt, dash of paprika, 1 tablespoon fresh lemon juice.
Tomato—½ cup butter, ¼ teaspoon salt, dash of pepper, chopped pulp of 2 firm tomatoes. Force through a fine sieve.

CANAPÉ SPREADS

Almond-Olive—¼ pound salted almonds, finely chopped, ¼ cup chopped stuffed olives, 2 tablespoons mayonnaise, 1 teaspoon French dressing.
Bologna—1 cup minced bologna, 2 teaspoons minced onion, 2 tablespoons minced celery, mayonnaise to bind.
Celery-Pickle—½ cup minced celery, ¼ cup chopped sweet pickle, ¼ cup chopped pimiento, 3 tablespoons mayonnaise.
Cheese-Deviled Ham—¾ cup grated Cheddar cheese, ⅓ cup deviled ham, ½ teaspoon Worcestershire, ¼ cup heavy cream.
Cheese-Pickle—1 cup grated Cheddar cheese, ¼ cup chopped sweet pickle, mayonnaise to moisten.
Chicken Liver-Bacon—1 cup mashed cooked chicken livers, 2 tablespoons minced cooked bacon, 4 drops of hot pepper sauce, 1 tablespoon fresh lemon juice.
Chicken Liver-Shrimp—½ cup ground cooked chicken livers, ½ cup ground cooked shrimps, 2 tablespoons minced onion, ¼ cup minced green pepper, chili sauce to bind.
Chicken-Pineapple—¾ cup minced cooked chicken, ⅓ cup crushed pineapple, 3 tablespoons mayonnaise.
Cottage Cheese, Celery, and Olive—½ cup cottage cheese, ⅓ cup minced celery, 8 minced green olives, ⅓ cup minced green onion, and salt, pepper, paprika to taste.
Crabmeat-Horseradish—1 cup of minced cooked crabmeat, 2 tablespoons cream, 1 tablespoon prepared horseradish.
Cream Cheese-Olive—3 ounces cream cheese, ½ cup minced stuffed olives, ¼ cup mayonnaise, 1 tablespoon prepared mustard, 1 teaspoon minced onion.
Cream Cheese-Roquefort—3 ounces cream cheese, 1½ ounces Roquefort cheese, ½ cup heavy cream, ⅛ teaspoon salt. Blend. Fold in ¼ cup heavy cream, whipped.
Deviled Ham-Egg—¾ cup deviled ham, 1 chopped hard-cooked egg, 1 tablespoon mayonnaise, 1 tablespoon chili sauce.
Dried Beef, Cheese, and Celery—¾ cup ground dried beef, ¼ cup grated cheese, ¼ cup minced celery, mayonnaise to bind.

Egg-Caviar—8 hard-cooked eggs, pressed through ricer, ¼ cup soft butter, 2 tablespoons caviar, salt and pepper to taste. Spread on slices of cooked celery root.
Egg-Nut—4 hard-cooked eggs, minced, ¼ cup ground walnuts, almonds, or filberts, 3 minced sweet cucumber pickles or ¼ cup pickle relish, 2 tablespoons mayonnaise.
Egg-Pickle—3 hard-cooked eggs, mashed, 6 sweet pickles, minced, 1 tablespoon peanut butter, prepared mustard, pickle juice to moisten.
Egg-Watercress—4 hard-cooked eggs, mashed, few sprigs chopped watercress, mayonnaise to moisten.
Ham-Chutney—½ cup minced cooked ham, ½ cup minced chutney.
Liverwurst—1 cup mashed liverwurst, 2 tablespoons mayonnaise, 1 tablespoon fresh lemon juice, ¼ teaspoon pepper.
Lobster—1 cup minced lobster, 1 tablespoon fresh lemon juice, ⅛ teaspoon pepper, ¼ teaspoon salt, 1 tablespoon mayonnaise, 1 tablespoon French dressing.
Pimiento Cheese-Bacon—½ pound pimiento cheese, 2 tablespoons chopped sweet pickle, 4 slices of broiled bacon, minced.
Salmon—1 cup flaked salmon, ¼ cup mayonnaise, 3 tablespoons chopped sweet pickle, salt and pepper to taste.
Sardine-Beet—1 cup mashed sardines, 3 tablespoons mayonnaise, ¼ cup chili sauce, ⅓ cup chopped pickled beets.
Spicy Ham—1 cup minced cooked ham, ¼ teaspoon ground cloves, ¼ teaspoon ground mace, dash of salt, ¼ cup heavy cream.
Tuna—½ cup mashed tuna, 2 tablespoons mayonnaise, 1 tablespoon fresh lemon juice, 2 tablespoons chopped stuffed olives, dash of Worcestershire.

MELBA TOAST

Cut bread into ⅛-inch slices and then into desired shapes for canapé. Put on cake racks. Pile cake racks one on top of the other with one empty rack on top. Put stack in a very slow oven (250°F.) and leave in oven until bread is dry and delicately browned.

To prevent toast from becoming soggy when using moist toppings, dip each piece of toast into a little raw egg white. Put in a warm oven for a few minutes.

BARQUETTES

Roll a flaky pastry made with butter or margarine to ⅛-inch thickness on floured board. Line tiny boat-shape barquette or round tart pans with pastry. Fill centers with rice to prevent overbrowning. Bake in preheated hot oven (425°F.) until lightly browned. Discard rice.

If barquette pans are hard to find, roll out pastry thinly on top of heavy-duty aluminum foil. Cut foil and pastry with scissors into ovals 3 × 2 inches. Moisten ends of oval pastry with water and pinch ends together using foil to shape pastry. Leave foil on pastry. Bake as above. Remove foil.

CANAPÉ

Clam Barquettes

- 1 can (10½ ounces) minced clams, drained
- 1 tablespoon instant minced onion
- ¼ cup minced green pepper
- 1 egg
- ½ cup heavy cream
- 2 tablespoons minced celery and leaves
- ½ cup fine dry bread crumbs
- 1 tablespoon butter, melted
- Dash of cayenne
- ¾ teaspoon salt
- ¼ teaspoon pepper
- 24 baked Barquettes or tiny tart shells

Blend all ingredients except pastry shells. Fill shells and broil until golden brown. Serve at once. Makes 2 dozen.

BRIOCHE FOR CANAPÉS

- 2 tablespoons water*
- 1 teaspoon (about ½ package) active dry yeast or ½ cake compressed yeast
- ⅓ cup milk, scalded and cooled to lukewarm
- ⅓ cup soft butter or margarine
- 1 egg
- 2 egg yolks
- 1 tablespoon sugar
- ½ teaspoon salt
- 2¼ cups sifted all-purpose flour

*Use very warm water (105°F. to 115°F.) for dry yeast; use lukewarm (80°F. to 90°F.) for compressed. Sprinkle yeast or crumble cake into water in large bowl. Let stand for a few minutes, then stir until dissolved. Add next 6 ingredients and 1¼ cups flour. Beat for 10 minutes by hand or for 3 minutes at medium speed of electric mixer. Add 1 cup flour and beat well. Let rise at room temperature for 3 hours. Punch down, cover, and chill overnight, or for at least 3 hours. Shape into a loaf and put in greased loaf pan, 9 × 5 × 3 inches. Let rise until light. Bake in preheated moderate oven (350°F.) for about 10 minutes. **Note:** This bread is baked in a loaf pan so that it can easily be sliced for canapés.

Brioche Canapés

Cut loaf of Brioche (above) into ¼-inch slices. Cut into small rounds with a canapé cutter of biscuit cutter. Spread half of rounds with one of Canapé Butters and top with a second slice of Brioche. Roll the edges first in mayonnaise and then in minced parsley.

PUFF PASTE

- 1 pound unsalted butter
- 4 cups all-purpose flour
- 1 teaspoon salt
- 1 tablespoon fresh lemon juice
- 1¼ cups cold water (about)

Shape butter into a brick about 3 × 5 × ¾ inches.
Roll butter in 3 tablespoons of the flour, coating all sides. Wrap in wax paper and chill.
Put remaining flour in a large bowl. Make a well in the center. Add salt and lemon juice. Gradually add water, using only enough to make a rather firm, slightly sticky dough.
Knead dough thoroughly on floured board for 20 minutes. Pound it on the table at intervals to achieve the right consistency. It should be very elastic and smooth. Form it into a ball; place on well-floured cloth.
With a rolling pin make the ball of dough into the shape of a four-leaf clover. Roll ends out, leaving the center thick. Well rolled, the dough will have a thick cushion in the center and 4 thinner "petals."
Put brick of butter in center of four-leaf clover. Fold petals over dough by stretching them over butter and sealing all edges so that butter is completely enclosed. Wrap in wax paper and chill for 20 minutes.
On a well-floured cloth gently roll out block of dough as evenly as possible into a rectangle slightly less than ⅓ inch thick and about 3 times as long as it is wide. Do not roll over ends in the length, but when dough is long enough, roll it lightly in the width, flattening ends to same thickness as the rest of the dough. Fold dough into thirds, making 3 layers, and chill for 20 minutes. Turn folded sides toward you and roll out dough; fold again into thirds. (Rolling, folding, and turning is called a "turn.") It is necessary to make a total of 6 turns, after which the dough is ready for use. The dough should be chilled between each turn and again after cutting.

Bouchées

Roll Puff Paste to ¼-inch thickness. Cut with a round scalloped cutter of the size desired. Cut small rounds from the centers of half the pieces. Brush rings and whole rounds with water and press gently together. The tiny centers can be baked and used for canapé bases or for cheese puffs if sprinkled with grated Parmesan or Swiss cheese. Put rounds on a cookie sheet and bake in preheated extremely hot oven (500°F.) for 5 minutes. Reduce heat to 450°F. and bake until browned, reducing heat 50° every 5 minutes down to moderate (350°F.). Cool; fill with any creamed or curried meat, fish, or poultry. (Ingredients should be chopped fine.) Finely chopped sautéed chicken livers with onion also make a good filling for Bouchées.

Cheese Allumettes

Cut rolled Puff Paste into strips 1 × 3 inches. Cover with thin strips of Swiss cheese and bake in preheated hot oven (425°F.) until well browned.

CANDY COOKBOOK

CANDY—"Sweets to the sweet," said Hamlet, and who can resist? It is a rare person who is born without a sweet tooth. Our word candy comes from the Persian word *qand,* or "candy," and although there is no one ingredient necessary to its making, the end result must be sweet. Egyptians used that age-old sweetener, honey, to which they added figs, dates, nuts, and spices. These early confections were made in various shapes and sometimes colored. The Arabs and Chinese also made a sweet consisting of different fruits, juices, and honey. It was the Arabs who made the biggest contribution to candy-making: the early refining and processing of sugar. They spread the knowledge of sugar cane from Persia to the Mediterranean, although it was not until after the Crusades, in the 14th century, that the acquaintance with sugar became widespread. Venice, that aristocratic lady of the Adriatic, carried on an extensive sea trade, and it was to this port that sugar was brought and made into tasty confections.

From Italy, as well as from the Arab influence in Spain, the use of sugar spread throughout Europe. For a time European candy-making remained in the hands of the apothecaries. Soothing and beneficial properties were ascribed to its consumption. Caraway comfits, sugar-coated caraway seeds, were considered a most pleasurable way of settling the stomach after a large medieval feast. The sugar-coated pill was an early invention: Greek and Roman physicians had once advised smearing the rim of a cup holding a bitter draught with honey. Now medicine could be made palatable by the coating of sugar.

SUGAR AND CANDY IN AMERICA

Columbus brought sugar to the New World, specifically San Domingo, on his second voyage in 1493. By 1511, growing sugar cane was an established practice in Cuba, and from there it spread to most of the West Indian islands and to Central and South America. Sugar was one of the important early imports into the Colonies. Again it was the druggist who had charge of candy-making. Candy drops containing peppermint, hoarhound, and wintergreen were healing as well as tasty. At home, children depended on molasses, honey, maple, or jam to satisfy their sweet tooth. The nearest thing to candy was a type of "sugar candy" made by boiling sugar in water and letting it crystallize. The first real candy was made in the form of stick candy. Later additions were molasses taffy and the sugar plum (not a plum at all but a plum-shape bonbon).

By 1845 the candy trade in this country had not grown to any appreciable extent. In Europe, too, candy-making as an industry moved slowly. The introduction of machinery, around 1840, gave impetus to the trade throughout Europe. Although, on a nutritional level, there seems no earthly reason to justify the pleasure of eating candy, it does supply quick energy for physical exercise. Admiral Richard E. Byrd took two and a half tons of candy to the South Pole on one of his expeditions.

Today, candy-making is an important industry in the United States. But most good cooks enjoy turning out their own occasional batch of fudge to please the youngsters, or to recapture the nostalgia of olden days, when the fragrance of homemade candy brought old and young to the kitchen.

In general, candies fall into two classes: creamy or crystalline, and amorphous or noncrystalline.

CREAMY OR CRYSTALLINE

Creamy candies include fondant, fudge, penuche, divinity, and seafoam. When making creamy candies, the chief concern is to control the mixture so that the sugar crystals in the finished candy are so small they cannot be seen or felt when eaten. The texture must be smooth and creamy, never gritty or sugary.

Nutritive Food Values
Fondant, 3½ ounces = 364 calories
Fudge, vanilla, with nuts, 3½ ounces = 424 calories
Fudge, chocolate, 3½ ounces = 400 calories
Fudge, chocolate, with nuts, 3½ ounces = 426 calories

AMORPHOUS OR NONCRYSTALLINE

Chewy or hard candies such as caramels, butterscotch, taffy, lollipops, nougat, brittles, gumdrops, and marshmallows become a solid mass as the candy hardens.

Nutritive Food Values
Caramels, plain or chocolate, 3½ ounces = 403 calories
Butterscotch candy, 3½ ounces = 397 calories
Nougat, chocolate coated, 3½ ounces – 416 calories
Brittle, peanut, 3½ ounces = 421 calories
Marshmallows, 3½ ounces = 315 calories
Gumdrops, 3½ ounces = 347 calories
Hard candy, 3½ ounces = 385 calories

SUGGESTIONS FOR CANDY MAKERS

Follow recipes carefully. Use a heavy saucepan—one larger than you think you'll need. Use a candy thermometer if possible. Always make sure the thermometer bulb is in the boiling mixture but does not touch bottom of the pan. Read the thermometer with your eye in a direct line with the upper level of the mercury. During cooking wash down the sides of the pan with a wet pastry brush or damp paper towel to make sure all sugar dissolves. For all candy except fondant, grease pans or slabs that are to be used. For fondant, moisten the slab with cold water. Grease hands before pulling taffy. Many mixtures with milk or cream, or those cooked to a higher temperature, will burn easily. Watch candy carefully, especially during the last few minutes of cooking. Temperatures rise quickly at the end. For best results, don't double or make substitutions in the ingredients. Finally, allow plenty of time when making most candies. Many, such as caramels, take long cooking and stirring.

If you do not have a candy thermometer, see the chart on Candy-Making Tests, for tests you can use to determine the approximate temperature of the sugar syrup.

Fondant—This is the foundation for most mints, bonbons, and the creamy centers for chocolates. Many short-cut recipes have been devised but anyone who really enjoys candy-making should try a real fondant at least once.

The chief ingredients are sugar and water, plus corn syrup or an acid such as cream of tartar to aid in keeping sugar crystals small, so that the candy will be smooth. After cooking, the candy is beaten, then kneaded. It needs a ripening period of 12 to 24 hours to make it easier to handle.

Fudge—A creamy, smooth confection which is the pride and joy of all youngsters in their first candy-making adventure. In fudge, milk and some agent such as corn syrup are used to help keep the texture smooth. The candy is also beaten after a cooling period. An important point to watch is the temperature before beating. If stirring or beating is started too soon, the candy will be less smooth. Once beating is started, it should not be interrupted. In the beating process, the candy will go through interesting changes in appearance. At first it will be shiny and quite thin. As beating continues, the shininess will begin to disappear and by the end of the beating period, it will be lusterless and, of course, thick.

There are many varieties of fudge: chocolate, cocoa, or peanut butter, plain, or with nuts, fruits, or spices added.

The same general method is used for making Penuche and Pralines.

Divinity and Seafoam—Fluffy, porous candy is made by boiling sugar, water, and corn syrup to the firm or hard-ball stage, then slowly beating this syrup into egg whites, and beating constantly until the mixture is very stiff. The candy is then dropped by spoon onto wax paper, cut when firm, or sometimes kneaded.

Caramel—It is characterized by its chewy consistency. This is achieved by the high fat content of butter and/or cream and corn syrup, or molasses. Candies containing milk or cream must be stirred constantly while cooking but, in many cases, not at all after removing from heat. They are poured to desired thickness, cooled, and cut into pieces with scissors or knife.

Butterscotch—A butter-flavored caramel which can be poured into a pan and cut into squares. If cooked a little longer, it can be dropped by a spoon onto wax paper and used as a hard candy.

Taffy—A syrup cooked without stirring until it reaches the hard-ball or soft-crack stage; then the mixture is allowed to cool until it can be pulled with the hands. Here, as with fudge, the temperature of the candy is important.

Nougat—Chewy candy made by adding syrup to stiffly beaten egg whites, then stirring in nuts, usually chopped almonds. Commercially made nougats are poured onto and covered with wafer paper, then pressed to form smooth surfaces. Since wafer paper is not always readily available to homemakers, a light dusting of cornstarch may be substituted. Nougats should stand for several hours before cutting.

Brittle—There are two ways of making this hard candy. One is to caramelize sugar in a skillet over low heat until melted and golden brown, then add nuts. A second way is to cook syrup in a saucepan to the hard-crack stage, then add butter and soda to make a tender, more porous brittle. In either case nuts are added when cooking is completed. Mixture is poured immediately so that the candy is 1/8 to 1/4 inch thick; sometimes it is pulled even thinner as it begins to harden. When hard, it is cracked into pieces.

Marshmallows—These are very simple to make because there is no cooking involved. However, the mixture must be beaten for 15 minutes and a good electric mixer is necessary. It is almost impossible to beat the mixture with a rotary beater.

Storage—Keep different types of candy separately. Brittles soften if stored with creamy candies. Air tight storage in a cool place is best. Some candies may be frozen, but avoid freezing those made with fruits and nuts.

FONDANT

3 cups sugar
1 1/3 cups water
1/4 teaspoon salt
1/3 cup light corn syrup

Mix all ingredients in large saucepan. Bring to boil, stirring. Cover; boil for 3 minutes. Remove cover and cook until a small amount of mixture forms a soft ball when dropped into cold water (238°F. on candy thermometer). Wash down sides of pan several times with a fork covered with cheesecloth and dipped into water, using an up-and-down motion. Pour out onto ungreased platter. Cool to lukewarm (110°F.). Beat with fondant paddle or spatula until mixture turns cloudy. Gather into a ball and knead with lightly buttered hands until smooth and creamy. Put away in crock glass jar and allow to "ripen" for 2 or 3 days before using. Makes about 2 1/4 pounds.

Fondant Patties
[Mints]

Melt small amount of Fondant (about 1 cup) at a time over hot water. Keep water in bottom of double boiler just below boiling point. Stir melted fondant enough to blend. Add coloring, if desired, and a few drops of flavoring oil such as peppermint, wintergreen, or spearmint. Drop patties from tip of teaspoon onto wax paper. As soon as firm, loosen and lift. Decorate if desired.

Bonbons

Using two thirds of Fondant planned for any one flavor of bonbon, work in desired flavoring and coloring, a little at a time. Shape into 3/4-inch balls for centers. Bits of nuts, candied or dried fruits, or coconut can be added on wax paper, covered overnight. Next day, melt remaining third of the fondant set aside for this batch in top part of metal double boiler over boiling water. Add flavoring and coloring to match fondant centers. Remove from heat. Set pan in cold water for a moment and then put over hot, not boiling, water to keep fondant warm and soft. With dipping fork, or other fork, dip bonbon centers, one at a time, into melted fondant to cover. Stir after each bonbon is dipped to keep crust from forming on top. If this fondant becomes too thick, reheat or add a few drops of hot water. Tip bonbon over onto wax-paper-covered tray. Decorative circles can be made by holding dipping

CANDY

fork on top of bonbon for a moment. Decorate at once with bits of nuts, candied fruits, silver shot, or colored sugar, as desired. Leftover dipping fondant can be dropped onto wax paper to make patties. Store, covered, in cool dry place.

CANDY-MAKING TESTS

Temperature-Degrees F.- of syrup at sea level (indicating concentration desired)	Stage	Description of Test
230 to 234	Thread	Syrup spins a 2-inch thread when dropped from fork or spoon.
234 to 240	Soft ball	Syrup, when dropped into very cold water, forms a soft ball which flattens on removal from water.
244 to 248	Firm ball	Syrup, when dropped into very cold water, forms a firm ball which does not flatten on removal from water.
250 to 266	Hard ball	Syrup, when dropped into very cold water, forms a hard ball which holds its shape, yet is plastic.
270 to 290	Soft crack	Syrup, when dropped into very cold water, separates into threads which are hard but not brittle.
300 to 310	Hard crack	Syrup, when dropped into very cold water, separates into threads which are hard and brittle.

UNCOOKED FONDANT

⅓ cup soft butter or margarine
⅓ cup light corn syrup
½ teaspoon salt
1 teaspoon vanilla extract
3½ cups (1 pound) sifted confectioners' sugar

Blend all ingredients but sugar; mix in sugar; knead until blended. Makes about 1⅓ pounds.

Candied-Fruit Squares

Substitute rum extract for the vanilla in Uncooked Fondant recipe. Add ½ cup finely chopped candied fruit (cherries, pineapple, orange and lemon peels). Roll ½ inch thick; cut into squares.

Peanut Squares

Add ¾ cup chopped unsalted peanuts to Uncooked Fondant recipe. Roll about ½ inch thick. Cut into squares.

Mocha Logs

Add 2 teaspoons instant coffee to Uncooked Fondant recipe. Shape into rolls ½ x 2 inches. Roll in chocolate sprinkles.

OPERA CREAMS

2 cups sugar
2 tablespoons light corn syrup
1 cup light cream
⅛ teaspoon salt
1 teaspoon vanilla extract
½ cup broken nuts

Mix all ingredients except last 2 in saucepan. Bring to boil and cook, without stirring, until a small amount of mixture dropped into cold water forms a soft ball. (236°F. on candy thermometer). Remove from heat and let stand until lukewarm (110°F.). Add vanilla and nuts; beat until mixture is thick and loses its gloss. Drop by dessertspoon onto wax paper and let stand until firm. Makes about 20 creams.

Opera Fudge

Make Opera Creams and pour candy into buttered 8-inch square pan. When firm, cut into squares.

CHRISTMAS FUDGE

⅔ cup (1 small can) undiluted evaporated milk
2 tablespoons butter or margarine
1⅔ cups sugar
½ teaspoon salt
2 cups (4 ounces) miniature marshmallows
1½ cups (9 ounces) semisweet chocolate pieces
½ cup chopped pistachio nuts
¼ cup crushed peppermint candy sticks

Mix first 4 ingredients in saucepan. Bring to boil and cook 4 to 5 minutes, stirring constantly. (Begin timing when mixture bubbles.) Remove from heat and add marshmallows, chocolate and nuts; stir hard until marshmallows are melted. Pour into buttered 8-inch square pan and sprinkle with crushed candy. Cool thoroughly and cut in squares. Makes about 2 pounds.

CHOCOLATE DAINTIES

7 ounces semisweet chocolate
7 tablespoons vegetable shortening
2 eggs, beaten
Grated rind of 1 orange (optional)
Chocolate shot, chopped nuts or candied violets

In top part of double boiler, melt chocolate and shortening over hot water. Remove from heat, blend well and let stand until cold but not hard. Gradually add to eggs, beating vigorously with electric mixer or whisk until mixture holds its shape in stiff peaks. Add orange rind, if desired. Using a No. 3 rose pastry tube, pipe rosettes of the mixture into tiny foil cups. Decorate as desired and chill until firm. Store in refrigerator. Makes about 1 pound.

BROWN SUGAR FUDGE

- 1 pound light-brown sugar
- 1 cup granulated sugar
- 2/3 cup milk
- 1/8 teaspoon salt
- 2 tablespoons each peanut butter and marshmallow cream
- 1 teaspoon vanilla extract

Mix sugars, milk and salt in saucepan, bring to full boil and boil 2½ minutes. Remove from heat and add remaining ingredients. Beat until mixture starts to thicken, then turn into a buttered 8-inch square pan and let stand until firm. Cut in squares. Makes about 1½ pounds.

OLD-TIME PENUCHE

- 4½ cups (2 pounds) firmly packed light brown sugar
- 1 cup undiluted evaporated milk
- ½ cup butter or margarine
- ¼ teaspoon salt
- 1 teaspoon vanilla extract
- 2 cups chopped walnuts

In large saucepan mix sugar, milk, butter, and salt. Cook, stirring, until sugar is dissolved. Continue cooking until a small amount of mixture dropped into cold water forms a soft ball. (238°F. on candy thermometer). Remove from heat and let stand until lukewarm (110°F.). Add vanilla and walnuts. Beat until mixture is thick and loses its gloss. Pour into buttered 9-inch square pan. When firm, cut into squares. Makes about 3 pounds.

DIVINITY

- ½ cup light corn syrup
- 2½ cups sugar
- ¼ teaspoon salt
- ½ cup water
- 2 egg whites
- 1 teaspoon vanilla extract
- 1 cup coarsely chopped nuts

In saucepan mix corn syrup, sugar, salt, and water. Cook, stirring, until sugar is dissolved. Continue cooking, without stirring, until a small amount of mixture dropped into cold water forms a firm ball (248°F. on candy thermometer). Beat egg whites until stiff but not dry. Pour about half of syrup slowly over whites, beating constantly. Cook remainder until a small amount of mixture dropped into cold water forms hard but not brittle threads, the soft-crack stage (272°F. on candy thermometer). Add slowly to first mixture and beat until mixture holds its shape. Add vanilla and nuts and drop by dessert-spoonfuls onto wax paper, or spread in buttered 9-inch square pan. When firm, cut into squares. Makes about 1½ pounds.

Seafoam

Follow Divinity recipe, substituting light brown sugar for granulated sugar.

Chocolate Divinity

Follow Divinity recipe. Beat until mixture begins to hold its shape; then add vanilla, one 6-ounce package semi-sweet chocolate pieces and 1 cup nut halves. Beat until well blended.

Holiday Divinity

Follow Divinity recipe, adding ¼ cup each of chopped candied cherries and pineapple with the nuts.

Ginger Divinity

Follow Divinity recipe, using 6 tablespoons water and 2 tablespoons preserved-ginger syrup for the liquid. Add ½ cup finely diced ginger with the nuts.

VANILLA CARAMELS

- 2 cups sugar
- 2 cups light cream, warmed
- 1 cup corn syrup
- ½ teaspoon salt
- ⅓ cup butter or margarine
- 1 teaspoon vanilla extract
- ½ cup broken nuts

Mix sugar, 1 cup of the cream, the corn syrup, and salt in large saucepan. Cook, stirring, for about 10 minutes. Add remaining 1 cup cream very slowly so that mixture does not stop boiling. Cook for 5 minutes longer. Stir in butter, 1 teaspoon at a time. Cook slowly, stirring, until a small amount of mixture dropped into cold water forms a firm ball (248°F. on candy thermometer). Remove from heat; add vanilla and nuts and mix gently. Pour into buttered 8-inch square pan, and cool. Turn out on board, mark off ¾-inch squares, and cut. Wrap in wax paper. Makes about 2 pounds.

Chocolate Caramels

Follow recipe above, adding 3 or 4 ounces (3 or 4 squares) unsweetened chocolate to mixture before cooking.

CHOCOLATE-COCONUT CLUSTERS

Heat 1 package (8 ounces) semisweet chocolate squares over hot water until partially melted. Remove from heat and stir until completely melted. Add 1 cup flaked coconut and mix well. Drop by teaspoonfuls onto waxed paper and let stand until firm. Makes 2 dozen.

Mints Butterscotch Opera Creams

Penuche Pecan Roll Rum Balls

Popcorn Balls Molasses Taffy Pralines

Truffles	Divinity	Chocolate Fudge
Raisin-Peanut Clusters	Toffee	Candied Peel
Nougat	Peanut Brittle	Caramels

CANDY

NO-COOK CHOCOLATE CHEWS

2 tablespoons butter
½ cup corn syrup
2 ounces unsweetened chocolate, melted
1 teaspoon vanilla extract
3 cups sifted confectioners' sugar
¾ cup dry nonfat milk powder

Blend butter and corn syrup, then stir in chocolate and vanilla. Mix sugar and dry milk. Gradually stir into first mixture, then knead until thoroughly blended. Shape in ¾-inch rolls and cut in 1-inch pieces. Makes about 1½ pounds.

PECAN PRALINES

1 cup granulated sugar
2 cups firmly packed light brown sugar
¼ cup light corn syrup
⅛ teaspoon salt
1¼ cups milk
1 teaspoon vanilla extract
1½ cups unbroken pecan halves

Combine sugars, corn syrup, salt, and milk in saucepan. Bring to boil and cook, without stirring until a little of mixture dropped into cold water forms a soft ball (236°F. on candy thermometer). Remove from heat and let stand until lukewarm (110°F.). Add vanilla and pecans and beat with spoon until mixture begins to thicken and loses its gloss. Drop from tablespoon onto wax paper and spread to form patties about 4 inches in diameter. Let stand until firm. Then wrap individually in moistureproof paper. Store in airtight container. Makes 12 pralines.

Vanilla Pralines

Use 3 cups granulated sugar in place of white and light brown sugars in Pecan Praline recipe.

BUTTERSCOTCH DROPS

2 cups granulated sugar
1 cup firmly packed light brown sugar
¾ cup water
¼ cup light corn syrup
1 teaspoon cider vinegar
½ teaspoon salt
1 package (6 ounces) butterscotch pieces
¾ cup coarsely chopped nuts

Put first 6 ingredients in 2-quart saucepan and bring to full boil, stirring. Boil 3 minutes, without stirring, over high heat. Remove from heat, add butterscotch pieces and stir until melted (mixture will be thin). Add nuts and drop by teaspoonfuls on ungreased foil. If mixture becomes too thick to drop, add a little hot water, beginning with 1 teaspoon. Let stand until set. Makes about 1¾ pounds.

COCONUT CONFECTIONS

2 cups sifted confectioners' sugar
1 package (7 ounces) fine grated coconut
3 tablespoons butter or margarine, melted and cooled
1 egg white
1 tablespoon light cream
½ teaspoon almond extract
    Melted unsweetened chocolate
    Green or red food coloring
    Tiny candy sprinkles or tinted fine grated coconut

Mix first 6 ingredients, working well with hands to form a paste. Using a level teaspoonful, shape pieces in round balls. Make a small deep depression in center of each and fill with melted chocolate. Chill until firm. Or tint mixture desired color, shape in balls and decorate with sprinkles. Or tint mixture and press out to a square ½-inch thick. Cut in ¾-inch squares or other desired shapes and decorate tops with tinted coconut. Chill. Store all candies airtight. Makes about 1 pound.
Note: If paste is too sticky to handle, rub hands with confectioners' sugar.

PULLED MINTS

3 cups granulated sugar
1 cup water
2 tablespoons light corn syrup
¼ teaspoon salt
10 drops oil of peppermint or spearmint
1 cup sifted confectioners' sugar
½ cup cornstarch

Combine granulated sugar, water, corn syrup, and salt in saucepan. Put over heat and stir until sugar is dissolved. Bring to boil; cover and boil for 2 minutes. Uncover and continue cooking, without stirring, until a little of mixture dropped into cold water forms a very hard ball (265°F. on candy thermometer). Remove from heat and pour out onto large platter. Cool until comfortable to handle (mixture should still be quite warm). Add oil of peppermint. Then pull with fingers until light-colored and glossy. Stretch into long rope about ½ inch in diameter. Cut into 1-inch pieces and put at once into mixture of confectioners' sugar and cornstarch. Let stand in warm place overnight to allow mints to mellow. Then shake in strainer to remove excess sugar mixture. Store in airtight container. **Note:** Red or green vegetable coloring may be added with the oil of peppermint or spearmint. If more than one color is desired, make recipe twice, or make half of recipe twice, as all of candy must be pulled at one time.

BUTTERSCOTCH CANDY

2 cups sugar
⅔ cup dark corn syrup
¼ cup water
¼ cup light cream
¼ cup butter or margarine

CANDY

Cook, stirring often until a small amount of mixture dropped into very cold water forms a hard ball (260°F. on candy thermometer). Add butter and cook, stirring, until a small amount of mixture dropped into very cold water separates into threads which are hard but not brittle, or the soft-crack stage (280°F. on candy thermometer). Pour into buttered 8-inch square pan. When almost set, cut into squares. When cold, break apart. Makes about 1¼ pounds.

ALMOND NOUGAT

- 1½ cups light corn syrup
- 2 cups sugar
- ¼ teaspoon salt
- ¼ cup water
- 2 egg whites
- ½ teaspoon almond extract
- Red or green food coloring
- ¼ cup soft butter or margarine
- 1 cup chopped toasted almonds
- ¼ cup chopped candied cherries

Mix first four ingredients in heavy saucepan. Cook, stirring, until sugar is dissolved. Cook, without stirring, until a small amount of mixture dropped into cold water forms a hard ball (250°F. on candy thermometer). Beat egg whites until stiff but not dry in large bowl of electric mixer. Gradually beat in about one fourth (not more) of the syrup and continue beating until mixture holds its shape. Cook remaining syrup until a small amount of mixture dropped into cold water separates into hard and brittle threads (300°F. on candy thermometer). Gradually beat into first mixture and continue beating until mixture begins to hold its shape. Add flavoring and food coloring to tint a delicate shade. Beat in butter; continue beating until very thick and satiny. Stir in nuts and cherries. Press into a buttered 8-inch square pan and smooth top. Let stand until firm. Turn out of pan and cut into pieces 1 x 1½ inches. Wrap each piece individually in wax paper. For best flavor, store for several days in a cool place before serving. Makes about 2 pounds.

PEANUT BRITTLE

- 2 cups granulated sugar
- 1 cup firmly packed light brown sugar
- ½ cup light corn syrup
- ½ cup water
- Pinch of salt
- ¼ cup butter or margarine
- ⅛ teaspoon baking soda
- 1½ cups peanuts

Combine sugars, corn syrup, and water in saucepan. Cook, stirring, until sugar is dissolved. Cook, without stirring, until a little of mixture dropped into cold water becomes very brittle (300°F. on candy thermometer). Remove from heat; add salt, butter, and soda and stir just to mix. Add nuts and turn into shallow greased pan. Let stand for a minute or so and then pull quite thin. When cold, break up. Makes about 1½ pounds.

OLD-FASHIONED MOLASSES TAFFY

- ½ cup butter or margarine
- 2 cups sugar
- 1 cup molasses
- 1½ cups water
- ¼ cup light corn syrup

Combine all ingredients except butter in a saucepan and bring to a boil, stirring. Cook, stirring often until a small amount of mixture dropped into very cold water forms a hard ball (260°F. on candy thermometer). Add butter and cook, stirring, until a small amount of mixture dropped into very cold water separates into threads which are hard but not brittle, or the soft-crack stage (280°F. on candy thermometer). Pour into buttered 8-inch square pan. When almost set, cut into squares. When cold, break apart. Makes about 1¼ pounds.

TOFFEE

- 1⅔ cups sugar
- ⅔ cup dark corn syrup
- ⅓ cup light cream
- ¼ cup butter or margarine
- ½ teaspoon vanilla extract
- ⅔ cup chopped nuts

Combine sugar, syrup, and cream in heavy saucepan; cook over medium heat, stirring constantly, until sugar is dissolved. Add butter. Turn heat low and cook, stirring occasionally, until a small amount of mixture dropped into cold water forms a hard ball (260°F. on candy thermometer). Remove from heat and stir in vanilla and ⅓ cup nuts; stir for 2 minutes longer. Pour into buttered 8-inch square pan and sprinkle with remaining nuts. When almost set, mark into squares with knife. When cold, cut or break into squares as marked. Makes about 1⅓ pounds.

MARSHMALLOWS

- 1 envelope unflavored gelatin
- ⅓ cup cold water
- Sugar
- ⅔ cup light corn syrup
- ½ teaspoon vanilla extract
- Cornstarch

Soften gelatin in cold water and dissolve over hot water or low heat. Add ½ cup sugar, and stir until dissolved. Put in large mixer bowl with the corn syrup and vanilla. Beat at high speed for 15 minutes, or until mixture is very thick and of marshmallow consistency. Cover bottom of 9 x 9 x 2-inch pan with equal parts of sugar and cornstarch. Pour in mixture, and smooth top. Let stand in cool place for 1 hour, or until set. Loosen from pan, and turn out on board sprinkled with mixture of equal parts cornstarch and sugar. Cut in squares with knife wet with cold water. Roll in cornstarch and sugar. Makes 1 pound.

CANDY

CREAMY CARAMEL MIXTURE

- 2 cups light cream
- 2 cups sugar
- 1 cup light or dark corn syrup
- ½ teaspoon salt
- ⅓ cup butter or margarine
- 1 teaspoon vanilla extract

Heat cream to lukewarm in large, heavy saucepan. Pour out 1 cup and reserve. Add sugar, corn syrup and salt to cream in saucepan. Cook, stirring, until mixture boils. Add reserved cream very slowly so mixture does not stop boiling. Cook 5 minutes, stirring. Stir in butter, about 1 teaspoon at a time. Reduce heat and cook, stirring almost constantly, until a small amount of mixture forms a firm ball when dropped in very cold water (248°F. on a candy thermometer). Remove from heat and gently stir in vanilla and cool slightly.

Note: Only occasional stirring will be necessary if final cooking is done on a thick asbestos mat.

OLD-FASHIONED MARZIPAN

- ½ pound (about 2 cups) sifted confectioners' sugar
- 2 cans (8 ounces each) almond paste
- 1 tablespoon strong rose water
- Food colorings
- 8 to 10 whole cloves

Put sugar in bowl and break in paste. Sprinkle with rose water. Cut mixture together with pastry blender. When pieces are the size of peas, knead mixture with hands until very smooth and pliable. Divide in 8 parts. Tint each piece a different color as follows: for apple, use 2 drops yellow coloring; for peach, 1 drop red, 1 drop yellow; for orange, 1 drop red, 10 drops yellow; for lemon, 5 drops yellow; for lime, 1 drop yellow, 1 drop green; for banana, 7 drops yellow; for pear, 1 drop yellow; for strawberry, 10 drops red, 2 drops yellow. Rinse hands after coloring each piece. Working with one part at a time, cut each in 6 even pieces. Keep remaining mixtures in plastic bag until ready to use to avoid drying out. Shape fruits. To make dimples in strawberries and citrus fruits, roll fruits gently over smallest teeth in food grater as soon as fruits are shaped. For apples and pears, insert a whole clove in blossom end. Using plastic leaves, insert a small piece of the stem with attached leaves in apples, pears and peaches. Put all fruits on a tray and cover with waxed paper. If desired, fruits can be painted with diluted food coloring and a small paintbrush. Let fruits stand at least 2 hours before painting. Store, covered with waxed paper, in airtight container at room temperature. Makes about 1½ pounds.

Note: Marzipan can be divided in 3 equal parts and tinted light green, pink and yellow. Press each part in a square and arrange in layers. Cut in squares, fingers or diamonds.

CRUNCHY CEREAL PATTIES

- 5 cups assorted unsweetened crisp ready-to-eat cereals
- 4 cups miniature marshmallows
- ⅓ cup peanut butter
- ¼ cup butter
- ½ cup semisweet chocolate pieces

Put cereals in large greased bowl. Melt together next 3 ingredients in top part of double boiler over hot water, stirring occasionally until smooth. Pour over cereal, stirring until evenly coated. With buttered hands, shape mixture in fifteen 3-inch patties; put on waxed paper. Melt chocolate and decorate tops. Chill until set.

POPPED CORN CRACKLE

- 2 quarts popped corn
- ½ cup salted peanuts
- 1 cup sugar
- ¼ cup light corn syrup
- ½ cup water
- ¼ teaspoon salt
- 3 tablespoons light molasses
- 2 tablespoons butter or margarine
- ¼ teaspoon baking soda

Put corn and peanuts in large bowl and set aside. Mix next 5 ingredients in heavy saucepan. Put over low heat and stir until sugar is dissolved. Cover and cook 3 minutes. Uncover and cook over medium heat until small amount of mixture forms hard but not brittle threads when dropped in very cold water (265°F. on a candy thermometer). Reduce heat and cook, stirring constantly, until small amount of mixture forms hard brittle threads when dropped in very cold water (290°F.). Remove from heat and blend in butter and soda. Pour over corn and peanuts, mixing to coat evenly. Press into buttered 15 x 10 x 1-inch pan. Cool and break in pieces. Makes about 1½ pounds.

POPCORN BALLS

- 1 cup molasses
- 1 cup corn syrup
- 1 teaspoon cider vinegar
- 3 tablespoons butter
- ½ teaspoon salt
- 2 quarts freshly popped corn

In saucepan combine molasses, syrup, and vinegar. Cook until a small amount of mixture dropped into cold water forms a hard ball (266°F. registers on candy thermometer). Stir in butter and salt and pour slowly over popped corn, stirring so that each kernel is coated. Butter hands slightly and shape into 3-inch balls. Cool; wrap balls individually in wax paper or plastic wrapping. Makes 6 balls.

TURTLETTES

2 cans (6 ounces each) pecans
1 recipe Creamy Caramel Mixture
1 package (12 ounces) semi-sweet chocolate pieces

Arrange groups of 4 pecan pieces on buttered cookie sheet. Spoon about 1 teaspoon caramel mixture in center of each group of nuts, half covering each nut, to resemble turtles. Let stand about 10 minutes. Melt chocolate and spread some on each turtlette. Let stand until set, then wrap in plastic. Makes about 4 dozen.

CANNING—Until a French confectioner opened the world's first vacuum-bottling plant in 1804, foods were preserved only by drying, smoking, salting or pickling, methods that changed the appearance, flavor, and nutritive values of food. Nicolas Appert believed that the absence of oxygen was what gave his hermetically sealed foods their keeping quality. Later research showed that it was really the destruction by heat of all organisms that might cause spoilage.

Before Nicolas Appert invented the process that won him a prize of nearly $250,000 from the emperor Napoleon, there was little variety to preserved food. Canning has made it possible to enjoy many fruits and vegetables out of season with little effort and with little change in the appearance or nutritive values of the foods canned.

Today, the foods most often canned at home are tomatoes, green beans, and peaches — home-grown or purchased at low seasonal prices. Millions of homemakers each year put up at least a few jars of an old favorite, using any of several canning methods depending on the kind of food canned.

There are potential hazards in canning and in eating foods improperly canned at home. To avoid such hazards, follow carefully the directions in this section.

CANNING EQUIPMENT

If only 3 or 4 small jars are to be canned, a large kettle with a lid will serve the purpose. A cake cooling rack on the bottom will keep the jars from touching the bottom.

For more ambitious efforts, the homemaker's investment in canning equipment will be determined by how much food is to be canned, and on how much storage space is available. The equipment can be expensive, and it can take up a good deal of space.

Canners

If space is limited, a steam pressure canner is more essential than a boiling water bath canner, although both have their uses.

Boiling Water Bath Canners are preferable when there is to be a great deal of canning and the food to be canned is acid (tomatoes, fruit preserves). Such canners are available in a 20-quart size, made of aluminum with a tight-fitting lid. Or they can be made at home using a large metal or enamelware kettle with a tight cover, or a clean wash boiler, or a large soup kettle. The canner must be deep enough so that boiling water will be 2 to 4 inches over the tops of the jars. The canner must be fitted with a rack of metal or wood to keep the jars from touching the bottom and with partitions to keep them from touching one another or falling against the side of the canner.

Steam Pressure Canners are available in 16- to 20-quart sizes. Made of heavy cast aluminum with gasket-sealed lids, they come equipped with racks. Some have pressure gauges, others have weighted gauges plus safety valve petcocks or vents, thus providing for the escape of air and steam when open. When petcocks or vents are closed, the steam is held inside, allowing pressure to build up so that foods may be heated at 240°F. The petcock may be in one unit with the safety valve, or each may be a separate part. The safety valve is so adjusted that steam will be released automatically should the pressure in the cooker rise too high. Drawing a string or narrow strip of cloth through the vents will keep them clean; this should be done before using the canner and should be repeated often. Check the pressure gauge to be certain that it can maintain pressure at 10 pounds. If the gauge is off by 2 pounds or less, you should be aware of it and should make adjustments accordingly. If the inaccuracy is greater than 2 pounds, you need a new gauge to maintain proper internal temperature. Accuracy in time and temperature is vital for safe canning especially of nonacid foods. When canning acid foods in a Steam Pressure Canner rather than a Boiling Water Bath Canner, just set the cover of your Steam Pressure Canner in place without fastening it; leave the safety petcock open to prevent pressure from building up.

Canning Containers

The Mason jar patented by a 26-year-old New York metalworker in 1858 was the grandddaddy of most modern glass canning jars. Many variations of John Landis Mason's jar are available today. The type you select is largely a matter of personal preference, but any jar used in pressure canning must stand up to heats of 240°F. and higher. Jars come in half-pint, pint, and quart sizes. Metal lids are generally easiest to use and the least fragile. Any lid must be airtight. To test, fill the jar with water, cap it properly, and turn it upside down. If there are no leaks the jar is safe. Keep jars and lids scrupulously clean. Different jars and lids require specific methods of handling and cleaning; follow the manufacturer's directions.

Rubber Rings—They must be clean, new, and of the right size. Rubber deteriorates. Using rings left over from last year can be dangerous. Even new rings should be tested: bend them in small pleats; if they crack, throw them away. If they are sound, wash them, rinse them, and keep them wet until needed. When filling a wire-bail type jar, the lip of the rubber ring must be on the side of the jar opposite the wire side. After filling a jar, wipe off the rubber ring and the jar rim with

CANNING

a clean, damp cloth. Put the lid on, making sure it rests on rubber, and seal. When opening glass-topped jars, it is best to pull the rubber out part way rather than prying up the top and possibly chipping the lid or jar.

Bottles—Some juices (tomato juice, apple juice, citrus juices) may be canned in bottles. Caps and sealers are available for this purpose.

Other Canning Equipment—A Timer is essential. Many other items are useful:

- Bowls
- Colander
- Chopping bowl and chopping knife
- Cutting board and slicing knives
- Sharp knives and parers for quick, neat work
- Fruit or vegetable press or food mill
- Household scales to check weights of food to be canned, sugar, and salt
- Measuring devices: 1-cup, 1-quart, and 4-quart measures, measuring spoons
- Jar filler and funnel for large hot foods and for juices
- Ladles and large stirring spoons: wood and metal, long and short handles
- Strawberry huller
- Spatula for removing air bubbles
- Large kettles with covers
- Wire basket or cheesecloth
- Vegetable brushes
- Jar tongs, a must if Boiling Water Bath Canner does not have a lifting rack
- Scissors
- Shallow pans or trays for sorting, transporting
- Potholders

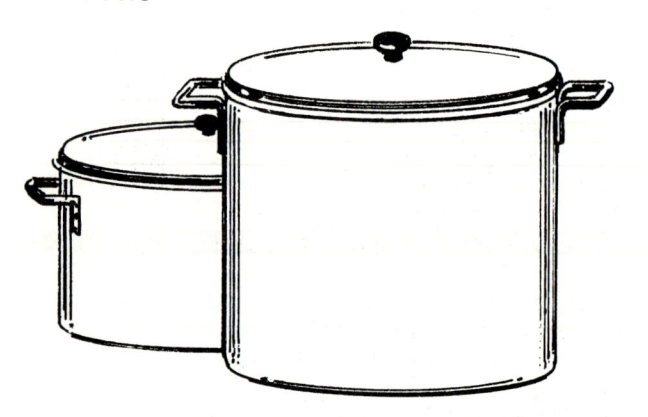

GENERAL CANNING DIRECTIONS

Foods

Fruits and Vegetables—Use only firm, fresh, unbruised and fully ripe fruits and vegetables. They must be mature enough to be fully flavored, yet firm enough to hold their shape during processing. Sort according to size for even cooking. Scrub and wash fruits and vegetables thoroughly, in small quantities at one time, under running water or in several changes of water. Don't let them soak or they will lose their flavor and some of their nutritive value.

Meat—Beef, veal, lamb, pork, and rabbit may be successfully canned at home. So can various kinds of poultry, chicken, duck, goose, guinea hen, squab, turkey. Meat of large game animals like deer and small game animals and birds may be canned. Wash poultry and game, but do not wash meats. Wipe them clean with a damp cloth.

Preparation—Get out all your equipment before starting to can. Make sure it is absolutely clean and in perfect working order. Read instructions carefully for use of equipment and canning. Make sure that your jars, lids, canner, and rack are absolutely clean.

Sterilization—In canning, the heat treatment used must be sufficient to destroy all enzymes and microorganisms present in the food. When the directions for method, heat, and time of processing are followed, the foods will be sterile and will remain so in their sealed containers until container is opened.

Consequently, the question often asked is, "Must jars and lids be sterilized before canning?" The answer, nowadays, is "no" if they are processed at least 15 minutes along with the food. Jars should be scrupulously clean and, to prevent breakage, they should be kept in hot water until filled.

Salt, Sugar, and Other Ingredients

Foods are often canned using salt and water, or sugar and water, or an acid such as lemon or vinegar. Foods may be canned safely without these if necessary for some diets or preference. Overripe tomatoes may be low acid, so add 1 tablespoon vinegar or lemon juice to each pint to prevent growth of the botulism organism after processing.

Salt—Any regular table salt may be used for canning and it is also used for flavor.

Sugar—To help canned fruits hold shape, color, and flavor, sugar is used.

For very juicy fruit, packed hot, sugar may be added without liquid. Add about ½ cup sugar to each quart of raw, prepared fruit. Heat to simmering (185°F. to 210°F.) in a kettle on top of the stove over low heat. Pack the fruit in the juice that cooks out.

Light corn syrup or mild-flavored honey may replace as much as half the sugar called for in canning fruit. Do not use brown sugar, or molasses, sorghum or other strong-flavored syrups; their flavors overpower the fruit flavor and they may darken the fruit.

CANNING

Sugar Syrup—Most directions call for canning most fruit with a sweetening in the form of a sugar syrup. To make sugar syrup: Mix sugar with water or with juice extracted from some of the fruit. Use thin, medium or heavy syrup to suit the sweetness of the fruit and your taste. The proportions are:

	SUGAR	WATER OR JUICE	YIELD
Thin	2 cups	4 cups	5 cups
Medium	3 cups	4 cups	5½ cups
Heavy	4¾ cups	4 cups	6½ cups

Boil sugar and water or fruit juice together for 5 minutes. Skim if necessary.

Three quarters to one cup sugar syrup is needed for each quart of fruit.

Canning Fruit Without Sugar—Fruit may be canned without sweetening, in its own juice, in extracted juice, or in water. Sugar is not needed to prevent spoilage and the processing is the same for unsweetened fruit as for sweetened.

Certain noncaloric sweeteners may be used by people requiring special diets. Consult package for amount to use in place of sugar.

Salt-Vinegar Solution—To prevent darkening of some fruits, like apples, drop pieces of peeled fruit into a salt-vinegar water solution (2 tablespoons salt and 2 tablespoons vinegar added to 1 gallon cold water). Drain before heating or packing raw.

Ascorbic Acid—This is used to keep fruits from darkening in the jars. To every quart of fruit add ¼ teaspoon ascorbic acid when syrup is added. An ascorbic-acid mixture may be used following the instructions on the package. Pure ascorbic acid (vitamin C) may be bought in drugstores. Ascorbic-acid compounds for home canning (and freezing) are available in grocery stores.

Canning Method

The two most common methods used in home canning are the *cold* or *raw pack,* and the *hot pack*. The word "pack" refers to the way in which food is put into containers.

Cold or Raw Pack—The food is placed raw or blanched into the jar without heating or cooking. When this method is used, the food is packed tightly into the containers because it will shrink during processing. Fruits are prepared and cut into desired sizes, packed in tightly, and covered with boiling hot syrup, juice, or water. Tomatoes, however, are pressed down in the containers so they form, and are covered by, their own juice; no other liquid is added. Vegetables are packed tightly and covered with boiling water. Do not add liquid to raw pack meals. This avoids overflow of grease from jars during processing.

Hot Pack—The food is cooked and packed hot into jars. Hot food should be packed fairly loosely, and it should be at or near boiling temperature when packed. Fruits are heated in syrup, water steam, or in extracted juice before packing. Some juicy fruits and tomatoes may be preheated without adding liquid and packed in the juice that cooks out. Vegetables are heated in water or steam, then packed hot into containers, and the boiling

CANNING

liquid or boiling water poured over them. The cooking liquid is recommended for flavor and because it may contain the minerals and vitamins dissolved out of the food. However, plain boiling water should be used when the cooking liquid is dark, gritty, or strong-flavored, or when there isn't enough.

Many fruits and vegetables should be packed to within ½ inch of the top. Sugar syrup should be filled to within ½ inch of the top.

Pack meats only to within 1½ inches of the top with 3 or 4 tablespoons of liquid added to each quart jar.

Starchy vegetables like Lima beans, peas, and corn, should be packed to within 1 inch of the top and filled with boiling water to within 1 inch of the top.

Release all air bubbles trapped in the food by running a long thin knife down the side of the jar and moving contents to release air.

Boiling Water Bath—This is the name of the procedure used in canning acid foods. Foods are packed, by the cold or hot pack method, in containers of glass, sealed partially or completely, then heated in a hot water bath for a given period of time until the contents reach a temperature of at least 170°F. To can by this method, see Step-by-Step Canning Directions for Tomatoes and Pickled Vegetables.

Steam-Pressure Canning—This is the name of the procedure recommended for the canning of low- or nonacid foods. These include most vegetables and all meat, poultry, and fish. Food is packed by cold or hot pack, in glass jars, and put in canner with 2 to 3 inches of boiling water. Canner is covered and locked. Over full heat and with the vent open, the steam is allowed to escape for 10 minutes. Then the vent is closed, the heat adjusted to hold even temperature, and the food processed according to the Step-by-Step Canning Directions for Vegetables, Meats, Poultry, and Game.

Open Kettle and Oven Canning—These two methods, once popular, are no longer recommended because the temperatures achieved are not high enough to guarantee the destruction of all spoilage organisms and because spoilage bacteria may also be introduced when the food is transferred from kettle to jar.

Labels—After glass jars are wiped clean and before storing, it is advisable to label with the date and, if more than one lot was canned the same day, the lot number.

Storing Home-Canned Foods—They keep a long time but not indefinitely. Once the jars have been tested to make sure that they are properly sealed, they should be stored in a cool, dry place at a temperature below 70°F., but well above freezing.

If the sterilization was not quite complete, warmer temperatures will encourage the growth of bacteria and possible spoilage. Warmth and light also may change the color and flavor of the food. Dampness may cause the jar closings to deteriorate.

Check stored jars and cans at regular intervals for spoilage. We cannot stress proper canning methods and storage strongly enough. If they are not followed, botulism, a serious and often deadly food poisoning, may result.

Warning—Do not use any jars or cans that leak or bulge at the top or bottom. After opening, check for off-odors, spurting liquid or gas bubbles, and pronounced or off color or texture changes.

It is possible for canned vegetables to contain the poison which causes botulism without showing signs of spoilage. There is no danger of botulism if a pressure canner was used where recommended and if the canner was in perfect order and if every canning step was done correctly. To be absolutely sure, boil home meats and canned vegetables before tasting. To do this: Bring food to a rolling boil, then cover and boil for at least 10 to 15 minutes. Boil spinach and corn 20 minutes. If the food looks spoiled, foams, or has an off-odor during heating, destroy it.

Spoilage—Spoilage in foods can be caused by enzymes and microorganisms. Enzymes are substances which are produced in the living tissues of plants and their activities often continue after harvesting. Unless controlled they can be responsible for chemical changes affecting the flavor and color of food, and are especially noticeable in the cut surfaces of some fruits. The enzymes can be destroyed by boiling water or steam (the processing of canned foods) or controlled by the addition of a citric acid (such as vinegar or lemon juice) or ascorbic acid.

The second group of spoilage agents are microorganisms and these include the bacteria, molds, and yeasts. They are, as the name indicates, tiny in size. Canning methods destroy these completely.

Bacteria are always present in the air, water, and soil. In order to avoid food spoilage caused by bacterial fermentation and putrefaction, keep the food and canning equipment scrupulously clean. Since many bacteria will survive in spite of this, they must be destroyed by heat in the processing of canned foods. The organism which causes botulism is one of these bacteria.

CANNING

Molds are microorganisms which reproduce by spores that are widely distributed in the air. When they lodge on food, spoilage soon occurs. They can be destroyed by heating the food to 150°F. to 180°F. In canned foods molds are easily detected for they can be seen. Dispose of all food with mold.

Yeasts are most troublesome and cause spoilage in sweet foods, sweetened canned fruits, jellies, and jams. They literally live on sugar and are tolerant to acids, hence must be destroyed by heat when canning or preserving. They multiply by budding, but perpetuate through spores with thick walls. Thus they can remain dormant without food or correct temperatures until these are supplied them, and then they will multiply rapidly.

Recanning—Many times people wish to know whether canned or frozen fruits purchased in large containers may be canned in smaller ones. It is possible in terms of safety, so long as the original directions for canning the fresh food are followed. However, it will be of much lower quality than if canned fresh.

Altitude—Processing times recommended and given in the charts which follow are only for foods prepared and packed at altitudes of 1,000 feet above sea level or less. So, those living and working at higher altitudes must increase the cooking (processing) time. (Recall the law of physics that water boils at 212°F. at sea level. At an altitude of 2,000 feet this goes down to 208°F. and at 5,000 feet water boils at only 203°F.)

Thus at altitudes of 1,000 feet or more, food must be processed in a Boiling Water Bath for a longer time. If your altitude is over 1,000 feet, increase processing time given in charts according to table below:

Altitude	If Time Given Is 20 Minutes or Less, INCREASE	If Time Given Is More Than 20 Minutes, INCREASE
1,000 ft.	1 min.	2 mins.
2,000 ft.	2 mins.	4 mins.
3,000 ft.	3 mins.	6 mins.
4,000 ft.	4 mins.	8 mins.
5,000 ft.	5 mins.	10 mins.
6,000 ft.	6 mins.	12 mins.
7,000 ft.	7 mins.	14 mins.
8,000 ft.	8 mins.	16 mins.
9,000 ft.	9 mins.	18 mins.
10,000 ft.	10 mins.	20 mins.

STEP-BY-STEP CANNING DIRECTIONS

Acid foods include tomatoes, pickled vegetables and fruits, and these are processed by the Boiling Water Bath method. Nonacid foods include all vegetables (except tomatoes), meats, poultry, and game, and these must be processed by the Steam Pressure method.

Process food according to directions and charts which follow. After processing, open the canner, turning the lid away from the face to prevent steam burns.

To remove the hot jars use the rack, if it has handles. If it does not, use tongs or a jar lifter. Place the hot jars on several thicknesses of towel or on a rack to prevent sudden cooling. Close lids by screwing cap tight or pushing the wire seal down. Leave it alone if the jar is a self-sealing type. Above all, do not open the jar after processing as this will contaminate the food.

After jars are cooled, but within 24 hours after processing, test the seal.

Label and store properly in cool dry place and check occasionally for signs of spoilage.

TOMATOES AND PICKLED VEGETABLES: COLD OR RAW PACK GLASS JARS
[Boiling Water Bath (212°F.) Method]

Select firm, ripe tomatoes. Examine for spots and cracks; use only the best. Wash just enough for one canner load if you are working alone. (Same general directions apply to fruits.)

Put tomatoes in a wire basket or large clean cloth; lower into a kettle of rapidly boiling water. Cover kettle. After about ½ minute, remove and dip into cold water about 1 minute. Drain. (Test ease of removing skins and adjust time in boiling water.)

Cut out stem ends of tomatoes and slip off skins.

Work rapidly at this point. Cut tomatoes in halves or quarters or leave whole. Put hot jar on heatproof surface or in a shallow pan filled with hot water. Pack tomatoes into hot jars, pressing down gently until all spaces fill to ½ inch from top.

Add ½ teaspoon salt to each pint, 1 teaspoon salt to each quart. Run a knife or rubber bottle scraper down inside between tomatoes and jar to release air bubbles. Wipe jar rim with clean, damp cloth. Put lids with sealing compound on jar, or put on washed rubber rings. Screw on bands or tops, or put glass top in place.

Place filled sealed jars on rack in boiling water. Make sure jars are spaced out and do not touch. Pour in boiling water if needed, enough to cover tops of jars by 1 to 2 inches. Do not pour water directly on jars.

At sea level, process pint jars of tomatoes 35 minutes, quart jars 45 minutes. Keep heat regulated so water boils gently but steadily.

When time is up, remove jars from hot water immediately. Complete seal on those which require it; do not adjust jars with metal lids with sealing compound. To cool, place jars on a wooden surface or on towels or newspapers, spaced out and away from drafts. Do not cover.

CANNING

FRUITS: HOT PACK GLASS JARS
[Boiling Water Bath (212°F.) Method]

Follow first 5 steps given for Tomatoes, Cold Pack.

Prepare syrup. See Sugar Syrup. Heat to boiling. Drain fruit which may have been put in a solution to prevent darkening. Put fruit into syrup, heat through, but do not cook until soft.

Pack fruit loosely in hot jars. Peaches, pears, and other fruits with pits removed should be packed in overlapping layers, cavity side down. Leave ½ inch of space at top of jar. (Put on rubber ring if this type of jar is used.)

Cover fruit with boiling syrup, leaving the required amount of headspace at top of jar. It will take about ¾ to 1 cup syrup for each quart.

Run bottle scraper or similar nonmetal utensil between fruit and jar to release air bubbles. Add more syrup if needed. Wipe top and threads of jar, adjust lids and tops. Seal as required.

VEGETABLES, MEATS, POULTRY, AND GAME: COLD OR RAW PACK OR HOT PACK
[Steam-Pressure Canner (240°F.) Method]

Read manufacturer's directions for use of the canner and follow *specific* directions given there. The following are *general* directions for the steam-pressure canner.

Get the canner ready; check the gauge, petcock, and other points needed. Have all canning containers ready. Prepare vegetables according to directions given on chart.

For *cold* or *raw pack* have boiling water ready. Pack prepared vegetables in hot jars, add salt, and fill jars as directed with boiling water. For *hot pack* prepare and precook according to chart given by manufacturer. Pack in jars, add salt, and fill jars, as directed, with boiling liquid or water. Seal or otherwise prepare for processing.

Have 2 or 3 inches of water boiling in the bottom of canner (more may be required if the weight-type gauge is used). The total amount of water required will depend on size and shape of canner.

Put rack in bottom of canner, arrange filled glass jars on it so they will not touch each other or the sides, and thus allow steam to flow around and between them. If a second layer is to be put in, put rack in place and stagger the jars.

Put on cover and fasten securely so no steam can escape except through vent (petcock or weighted gauge opening).

Put on heat and watch until steam pours steadily from vent. Let it escape for 10 minutes to force the air out of cooker and allow gauge to register correctly. Then close petcock or put on weighted gauge. Let pressure rise to 10 pounds: the temperature will then be 240°F. at sea level. Immediately start counting processing time. Watch heat and regulate to keep pressure constant; do not lower pressure by opening petcock. Keep drafts from blowing on canner. Pressure cookers that maintain 15-pounds pressure can be used for a few jars. Follow manufacturer's directions.

For additional information, on home canning of foods, write manufacturers of canning equipment or consult special canning books, or contact the extension services of the Agriculture Department of your state and of your state university, or contact your county agent. "Home Canning of Fruit and Vegetables" and "Home Canning of Meats" are two worthwhile publications. To learn how to obtain them, write to Consumer Product Information, Public Documents Distribution Center, Pueblo, Col. 81009.

CANTALOUPE—This is a variety of the muskmelon, with a sweet and fragrant taste. The cantaloupe was named for a castle in Italy. Like all melons, it originated in Asia, and was well known to the ancient Romans and other Mediterranean peoples.

Availability—May to December, peak crop in the late summer. Crop comes from Arizona, California, Texas, and Mexico.

Frozen cantaloupe is available as melon balls, mixed with honeydew. Serve these partially thawed. If allowed to thaw completely, they become mushy.

Purchasing Guide—According to variety, the flesh of a cantaloupe may be salmon, pink, or green-colored. The salmon-colored are the most prevalent.

Sweetness, fine texture, and pungent aroma are the characteristics of a good cantaloupe, and are found only in the well-matured melons. It is difficult to distinguish a ripe melon; however, there are two clues worth observing. The outside or netting should be well raised, coarse, and grayish. The stem-end scar, where the melon was attached to vine, should be slightly sunken, smooth, and well-calloused. When only half the scar is slightly sunken and the other half is rough, the melon was picked at "half slip," or before it matured on the vine. The melon should have a fruity fragrance, with no soft spots in the skin.

CANTALOUPE

Storage—If melon is ripe, keep in refrigerator. Other melons should be kept at room temperature until ripening is completed.
Refrigerator shelf: 4 to 8 days
Refrigerator frozen-food compartment, prepared for freezing: 1 month
Freezer, prepared for freezing: 9 months

Nutritive Food Values—Cantaloupe is an excellent source of vitamin A and vitamin C.
½ melon, 5 inches in diameter = 60 calories

Basic Preparation—Cut into halves or wedges, remove seeds, and serve with slices of lime or lemon. Serve halves filled with other fruits or ice cream. Cut crosswise into 1-inch slices, remove rind, place on plates, and fill centers as above. Cut into wedges or chunks and combine with other fruits, fruit cups, or salads. The flesh may be pickled or made into preserves.
To Freeze—Use ripe firm melon. Cut into halves. Scoop out seeds. Peel. Cut into cubes or balls and pack in sugar syrup (2 cups sugar to 1 quart water). Use syrup to cover melon, allowing 1-inch headspace.

FRESH CANTALOUPE AND PINEAPPLE COMPOTE

Combine ¼ cup sugar, ½ cup water, and ¼ cup fresh lemon juice. Bring to boiling point. Remove from heat and cool for 15 minutes. Add ¼ cup fresh orange juice, 2 cups diced fresh cantaloupe, and 1 cup fresh pineapple wedges. Chill. Serve in sherbet glasses garnished with a sprig of fresh mint. Makes 6 servings.

MELON DELIGHT

- 1 medium cantaloupe
- 2 ripe peaches
- ⅓ cup sugar
- 2 tablespoons fresh lemon juice
- ½ teaspoon salt
- 2 tablespoons rosewater
- Crushed ice

Cut melon into halves. With a melon-ball cutter, scoop out melon. Place balls in a bowl. Add melon juice which collects while melon is being scooped. Peel peaches, pit, and slice thinly. Add to melon balls. Add sugar, lemon juice, and salt. Place in refrigerator and let chill for several hours. One half hour before serving, add rosewater and replace in refrigerator. When ready to serve, place mixture in sherbet glasses and top with very finely crushed ice. Makes 4 to 6 servings.

FRESH CANTALOUPE AND PROSCIUTTO APPETIZERS

Wrap bite-size wedges of fresh cantaloupe in thin slices of prosciutto. Serve on toothpicks as an appetizer.

Cantaloupe, Pineapples and Orange Slices

CAPER

FRESH CANTALOUPE AND GRAPE CUP

Combine 1½ cups diced fresh cantaloupe, 1½ cups green seedless grapes, 3 tablespoons fresh lemon juice, and 2 tablespoons sugar in a mixing bowl. Toss lightly and chill. Serve as a dessert, garnished with fresh mint and cantaloupe balls. Makes 5 or 6 servings.

FRESH CANTALOUPE AND SHRIMP LUNCHEON SALAD

Cut 3 cantaloupes into halves. Remove seeds. Fill with a mixture of 2 cups cold cooked deveined shrimps, 1 cup chopped celery, 1 tablespoon fresh lemon juice, ½ teaspoon salt, ⅛ teaspoon pepper, and ¼ cup mayonnaise. Toss lightly. Serve as a main-dish supper or luncheon salad. Makes 6 servings.

MELON ICE-CREAM SAUCE

Cut ripe cantaloupe into halves. Scoop out seeds. Peel. Sieve cantaloupe or whirl pieces of cantaloupe in a blender. When puréed, add fresh lemon or lime juice and sugar to taste. Chill, and serve over vanilla ice cream.

CAPERS
They are the unopened flowers of the caper bush, a shrub native to the Mediterranean but grown now in the southern part of the United States and cultivated in greenhouses in the North. During the flowering season, the buds are picked before the petals can expand and preserved in vinegar and salt. Those labeled "nonpareil" are the most expensive because they are the smallest, tenderest buds. Capers add liveliness to white and other sauces, to salads and creamed dishes, and, as condiments, to appetizers, meats, and seafood.

Availability—Bottled; may be in vinegar and salt solution or in salt only.

Storage—Keep covered in cool, dry place or in refrigerator.

Basic Preparation—Drain capers. Leave whole or chop finely.

EGG AND CAPER SAUCE

- ¼ cup butter or margarine
- 3 tablespoons all-purpose flour
- ½ teaspoon Worcestershire
- 1 teaspoon prepared mustard
- 1½ cups milk
- 3 hard-cooked eggs, diced
- 1 tablespoon capers

Melt butter in a saucepan. Blend in flour and seasonings. Add milk and cook until thickened, stirring constantly. Add eggs and capers. Especially good on hot cooked vegetables, poached, fried or baked fish. Makes about 2 cups.

TUNA IN CAPER SAUCE

- 1 cup diced celery
- 2 tablespoons butter
- 2 tablespoons all-purpose flour
- ¾ teaspoon salt
- ⅛ teaspoon pepper
- 1½ cups milk
- 1 can (about 7 ounces) tuna, drained and flaked
- 2 tablespoons capers
- Chopped parsley
- Hot cooked rice or noodles

Cook celery in small amount of boiling salted water for 5 minutes; drain. Melt butter; blend in flour, salt, and pepper. Gradually add milk, stirring constantly; cook until thickened. Add tuna, celery, and capers; heat thoroughly. Put in serving dish and sprinkle with parsley. Serve on rice. Makes 4 servings.

CAPON
Capons are male chickens which have been castrated at six to eight weeks of age to produce birds with more tender flesh and a generous fat covering. They are sold at seven to ten months of age. Even though more expensive than roasting chicken, capons are a good buy for a large group of people. Capons can be roasted or braised. Roast capons for twenty-two to thirty minutes per pound.

MIDDLE-EAST ROAST STUFFED CAPON

- 1 capon (about 6 to 7 pounds)
- Salt and pepper
- ⅓ cup melted butter or margarine
- 1 large onion, chopped
- 1½ cups cooked white or brown rice
- ½ cup chopped blanched almonds
- ½ cup golden raisins
- ⅓ cup chopped dried apricots
- 1 small sweet apple, cored and diced
- 1 teaspoon salt
- ½ teaspoon dried thyme
- ¼ teaspoon white pepper
- Spice Mixture

Wash capon and pat dry. Sprinkle inside and out with salt and pepper. Melt butter. Sauté onion in butter until golden brown. Combine sautéed onions and butter with remaining ingredients except spice mixture. Stuff body and neck cavities of capon, sew openings. Place capon on a rack in a shallow roasting pan. Roast in preheated moderate oven (325°F.) for 1½ hours. Sprinkle capon with Spice Mixture and roast for 1½ hours longer, basting capon with pan drippings. Makes 6 servings.

Spice Mixture

Combine ¼ teaspoon each of ground cinnamon, nutmeg, allspice, salt, and white pepper. Blend well; sprinkle on capon.

CAPSICUM

—Red pepper is another name for this pod-bearing plant which is native to tropical America and one of the most important spices.

The capsicum family is a very large one, and its fruits vary in size, shape, color, and pungency. The family includes such varieties as sweet or bell peppers, chilies, paprika, and pimientos.

Capsicum is not related to black or white pepper, which is a berry that grows on a tropical vine.

Capsicum peppers have been used in the New World since pre-Inca days: green, ripe, or dried, whole or ground. The Spaniards brought the seeds of the capsicum pod back to Europe, and by 1600 it had reached the eastern tropics.

To this day red pepper is widely used, either crushed or ground, to give zest to foods that are often heavy and starchy. The pods are available whole (to be crushed and seeded before using) or commercially packed in crushed or ground form. The spice may be labeled *"pepperoni rosso,"* "pizza pepper" or "cayenne red pepper."

Used with discretion, capsicum adds a great deal of zest to sauces, egg and cheese dishes, vegetables, and all foods that are bland, as well as to Italian and Mexican dishes.

PEPPY PORK SAUSAGE

- 1 pound ground lean pork
- 1 pound ground pork fat
- 2 tablespoons water
- 2 teaspoons salt
- 1 tablespoon dried sage
- ½ teaspoon dried thyme
- ½ teaspoon crushed red pepper
- ¼ teaspoon black pepper
- Dash of garlic powder

Mix lean pork and pork fat. Add water and seasonings. Mix; put through a meat grinder or food chopper, using the fine blade. Let stand in refrigerator overnight for flavors to blend. Shape into patties. Brown on both sides in a hot skillet. Makes 6 servings.

CARAMEL, CARAMELIZE

—The word "caramel" has two meanings. It describes a candy with a chewy consistency and it is also a culinary term that refers to burnt sugar by itself or thinned with water. In the latter sense it is used by cooks to add color, flavor, and style to various foods, from stews and gravies to desserts. To caramelize a mold is to coat it with sugar in the caramel stage.

The more sugar is caramelized, the less its sweetening power. To caramelize sugar, melt 1 cup granulated sugar in a mold or heavy skillet and cook over medium heat to 338°F. Use a candy thermometer to check heat. Cook, stirring constantly, until sugar forms a golden-brown syrup. Remove from heat immediately. Use this type of syrup to coat molds for custards and ice cream and as a glaze over caramelized custards and small cream puffs. When caramelizing a mold, rotate the sugar in it in all directions to coat the inside of the mold evenly.

To make a thick syrup, add ¼ cup very hot water slowly to hot sugar syrup. Stir constantly and heat for another 8 to 10 minutes over very low heat. Store in container for later use. If the syrup hardens in the container, place the container in hot water until the syrup melts. If a thinner syrup is desired, add more water.

To obtain a *croquant,* or "brown nougat," add 1 tablespoon water to the sugar when it is straw-colored. Cook, stirring, for 8 to 10 minutes. Cool; when hardened, crack, then roll into small pieces. Use for sprinkling over cakes, into puddings, and as flavorings in many other desserts to add a stylish touch.

To burn sugar for coloring: heat 1 cup granulated sugar over low heat until black and smoky. Add, drop by drop, 1 cup boiling water. Stir over low heat until completely dissolved. Use for coloring gravies. Can be stored indefinitely.

CARAMEL SYRUP

Put 1 cup sugar in a heavy skillet over low heat; stir constantly until it has melted to a brown liquid. When it bubbles over the entire surface, remove from heat; very slowly add 1 cup boiling water, stirring constantly. Pour into containers, and cool. Cover and store at room temperature. The syrup is now ready for use in the following recipes. Makes 1½ cups.

CARAWAY

CARAMEL CAKE

½ cup shortening
1¼ cups sugar
¼ cup Caramel Syrup
2 cups sifted all-purpose flour
2 teaspoons baking powder
½ teaspoon salt
⅔ cup milk
2 eggs

Cream shortening; add 1 cup sugar gradually, beating until light and fluffy. Beat in syrup. Sift flour, baking powder, and salt, and add to creamed mixture alternately with milk. Beat for 3 minutes. Beat eggs until foamy; add remaining ¼ cup sugar and beat until there is a fine spongy foam. Stir into cake batter until blended. Bake in 2 greased and wax-paper-lined 8-inch layer-cake pans in preheated moderate oven (375°F.) for about 20 minutes.

CARAMEL SQUARES

¼ cup butter or margarine
1 cup sugar
2 eggs
1 cup sifted all-purpose flour
¼ teaspoon salt
1 teaspoon baking powder
¼ cup Caramel Syrup
¼ cup chopped nuts

Cream butter and sugar until light and fluffy. Add eggs and beat well. Sift together dry ingredients and add to creamed mixture alternately with syrup, beginning and ending with dry ingredients. Add nuts. Pour into greased and floured pan, 9 x 9 x 2 inches, and bake in preheated hot oven (400°F.) for about 20 minutes. Cut into squares and let cool in pan.

CARAMEL FROSTING

⅓ cup Caramel Syrup
3 cups sugar
⅛ teaspoon salt
½ cup light or dark corn syrup
1 cup heavy cream or undiluted evaporated milk
2 tablespoons butter or margarine

Put caramel syrup, sugar, salt, corn syrup, and cream in saucepan. Bring to a boil and cook, stirring, until a small amount of syrup dropped into very cold water forms a soft ball (235°F. on a candy thermometer). Let cool to lukewarm (110°F.). Add butter. Beat at low speed with an electric mixer, or by hand, until slightly creamy. At this stage, the frosting has not completely crystallized and has the consistency of thick syrup. *Refrigerate for 6 to 8 hours before using.* Makes about 3 cups. **To use**—Put frosting needed in top part of double boiler over boiling water to soften. Stir constantly and remove as soon as it reaches spreading consistency (should not take more than 2 minutes). **Note:** This frosting may curdle, especially if made with evaporated milk, but it blends together when beaten. Frosting can be stored in a covered container in refrigerator for several weeks.

CARAWAY [*Carum carvi*] — This oval-shape brown seed was named after the ancient district of Caria in Asia Minor, demonstrating once more the antiquity of food seasonings. The caraway plant grows to a height of about two feet, with lovely feathery green leaves and yellow-white flowers that resemble Queen Anne's Lace. It is widely cultivated and grows well from Bulgaria to Morocco, Russia to Japan, and in various parts of the United States. Caraway has become one of the commonest field herbs in Maine, brought there by German settlers in the 18th century.

A most ancient herb, caraway was known to the Neolithic Swiss Lake Dwellers. Its medicinal properties were mentioned in the Medical Papyrus of Thebes, dating from 1552 B.C. Greeks and Romans appreciated its culinary values as well. Caraway was cultivated in the 8th century gardens of Charlemagne. This aromatic herb seems never to have lost favor. Cooks of the Middle Ages used the feathery leaves in soups and salads and the seeds in breads and sweetmeats. Tasty, good for the stomach, it also "restoreth hair where it has fallen away." Shakespeare, in the second part of Henry IV, speaks about "a dish of caraways." The Germanic and Slavic peoples, in particular, have always greatly favored the seed.

The uses of caraway are as varied today as they were hundreds of years ago. Fresh young leaves add a delicious flavor to soups, salads, cheeses, vegetables, and meat, especially pork. The roots may be steamed and eaten as a vegetable. Caraway seeds are used to season soups, meats, vegetables, breads such as rye, cakes, and pastries. Oil extracted from the seed provides the distinctive flavor of the liqueur kümmel.

CARAWAY PORK CHOPS

- 2 teaspoons crushed caraway seeds
- 1 teaspoon ground sage
- ½ teaspoon garlic salt
- ⅛ teaspoon salt
- ¼ teaspoon pepper
- 4 large pork chops
  Water
- ½ cup dry white wine

Combine herbs and seasonings. Rub mixture on both sides of chops and put chops in skillet. Pour water over chops to cover. Cook, covered, over low heat for about 1 hour. When the water has evaporated, chops will begin to brown. Turn several times until browned on all sides. When chops are browned, add wine. Bring to boil and remove from heat. Put chops in heated serving dish; pour sauce over top. Makes 4 servings.

CARAWAY COTTAGE OR CREAM CHEESE

- 1 cup cottage or cream cheese
- 2 tablespoons light or heavy cream
- ½ teaspoon salt
- 1½ teaspoons caraway seeds
- ⅛ teaspoon instant minced onion or onion salt
- ⅛ teaspoon cayenne

Blend cheese with cream until smooth. Add other ingredients and mix thoroughly. Serve as a salad or spread on dark bread. Makes about 1 cup.

CARBONATED—The term is applied to beverages made sparkling, bubbling, or fizzing by charging them under pressure with a gas called carbon dioxide. Soda water is the best known carbonated beverage. The term does not apply when the gas is produced within the beverage itself by the natural process of fermentation.

Carbonated beverages are flavored by syrups, cola, spices, and aromatic roots. Some are heavily sugared, others are made with low-calorie sugar substitutes. All carbonated beverages enjoy enormous popularity with old and young. Flavorful carbonated beverages can be served with ice cream as sodas, with fruit juices in punches, with fruit garnishes, with sherbet, with flavored syrups, or as a mixer for alcoholic beverages.

CARDAMOM [*Elettaria cardamomum*] — The plant grows to a height of eight to twelve feet, and the seeds which we use as a flavoring grow in groups within a pod that resembles a capsule. The capsules are sun-dried and marketed whole. The cardamom is a native of India and is used as a seasoning, but the name is also given to the seeds of other species that grow in Asia, Africa, and the Pacific Islands. These are more bitter in taste and serve as a substitute for pepper.

CARDAMOM

Cardamom is said to be the world's second most precious spice, the costliest one being saffron. An acre of land will yield only about 250 pounds of cardamoms, and their harvesting requires a good deal of hand labor.

Cardamom seeds are brown, and they have an aromatic odor and a warm, spicy taste. They turn up in curries and in such meats as frankfurters and sausages, in pickling-spice blends, and in baked foods. The spice is sold either whole in the form of bleached white pods, or ground.

Cardamoms have been used in the western world for at least 2,000 years. The word is Greek, and Dioscorides, the Greek authority on medicinal herbs (41-68 A.D.), mentions them as the best of a group of aromata.

Cardamom is the spice preferred in Scandinavia where it is used in a most imaginative manner, especially at Christmas time, in spiced cakes, sweet pastries, and cookies as well as in ground meat dishes. In India, it is an age-old practice to chew cardamom seeds like candy. In drug preparations the pleasant flavor of the seed is used to cover up the taste of certain medicines.

Whole cardamom pods must be crushed before using. When they are to be added to such dishes as soups, curries, or stews, the crushed outer shell pieces of the pod need not be removed. They will disintegrate and disappear during the cooking.

When whole cardamom is to be used in baking, it is advisable to pick out the little black seeds from the crushed outer shell and crush these seeds as well. All the crushing can be done either in a mortar and pestle, or by placing either pods or seeds in a paper bag or between two sheets of wax paper and pounding them with the back of a plate, a rolling pin, or a mallet or hammer.

One word of caution: use cardamom with a light hand since a little goes a long way. Also, it should not be stored for too long since it rapidly loses its flavor.

CARDAMOM SUGAR

It is delicious sprinkled over baked apples and cooked fruit, or fresh-fruit compotes. Combine ⅛ to ¼ teaspoon ground cardamom with ½ cup sugar in jar and shake well to blend. Or whirl together in electric blender ¼ teaspoon ground cardamom and ½ cup sugar.

CARDOON

CURRIED LAMB, INDIAN STYLE

- 3 tablespoons instant minced onion
- Water
- 2 tablespoons shortening or salad oil
- 1 tablespoon ground coriander seed
- ¾ teaspoon ground cuminseed
- ½ teaspoon each of ground cardamom, turmeric, and ginger
- ¼ teaspoon instant garlic powder
- ⅛ teaspoon each of ground red and black pepper
- 1 cinnamon stick
- 1½ pounds boneless lean lamb stew meat
- ¾ teaspoon salt
- ¼ cup tomato purée
- 2 tablespoons plain yogurt or dairy sour cream

Soak onion in 3 tablespoons water for 5 minutes. Heat shortening in a skillet. Add onions and spices and sauté for 5 minutes, or until onions are limp and transparent. Trim excess fat from the lamb, cut into 1-inch cubes, and add. Cook lamb until lightly browned, about 10 to 15 minutes, over moderate heat. Add 1¼ cups water, salt, and tomato purée and blend with mixture. Simmer for 30 to 40 minutes, or until sauce has thickened. Add yogurt just before removing from heat. Serve with hot cooked rice and chutney. Makes 4 servings.

CARDAMOM SOUR-CREAM WAFFLES

- 1 cup all-purpose flour
- ½ teaspoon salt
- 2 tablespoons granulated sugar
- 1 teaspoon crushed cardamom seed
- 2 eggs
- 2 cups dairy sour cream
- Confectioners' sugar, or whipped cream and canned whole-cranberry sauce

Combine first 4 ingredients in mixing bowl. Beat eggs and sour cream until blended. Add to dry ingredients and mix until blended. Spread one third (about 1 cup) batter at a time in hot waffle iron and bake until golden. Serve warm or cold, sprinkled with confectioners' sugar. Or serve with whipped cream flavored to taste with cranberry sauce. Makes three 9-inch waffles.

CARDOON—This thistlelike, silvery-green, prickly plant is closely related to the artichoke but it looks more like an outsize stalk of celery since its average length is four to five feet. Cardoons are grown for the leafy midribs of the plant, which are fleshy and tender. The flavor is delicate and resembles that of the artichoke and the oyster plant.

Cardoons are a favorite French and Italian winter vegetable. In America, they are grown in California, mostly for Italian markets. They are well worth eating and easy to prepare. However they are to be served, they must be boiled first.

Basic Preparation—Remove tough outer stalks and wilted stalks. Strip tender inner stalks free of leaves. Cut them into three-inch pieces. Drop at once into acidulated cold water (water with lemon juice or vinegar) to keep pieces from turning dark. Cook in boiling salted water over moderate heat until tender. Drain. Serve with melted butter and a little lemon juice or with a white sauce, a tomato sauce, or with hollandaise.

They can also be sautéed in olive oil, or dipped into egg yolk and bread crumbs and fried in deep fat.

CARIBBEAN STEWS
by SHIRLEY SARVIS

Concentrate on a Caribbean stew and you have the air of festivity innate in a foreign menu. You have the excitement of a new taste. You have the drama and color of tropical foods. You have almost the total menu in one dish.

Just a stew can stage all this because the stews of the Caribbean are exceptional and exotic. They are, for good reason. For the cuisine on each island is a culinary compilation of native dishes with the foods of whatever peoples crossed that island in the course of colonizing history: perhaps Dutch, Portuguese, British, French, Danish, Spanish, African, Indian, Chinese. The resulting stews are understandably unusual, combining strangely pleasing mixtures of fruits, meats, vegetables, and spices.

We have selected four such stews, each from a different Caribbean isle, as the focal point for a Caribbean Stew Party, a late supper, or informal dinner.

Choose any one for your party. Each is well suited to party giving, particularly when the hostess is the cook. Each stew is a hearty one-dish meal. You add only rice or bread, sometimes salad, to complete the major part of the meal. Dessert is concise and simple and served with dark-roast coffee, cream, and sugar. If you wish, serve rum cocktails before the meal and a favorite appropriate wine or beer with it; however, Caribbeans would most likely have only before-dinner rum cocktails and offer water with the meal.

Each stew can be prepared almost entirely ahead of time and is adaptable to large or small groups. You can multiply or divide the following recipes to suit your needs. Each recipe is authentic in origin, but available ingredients replace Caribbean specialties which are difficult to purchase in the United States.

You can easily set the scene and atmosphere for your Caribbean party with brightly colored table linens and table decorations of vivid flowers and tropical fruits; bananas, pineapples, papaya, oranges, limes, grapefruit, mangoes, coconuts. For background music, play recordings of steel bands or calypso or Latin meringues.

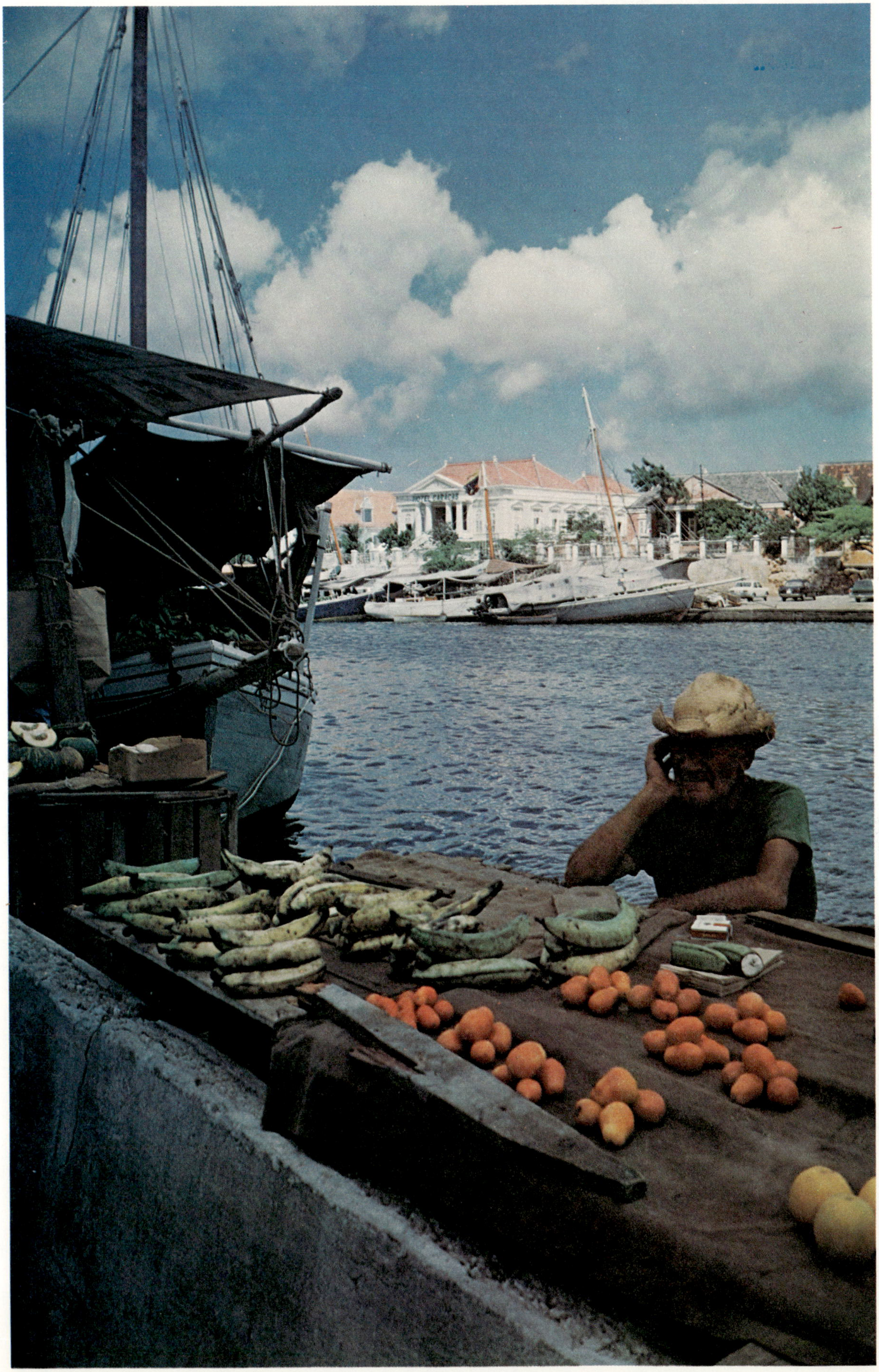

CARIBBEAN STEWS

CHICKEN SANCOCHO
[From the Dominican Republic]

Sancocho, often considered the national dish of the Dominican Republic, is presented in many forms. This Chicken *Sancocho* calls for chicken as the basic meat while other versions might use pork or beef. When served, each person has a wide soup-bowl serving, including a portion of chicken, ham, each vegetable, and plenty of broth, accompanied with an avocado and tomato salad on one side and an individual casserole of white rice on another. Part of the ritual of eating the stew is cutting the avocado into bites and dipping it into the stew broth.

Chicken Sancocho*
Steamed White Rice*
Guava Paste or Jam*
Cheese
Sesame-Topped Crackers

CHICKEN SANCOCHO

For simplest party preparation, we suggest that several hours before the party, you assemble the stew, cook it for the first 30 minutes, and prepare the vegetables. In time for serving, add vegetables and finish cooking.

- 1 large onion, finely chopped
- ¼ cup butter or margarine
- 1 large fresh tomato, peeled, seeded, and chopped
- 2 frying chickens (about 3 pounds each), cut into pieces
  Salt and pepper
- ½ pound lean boneless smoked ham, cut into ¾-inch cubes
- 2 cups water
- 2 garlic cloves, minced or mashed
- 1 bay leaf
- ¾ teaspoon dried oregano
- ½ teaspoon monosodium glutamate
- 2 medium-size white potatoes, peeled and cut into ½-inch crosswise slices
- ⅔ pound winter squash, peeled and cut into ¾-inch slices
- 3 medium-size carrots, peeled and cut into pieces about 4 inches long, ½ inch thick
- 3 tablespoons chopped fresh parsley

In a large kettle sauté onion in butter until limp. Add tomato. Sprinkle chicken pieces with salt and generously with pepper. Place in kettle. Add ham, water, garlic, bay leaf, oregano, and monosodium glutamate. Stir gently. Cover and simmer for 30 minutes. Add potatoes, squash, and carrots; cover and simmer for 30 minutes more, or until chicken and vegetables are tender. Taste broth and add salt and pepper to taste. Add parsley and simmer for 5 minutes more. Serve in heated wide soup bowls, arranging in each bowl a portion of chicken, ham, potato, squash, and carrot. Makes 6 servings.

STEAMED WHITE RICE

Steam raw long-grain white rice. Season with butter. Serve in individual heated casseroles or rice bowls. Garnish each with a strip of red pimiento.

GUAVA AND CHEESE DESSERT

Arrange on each dessert plate several sesame-topped crackers, a generous slice of guava paste (available in Puerto Rican, Spanish, and Mexican food stores and in some specialty food shops), and several slices of mellow natural light-colored cheese (California's Monterey Jack or Teleme are similar to the local cheese of the Dominican Republic, or use Muenster, Edam, or cream cheese). Serve with cheese or fruit knives. If guava paste is not available, you could assemble the cheese-and-crackers before serving, topping each cracker with a slice or spreading of cheese and a deep layer of chilled guava jelly.

STEW SHRIMP
[From Trinidad]

Out of perhaps the most cosmopolitan of all the cities of the Caribbean comes this fresh-tasting, delicate stew. Almost paradoxically, it is a simple dish, honoring the indigenous and utterly fresh foods of the island rather than any of the exotic foods from far-off parts of the world imported to the busy Port of Spain.

As the name indicates, the shrimps delicately "stew" with butter to a pungent juiciness. You serve them with brown rice cooked just-tender, so the grains are completely separate.

Stew Shrimp*
Ginger Brown Rice*
Watercress Salad Bowl*
French Bread and Butter
(Optional)
Brown-Sugared Roasted
Fresh Coconut Bites*

STEW SHRIMP

- 2 pounds large raw shrimps, shelled and deveined
- 3 tablespoons fresh lime juice
- 1 large sweet onion, very thinly sliced
- 2 medium-size tomatoes, peeled, seeded, and diced
- 1 large garlic clove, minced or mashed
- 1 tablespoon finely snipped chives
- ½ teaspoon each of salt and dried thyme
  Dried crushed red pepper to taste (begin with ¼ teaspoon)
- ⅛ teaspoon ground black pepper
- ¼ cup butter or salad oil
- ½ teaspoon each of monosodium glutamate and curry powder

CARIBBEAN STEWS

Sprinkle shrimps with lime juice and toss to mix. Add onion, tomatoes, garlic, chives, salt, thyme, red pepper, and black pepper. Toss gently to mix well. Allow to marinate for 30 minutes at room temperature, or for 1 to 3 hours covered and chilled. Just in time for serving, melt butter in a large frying pan. Stir in monosodium glutamate and curry. Add shrimps with marinating mixture. Cover and cook over medium heat just until shrimps turn pink and onion is slightly wilted, about 8 minutes; turn shrimps and stir gently once or twice. Serve immediately over Ginger Brown Rice. Makes 6 servings.

GINGER BROWN RICE

Cook raw brown rice just until tender, using chicken stock for the liquid, and seasoning with 1½ teaspoons grated fresh gingerroot or 1 teaspoon ground ginger and ¼ teaspoon pepper for each cup of uncooked rice.

WATERCRESS SALAD BOWL

Break tender crisp salad greens into salad bowl. Add a generous proportion of crisp sprigs of watercress and thin tomato wedges. Toss lightly with a mellow French dressing made simply of oil, vinegar, fresh lime juice, salt, pepper, dry mustard, and a pinch of sugar.

BROWN-SUGARED ROASTED FRESH COCONUT BITES

Cut the meat, with brown skin, from a fresh ripe coconut into bite-size triangles. Place, white side up, on baking sheet. Broil, about 3 inches from heat, just until edges turn light brown. Dot with butter. Sprinkle with raw sugar or brown sugar. Return to broiler just until butter and sugar melt. Arrange about 6 coconut triangles in a ring on each dessert plate. Eat with fingers.

CUCUMBER LAMB

[From Aruba]

This second island in the Antillean chain consistently offers *funchi* with its stew, too. But we find the character of cornmeal more appealing in toasted golden corn bread, served as toast points beneath the stew and as bread accompaniment.

This is a meaty stew; lamb cubes richly flavored in juices of sautéed onion, celery, garlic, and sweet and hot peppers. To "cool" the spicy hotness of the stew, you blend in shredded fresh cucumbers just before serving. Garnish the stew generously with overlapping paper-thin cucumber slices and a fat tomato wedge alongside so the garnish makes the salad. Serve guava jelly both as a stew condiment and a spread for toasted corn bread; its fruit sweetness also serves to counter the hotness of the stew.

Aruba Cucumber Lamb*
Cucumber Garnish
Tomato Wedges
Crisp Golden Corn Points*
Guava Jelly
Bananas in Rum Custard Sauce*
Lace Praline*

ARUBA CUCUMBER LAMB

You can make this stew as far ahead as the day before the party, if you wish, and reheat it in time to serve. Because fresh and dried hot chilies vary in their degree of hotness, you must add them according to taste. Begin with a very small amount and taste broth during cooking, adding more hot peppers as needed to make the stew just hot enough to be pleasing.

- 3 pounds lean boneless lamb shoulder, cut into 1½-inch cubes
  Salt and pepper
- 3 tablespoons salad oil
- 2 medium onions, thinly sliced
- 2 celery stalks, finely chopped
- 1 green pepper, finely chopped
  Finely minced fresh hot chilies or crushed dried red pepper to taste
- 2 garlic cloves, minced or mashed
  About 1½ cups water
- 2 cucumbers, peeled, seeded, and shredded
- 1 cucumber, peeled in alternating lengthwise strips and sliced paper-thin
  Tomato wedges

Season meat with salt and pepper. In a large kettle brown meat cubes well on all sides in salad oil. Remove meat and set aside. Discard from kettle any oil in excess of 3 tablespoons. Add to kettle onions, celery, green pepper, and fresh hot chilies (if you use them); sauté until limp. Return meat to kettle along with crushed dried red pepper (if you use it, begin seasoning by adding ⅜ teaspoon), garlic, ⅜ teaspoon black pepper, and water. Cover and simmer for 2 hours, or until meat is very tender. If necessary, add water, a few tablespoons at a time, during cooking. Taste and add salt and more hot chilies or crushed red pepper if necessary. Just before serving, stir in shredded cucumber; heat through. Serve stew over Crisp Golden Corn Points. Garnish each serving with a line of overlapping cucumber slices and a tomato wedge. Makes 6 servings.

CARIBBEAN STEWS

CRISP GOLDEN CORN POINTS

Make the corn bread ahead, cook, split, and butter; at serving time, broil-toast it.

Beat 2 eggs in a mixing bowl. Stir in 1 cup milk, ¼ cup melted butter, and 1 cup yellow cornmeal. Sift together into mixing bowl 1 cup all-purpose flour, 2 tablespoons sugar, 4 teaspoons baking powder, and 1 teaspoon salt. Mix just to blend. Pour into buttered baking pan (about 9 x 13 inches). Bake in preheated hot oven (400°F.) for 20 minutes, or until golden on top and browned at edges. Allow to cool. Cut into diamond shapes. Split; spread cut surfaces with butter. Before serving, slip under broiler to toast. Makes corn-bread points to accompany 6 stew servings.

BANANAS IN RUM CUSTARD SAUCE

Make the rum custard sauce far enough ahead so it can chill thoroughly; assemble desserts at serving time.

Beat together thoroughly in top of double boiler 4 egg yolks, 2 cups half-and-half (half milk and half cream), ¼ cup sugar, and ¼ teaspoon salt. Cook over hot water, stirring, until mixture thickens slightly and coats a silver spoon. Strain custard, add 1 tablespoon dark rum and 1 teaspoon vanilla; allow to cool, cover, and chill. At serving time, ladle over 6 thinly sliced bananas in 6 stemmed dessert glasses. Sprinkle generously with Lace Praline. Makes 6 servings.

LACE PRALINE

Thickly butter a chilled baking sheet. Sprinkle with ⅛- to ¼-inch layer of brown sugar rubbed through a strainer. Broil about 6 inches beneath heat until sugar bubbles; watch carefully. Cool until candy hardens slightly. Loosen and ease off sheet with a flexible spatula. Cool thoroughly. Break into large pieces and sprinkle over bananas in sauce.

BANANA STOBA
[From Curaçao]

In native form, this stew would be built upon the broth and flavors of smoke-cured pigs' feet or pigs' tails; the "bananas" would be both bananalike (but starchy) plantains and the sweet eating bananas we know. *Funchi,* a cornmeal-mushlike dish seemingly ever-present in local Curaçaoan cuisine, would be the accompaniment.

For a party here, we make the stew with meaty ham hocks, long simmered to tenderness and served to resemble individual little plump hams—one or two to a person. We use ripe but firm bananas, and *funchi* becomes crispy cubes of cheesed cornmeal floating in the stew broth as croutons.

Banana Stoba*
Cheese-Cornmeal Croutons*
Green-Pepper Strips*
Gingered Fresh Pineapple*

BANANA STOBA

Purchase meaty ham hocks for this stew, and ask your meatman to saw each into two or three serving pieces. You can make the stew as far ahead of time on the day of your party, or the day before, as you wish. Just be sure to add the vegetables only in time to cook to tenderness.

About 4 pounds smoked ham hock, cut into serving pieces
About 2 quarts cold water
1 whole onion, peeled
5 whole cloves
¼ teaspoon each of dried thyme and pepper
3 medium-size white potatoes, peeled and quartered
3 medium-size sweet potatoes or yams, peeled and cut into 1-inch crosswise slices
Salt (optional)
4 ripe but firm bananas, peeled and cut into 2-inch lengths
⅓ cup sliced green onions

Wash ham hock pieces and place in large kettle. Pour over ham enough cold water to cover. Stud onion with cloves and add to kettle along with thyme and pepper. Cover. Heat until boiling; reduce heat; simmer for about 1¼ hours. (At this point you could cool stew, chill, remove fat on top; reheat and add vegetables to cook before the party.) Add potatoes and simmer for 40 minutes more, or until vegetables are tender; skim off any excess fat on top of broth. Taste broth; add salt if needed. Add banana pieces and green onions and simmer for 5 minutes more, or until heated through. Serve immediately with a portion of all stew ingredients in each large shallow soup or stew bowl, or serve ham hock on a plate alongside the bowl of broth and vegetables. Pass Cheese-Cornmeal Croutons for each person to add to soup broth. Makes 6 generous servings.

CHEESE-CORNMEAL CROUTONS

You can make and mold the cornmeal mush, preparatory to making it into croutons, a day ahead. Brown the cubed cornmeal in butter before the party. Reheat in the oven in time to serve.

Combine in a saucepan ⅔ cup each of cold water and white *or* yellow cornmeal and ¾ teaspoon salt. Stir in 2 cups boiling water. Cook, stirring, until mixture thickens and boils. Reduce heat, cover, and cook over low heat for 10 minutes; stir frequently. Turn into a buttered loaf pan, about 5 x 9 inches. Chill until firm. Cut into 1-inch cubes. Coat each cube with flour. Sauté in butter until brown and crisp on all sides. Before serving, heap into heatproof serving bowl, sprinkle generously with shredded natural cheese (Edam, Gouda, or mild Cheddar). Place in oven or under broiler to heat and melt cheese. Makes croutons for 6 generous stew servings.

GREEN-PEPPER STRIPS

Pass a relish plate of cold and crisp green-pepper strips garnished with whole cherry tomatoes.

GINGERED FRESH PINEAPPLE

Generously sprinkle chunks or thin slices of fresh pineapple with chopped candied or preserved gingerroot. Chill for 1 hour or more. Serve chunks in stemmed sherbet glasses or overlapping thin slices on chilled dessert plates.

CARP [*Cyprinus carpio*] to give the scaly freshwater fish its ichthyological name, is a native of Asia that came to this country via Europe during the last century. It is a robust fish that thrives almost anywhere, preferring muddy waters. Carp in the United States reaches a length of two feet and may weigh as much as forty pounds. One of the hardiest and wiliest of fishes, carp is able to withstand extremes of temperature and lives to the ripe old age of twenty to forty years, but not to hundreds of years, as legend has it. Unfortunately the presence of carp in a lake or river tends to stir up mud, making the water uninhabitable for other fish.

Carp has been prized in Europe for hundreds of years, acquiring through the years a distinguished literary background. It still is one of the favorite fishes of French, Central European, and Slavic cooking. The monasteries of the Middle Ages all had their carp ponds, and so did the great French and English estates of the 17th and 18th centuries. In Europe's Catholic countries, carp is the traditional fish of the fast days preceding great holidays, such as Christmas and Easter.

The best time for eating carp is from November until April. In the summer they tend to develop a muddy flavor. Skinning the fish and soaking it in mild salt water helps remove this muddiness. The younger, smaller fish (up to seven pounds) are the best eating. They may be fried (if two to three pounds), poached, or baked.

Purchasing Guide—Carp is usually sold whole, weighing 2 to 8 pounds, or in fillets. Look for fish with pink gills, tight shiny scales, a bright skin, and firm flesh.

Storage—Fresh fish is very perishable and should be used within two days of purchase. Wrap cleaned and dressed fish in moisture-proof paper or place in a tightly covered dish and refrigerate immediately.

Nutritive Food Values—Carp is a lean fish. Fish is a good source of protein and contains iron, calcium, and B vitamins.
3½ ounces, raw = 115 calories

Basic Preparation—Rinse fish quickly in cold salted water. Let stand in ice water for 30 minutes to remove muddy flavor. Fresh carp may be baked, poached, stewed, or fried. Cook fish at low or moderately high temperatures, until it flakes easily with a fork. Handle fish carefully to prevent it from falling apart. If fish is overcooked it will become dry and tough.

CARP CASSEROLE

   2 garlic cloves
   1 tablespoon butter
   1 medium onion, thinly sliced
  ½ lemon, sliced
   2 bay leaves, crumbled
   1 tablespoon chopped chives
   1 tablespoon chopped parsley
   1 3- to 4-pound carp, cut into large pieces
   1 teaspoon salt
  ½ teaspoon pepper
   1 pint beer
   1 tablespoon butter
   1 tablespoon all-purpose flour
  ⅛ teaspoon ground cloves
     Dash of hot pepper sauce

Rub casserole with garlic and grease with butter. Place onion, lemon slices, bay leaves, chives, and parsley on bottom of casserole. Top with carp. Sprinkle fish with salt and pepper. Pour beer over fish. Bring to a quick boil. Simmer, covered, over low heat for 25 to 30 minutes. Remove fish to hot serving platter and keep hot. Strain pan liquid. Knead butter and flour together into balls the size of a pea. Reheat strained pan liquid and drop butter-flour balls into liquid, stirring constantly. Add cloves and hot pepper sauce. Cook, stirring all the time, until sauce is smooth and thickened. Pour over fish. Makes 4 servings.

Menus

50 Menus to help you plan more varied meals

BREAKFASTS OR BRUNCHES

Fresh Fruit Compote
Hot Sausage Slices
Corn Fritters
Orange-Ginger Marmalade

Crenshaw Melon
Deviled Ham Steak
Popovers
Honey

Canned Stewed Plums
Scrapple
Fried Apples
Currant Scones

Sliced Peaches and Cream
Ham Omelet
Toasted English Muffins
Apple Butter

Honeyed Grapefruit
Buttermilk Pancakes
Bacon
Maple Syrup

Papaya with Lime
Canadian Style Bacon
Waffles
Whipped Cream Cheese
Caramel Syrup

Whole Fresh Orange
Broiled Chicken Livers
Bacon
Creamed Eggs
Whole Wheat Toast

Strawberries with Orange Juice
Ham with Cream Gravy
Double Corn Muffins
Rose Hip Jelly

LUNCHEONS AND SUPPERS

Clear Tomato Soup
Luncheon Meat and Chick Pea Salad
Sliced Cucumbers
Pan Rolls
Prune Whip with
Custard Sauce

Prunes with Orange Chunks
Tuna and Walnut Salad
Bacon Batter Bread
Butter
Hot Chocolate

Quick Mushroom Broth
Ham and Tomato
on Potato Bread
Coconut Ice Cream

Chicken-Corn Chowder
Cheese Popovers   Butter
Hot Bacon Slaw
Fresh Fruit Compote

Tomato Juice
Cold Fried Chicken
Hearts of Palm Salad
Hot Potato Rolls
Strawberries in Wine

Manhattan Clam Chowder
Corn Sticks
Pineapple-Cream Cheese
Salad

Carrot and Celery Sticks
Apple-Buttermilk Waffles
Maple Syrup
Canadian Bacon
Jellied Cranberry Juice

Chopped Steak
Brussels Sprouts
in Browned Butter
Baked Potatoes
Green Salad
Baked Buckwheat
Pudding

Chop Suey Fried Noodles Rice Soy Sauce Lace Pralines	Jellied Vegetable Salad Caraway Cottage Cheese Bacon Batter Bread Jam Tarts	Fruit Salad Coconut Dressing Hard Rolls Butter Honey Ice Cream with Butterscotch Sauce	Fish Cakes Chili Sauce Creamy Slaw with Carrots Bread Sticks Nut Butter Cookies

---

DINNERS

London Broil Sauteed Mushrooms O'Brien Potatoes Panned Mixed Greens Rhubarb Fool	Corned Beef Hash with Poached Eggs Stewed Corn and Tomatoes Cottage Stuffed Celery Fresh Pear Pie	Cream of Celery Soup Fish Sticks with Tomato-Mushroom Sauce Chive Potatoes Marinated Green Beans on Lettuce Swedish Caramel Custard	Hamburgers Shoe String Potatoes Brussels Sprouts and Chestnuts Stewed Rhubarb and Strawberries
Jellied Consommé Madrilêne Southern Fried Chicken Cream Gravy Rice Escarole, Asparagus, Pimiento Salad Rainbow Cake	Sauteed Fish Fillets Tartar Sauce French Fried Potatoes Baked Sweet-Sour Brussels Sprouts Brownies à la Mode	Pork Chops Smothered with Sage Onions Candied Sweet Potatoes Dandelion Green Salad Melon with Ice Cream	Beef Pot Roast Onion-Seasoned Gravy Parsley Potatoes Broccoli with Sour Cream Pistachio Ice Cream Black and White Brownies
Spaghetti with White Clam Sauce Green Salad with Tomatoes Herb Breadsticks Melon with Lemon Ice Espresso	Lemon-Broiled Chicken Broccoli and Cheese Custard Rice with Parsley Kentucky Jam Cake	Broiled Tenderized Chuck Steak Hashed Brown Potatoes Broccoli Piquant Sherry Jelly Sugar Cookies	Apricot-Glazed Ham Slice Duchesse Potatoes Asparagus with Mock Hollandaise Crescents Butter Caramel Torte
Halibut Paysanne Potato Scallop Green Beans Avocado Salad with Orange Chunks Buttermilk Meringue Pie	Chinese Egg Rolls Mustard Sweet and Sour Meatballs Steamed Rice Chinese Vegetables Fresh Pineapple Fingers with Ginger	Frankfurters Sauerkraut with Apple and Caraway Boiled New Potatoes Mixed Fruit Bowl Gingersnaps	Cream of Watercress Soup Middle-East Roast Stuffed Capon Rice Pilaf Marinated Broccoli on Greens Canadian Rum Cake
Roast Lamb Shoulder Brown Gravy Anise Butternut Squash Simmered Barley Apple Crisp	Mixed Green Salad with Olives Hamburger Casserole French Bread Fruit Compote	Vegetable Cocktail Meatless Stroganoff Green Noodles Peas with Onions Chocolate Pudding	Hot Tomato Juice Chicken Livers en Brochette Rice with Peas Baking Powder Biscuits Carrot and Celery Sticks Coffee Ice Cream
Seafood Newburg Carrot Rice Asparagus with Vinaigrette Sauce Raspberries and Cream Nut Butter Cookies	Boeuf Bourguignon Buttered Noodles Romaine Salad Baked Apples Filled with Raisins	Tomato Bisque Salmon Loaf Hearts of Palm with Butter Sauce Parkerhouse Rolls Sliced Oranges with Coconut	Pain de Veau (Veal Loaf) Tomato Sauce Succotash Cheese Popovers Butter Lemon Pudding
Chicken Rosemary Panned Chinese Cabbage Raisin and Carrot Salad Chocolate Poundcake with Chocolate Sauce	Leftover-Lamb Stew with Mixed Vegetables Mashed Potatoes Melon Delight	Sauteed Lamb Patties Mint Jelly Home-fried Potatoes Curried Green Beans Cucumber Salad Sour Cream Dressing Daffodil Spongecake	Chicken Sancocho Fluffy Rice Avocado Tomato Salad Guava Shells with Cream Cheese
	Mixed Grill with Broiled Peaches Celery au Gratin Parsley New Potatoes Lettuce Hearts with French Dressing Butterscotch Cream Pie		Aruba Cucumber Lamb Crisp Golden Corn Points Bananas in Rum Custard Sauce

Table of Equivalents

few grains = less than 1/8 teaspoon (tsp.)

3 tsp. = 1 Tablespoon (Tb.)

4 Tb. = ¼ cup

8 Tb. = ½ cup

5 Tb. plus 1 tsp. = ⅓ cup

16 Tb. = 1 cup

1 cup = ½ pint (pt.)

2 cups = 1 pt.

4 cups = 1 quart (qt.)

4 qts. = 1 gallon

16 ounces (oz.) = 1 pound (dry weight)

16 oz. = 1 pt. (liquid measure)